FEMINIST RESEARCH METHODS

Recent Titles in
Bibliographies and Indexes in Women's Studies

Women in China: A Selected and Annotated Bibliography
Karen T. Wei

Women Writers of Spain: An Annotated Bio-Bibliographical Guide
Carolyn L. Galerstein and Kathleen McNerney, editors

The Equal Rights Amendment: An Annotated Bibliography of the Issues, 1976-1985
Renee Feinberg, compiler

Childbearing Among Hispanics in the United States: An Annotated Bibliography
Katherine F. Darabi, compiler

Women Writers of Spanish America: An Annotated Bio-Bibliographical Guide
Diane E. Marting, editor

Women in Ireland: An Annotated Bibliography
Anna Brady, compiler

Psychological and Medical Aspects of Induced Abortion: A Selective, Annotated Bibliography, 1970-1986
Eugenia B. Winter, compiler

Women Writers of Germany, Austria, and Switzerland: An Annotated Bio-Bibliographical Guide
Elke Frederiksen, editor

Immigrant Women in the United States: A Selectively Annotated Multidisciplinary Bibliography
Donna Gabaccia, compiler

Women and the Literature of the Seventeenth Century: An Annotated Bibliography Based on Wing's *Short Title Catalogue*
Hilda Smith and Susan Cardinale, compilers

Women and Mass Communications: An International Annotated Bibliography
John A. Lent

Sources on the History of Women's Magazines, 1792-1960: An Annotated Bibliography
Mary Ellen Zuckerman, compiler

FEMINIST RESEARCH METHODS

An Annotated Bibliography

Connie Miller
with
Corinna Treitel

Bibliographies and Indexes in Women's Studies,
Number 13

GREENWOOD PRESS
New York • Westport, Connecticut • London

Library of Congress Cataloging-in-Publication Data

Miller, Connie.
Feminist research methods : an annotated bibliography / Connie Miller, with Corinna Treitel.
p. cm.—(Bibliographies and indexes in women's studies, ISSN 0742-6941 ; no. 13)
Includes bibliographical references and index.
ISBN 0-313-26029-X (alk. paper)
1. Feminism—Research—Bibliography. 2. Women—Research—Bibliography. I. Treitel, Corinna. II. Title. III. Series.
Z7963.F44M54 1991
[HQ1180]
016.30542′072—dc20 91-3792

British Library Cataloguing in Publication Data is available.

Library of Congress Catalog Card Number: 91-3792
ISBN: 0-313-26029-X
ISSN: 0742-6941

First published in 1991

Greenwood Press, 88 Post Road West, Westport, CT 06881
An imprint of Greenwood Publishing Group, Inc.

Printed in the United States of America

The paper used in this book complies with the Permanent Paper Standard issued by the National Information Standards Organization (Z39.48-1984).

10 9 8 7 6 5 4 3 2 1

To Zsuzsa Koltay, who helped me see more

CONTENTS

1

INTRODUCTION

ORIGINS

A few years ago, about to begin a project comparing the speed with which my library received journal article photocopies from libraries and from commercial suppliers, I asked myself how I would make the research feminist. What differences would taking a feminist approach make? Were some methods more feminist than others? Could feminism and a project as prosaic as a comparative study of document delivery turnaround time have any possible relationship?

Librarian that I am, I sought the answers in a literature search. While articles and books on feminism and research were plentiful, no one source existed that would answer my questions. Many articles and books I could find focused on specific disciplines — sociology or history, for example. Often, criticisms of the traditional approach outnumbered suggestions for feminist alternatives.

I wanted one book that pulled all the articles and books on feminist research methods together, that showed what feminists in specific disciplines were saying about research and what principles were common across all disciplines. Assuming I couldn't be the only person wanting and needing such a book, I proposed Feminist Research Methods: An Annotated Bibliography to Greenwood Press.

DEFINITIONS

I define research methods broadly. My definition includes specific tasks, such as choosing research subjects, operationalizing variables, or designing questionnaires. It includes techniques, such as statistics. It also includes approaches, such as objectivity and the distance maintained between the researcher and the researched. Feminists in all disciplines have seen the need for changes in research tasks, techniques, and approaches.

No definition of feminism will satisfy everyone. But Liz Stanley and Sue Wise, in an article in Women's Studies International Quarterly, describe feminism in a way that captures what feminists, regardless of their subject areas, seem to be saying about research. "Feminism," Stanley and Wise say, "directly confronts the idea that one person or set of people have the right to impose definitions of reality on others."[1]

ORGANIZATION AND CONTENT

Feminist critics of traditional research prefer gray to black and white. The feminist model pulls down the barrier erected by tradition between objective experts and passive subjects. Researchers and research respondents act as partners, both with biases, both with insights. Feminists oppose the woodpile approach to history that chops human development into periods of progress, like the Renaissance, and periods of decline, like the Dark Ages. You can find progress and decline in all periods, they claim, depending on who you ask. Feminist researchers resist segmented knowledge, each discipline off on its own side trip, oblivious to the adventures and discoveries of the others. Understanding, like life, is interdisciplinary.

Then why, since I support the feminist inclination toward gray is my book full of compartments that look very black and white? Why are there separate chapters, for instance, on psychology, sociology, and anthropology? Unquestionably, these narrow compartments belie the behavior of the feminists squashed into them, most of whom draw on the ideas of thinkers from disciplines all over the map. I risked misrepresentation because I assume most users will approach the book with a subject-oriented research project in mind. Those interested only in history or economics can go directly to the relevant compartment, find what they need, and leave.

But the compartments, so hospitable to the expedient, need not stymie browsers and meanderers. A chapter called "General" gathers sources too interdisciplinary to cram into any one subject. Cross-references link sources separated by space, time, or topic. Indexes at the back of the book invade disciplinary hideaways to ferret out terms and authors of interest.

Each chapter contains annotations and an essay. The annotations of sources are arranged alphabetically by author name. The essays introduce the contents of the annotations and outline the consequences of the feminist critique, for particular disciplines in subject-oriented chapters, and for research generally in the "General" chapter.

Feminist Research Methods covers many, but not all, disciplines. Anthropology, sociology, psychology, economics, political science, and history merit chapters of their own. Architecture, urban planning, and geography, because they involve physical space, cluster into the "Geography" chapter. "Science" lumps together the so-called harder sciences (biology and physics, for example). The "Communication" umbrella encompasses media and mass communications, linguistics and speech, film studies, and art criticism. Omitted are the enormous body of feminist literary criticism — a book in itself — and philosophy, education, nursing, and medicine.

Feminist Research Methods includes only those sources that address explicitly how feminists practicing research behave differently from other researchers. It does not include sources that simply describe particular feminist research projects. The sources listed in the book are all in English; dates of publication range from the 1920s to 1990. Since I agree with Sue Scott [2] that women's experiences of oppression make their research feminist, male authors appear in the bibliography only when I couldn't justify leaving them out. Attempting to be comprehensive, I hunted, burrowed, and delved for sources, but inevitably, some got away; like the Fountain of Youth, irresistible, unreachable, these treasures beckon from an index I didn't search, a book I neglected to open, a library shelf I left undisturbed. Despite illusive gems, Feminist Research Methods will perform like a well-stocked outfitting post, equipping explorers with all they need to plan expeditions and make discoveries on their own.

HOW FEMINISM HAS CHANGED TRADITIONAL RESEARCH

No source I read while gathering material for Feminist Research Methods celebrated feminism's transformation of research. No source anticipated a celebration. Predictably, feminists are the primary consumers of other feminists' work, and articles about women or feminism tend to be published in journals devoted to that purpose. Ideas confined to feminist "ghettos" may create ripples but they won't redirect the mainstream.

The ripples vary in size, depending on the issue and the discipline. Feminists have changed the language of research. Despite die-hards, who continue to cry corruption, non-sexist language has become a standard, incorporated into the submission guidelines of many journals. Stabs of guilt and unwelcome awareness now haunt researchers who, in the past, studied men and, contentedly, drew conclusions about everyone.

Feminists in all disciplines have demonstrated that objectivity has about as much substance as the Emperor's new clothes. Women now parade through the annals of history; twenty years ago, they were lucky if they stood on the sidelines, clapping. Feminist anthropologists themselves are ambivalent about their successes, but feminists in other disciplines admire and envy their assault on tradition: because of feminism, the study of culture is much closer to being the study of gender.

DISAPPOINTMENTS

Many feminists seem disappointed. After almost twenty years of writing, politicking, and consciousness raising, researchers are behaving pretty much the same. Within feminism, factions have sprung up and proponents of one perspective are at the throats of proponents of another. Some advocates of feminist research have retreated and are reconnoitering: whatever alternatives feminism offers must account for the achievements of traditional research and patriarchal science.[3]

While gathering and annotating the sources for Feminist Research Methods, I became disappointed myself, but not because of what feminists haven't accomplished. The rudiments of feminism — consciousness raising, the personal is the political — seduced me into believing that I would understand feminist writers, even academic ones. I was convinced that feminists would write clear, accessible prose that would show, as well as tell, their nontraditional approach. Until I started reading. In the work of an undoubtedly brilliant, highly praised, and often quoted feminist theoretician, I read the following:

> "Having been objectified as sexual beings while stigmatized as ruled by subjective passions, women reject the distinction between knowing subject and known object — the division between subjective and objective postures — as the means to comprehend social life. Disaffected from objectivity, having been its prey, but excluded from its world through relegation to subjective inwardness, women's interest lies in overthrowing the distinction itself. Proceeding connotatively and analytically at the same time, consciousness raising is at once common sense expression and critical articulation of concepts."[4]

In the work of another feminist, as brilliant, as highly praised, and quoted as often as the first, I read:

> "This paper proposes a research strategy for doing a sociology for women.... This means...a method which does not begin with the categories of the discourse, approaching the actualities of the social world with a view to discovering in it the lineaments of the theoretical object. Rather it develops an inquiry which explores the everyday world not in itself but as it is articulated to the social relations of the larger social and economic process. A sociology for women must be able to disclose for women how their own social situation, their everyday world is organized and determined by social processes which are not knowable through the ordinary means through which we find out our everyday world."[5]

So much for clear, accessible writing.

Neither these quotations nor these authors are exceptional: the literature on feminist research methods teems with passages as opaque. Readers can, of course — I did, because I had to write annotations — sift out some interpretation. But, mining those nuggets of meaning demands blasting away strongholds of crabbed erudition and hacking through layers of jargon. Most people simply won't bother.

Ironically, and tragically, feminists fault traditional research for its inaccessibility to anyone but researchers or their peers. They insist that feminist research do more than increase production from the academy or fatten a tenure dossier. Feminist research will distinguish itself from tradition, they claim, by evolving out of women's own experiences and by cycling back to improve women's daily lives. The author of the first passage quoted above (if my interpretation is correct) hails consciousness raising as the cornerstone of the feminist method. Consciousness raising means understanding politics and theory because they grow out of personal, lived experiences, and yet, nothing about my personal life (including years of graduate education) equips me to understand her prose.

I confessed my disillusionment and frustration to a scholar at the institution where I work, hoping she could justify feminist writers' failure to practice what they preach. But, the scholar simply shrugged, dismissing my naïveté with a wave of her hand. All social movements, she told me, have intellectual manifestations that operate on some removed plane. Look at Marxism, for example. And feminists, who want traditional researchers to pay attention, need to communicate in language the latter will respect, play ball with the boys, so to speak. I slunk, chastened, from her office, more realistic, more practical, but no less disappointed.

CONCLUSION

The feminist writers I read for Feminist Research Methods told me some answers to the question which began this introduction: "What would make my research on document delivery turnaround time feminist?" They told me, for example, to avoid exploiting research assistants or graduate students and give them credit and recognition for their work. They told me to listen to my material, to let the data speak to me, instead of imposing my interpretations on the data. And, they told me to report the research using language and a format that would allow librarians, document suppliers, and anyone else, for that matter, to understand what I did, why, and how it might change their lives. I wish that more of the feminists I read had shown as much as they told, had acted as examples as well as advisers.

NOTES

[1]Stanley, Liz and Sue Wise. "Feminist Research, Feminist Consciousness and Experiences of Sexism." Women's Studies International Quarterly 2:359-374 (1979). (see annotation in General chapter)

[2]Scott, Sue. "Feminist Research and Qualitative Methods: A Discussion of Some of the Issues." In Issues in Educational Research: Qualitative Methods, edited by Robert G. Burgess, pp. 67-85 (Philadelphia, Pennsylvania: Falmer Press, 1985). (see annotation in General chapter)
[3]This paragraph reflects my interpretation of ideas expressed at a colloquium by Evelyn Fox Keller (see annotations in Science chapter).
[4]MacKinnon, Catharine. "Feminism, Marxism, Method and the State: An Agenda for Theory." Signs 7(3): 515-544 (1982). (see annotations in Political Science chapter)
[5]Smith, Dorothy. "Institutional Ethnography: A Feminist Method." Resources for Feminist Research 15(1): 6-12 (1986). (see annotations in Sociology chapter)

2
GENERAL

INTRODUCTION

Feminists find traditional research incompatible with their principles. For Bowles and Duelli-Klein (1981), in fact, the feminist and traditional approaches differ so greatly they cannot comfortably apply the term social science to both. But identifying incompatibility is one thing; defining an effective alternative is another.

On several points, feminists agree. Contrary to tradition, which grants researchers superior status, feminists claim that researchers and their respondents are equals. Respondents have as much right as researchers to decide what should be researched, how the research should be done, and what should happen to the results (Light, 1979). "Distortions, lying, even farcical results" stem from a power imbalance (Gorelick, 1988)

Tradition views researchers as uninvolved spectators. Gergen (1988) speaks for most feminists when she exposes researchers' personal interpretations and linguistic constraints. Harding, ("The Method Question," 1987) asks how, if the scientific method is supposed to be objective, sexist and androcentric biases have gone undetected. Feminists replace the myth of value-free research with a reality where researchers' partiality becomes part of the data (Mies, 1981).

Traditional researchers isolate variables in order to study them. Feminists call such isolation "context-stripping" (Duelli-Klein, 1980) and connect it with inaccurate assumptions and results. To earn the description feminist, research must emerge out of the actual experiences and concerns of women (Du Bois, 1981; Duffy, 1984).

Just as research questions must flow out of women's experiences, research results must improve women's lives. Bowles and Duelli-Klein (1981) identify the unique "heart" of the feminist approach as an emphasis on research for women rather than for the academy or the funding agency. Traditional researchers communicate their research results in professional literature. Feminists must find ways to share their results with the women who the findings will benefit and with institutions responsible for social policies (Bristow and Esper, 1984).

But suppose a feminist researcher actually does treat her respondents as equals, acknowledge her own preconceptions, biases, and values and factor them into the data, study her respondents while participating in their daily lives, and involve each respondent in a discussion of the results. What has she actually accomplished? Has she, as Nielsen (1990) and Roberts (1980) claim, initiated a paradigm shift? Or has she simply challenged pervasive male bias (Duffy, 1985)? Has she managed to avoid using research as an instrument of oppression (Mies, 1981)? Or has she just lessened the inevitable contradictions in the relationship between the researcher and the researched (Acker, Barry, and Esseveld, 1983)?

Many feminists advocate a particular method as the cure for what ails traditional research. McCormack (1981) promotes simulation; Reinharz (1981) describes a new method she calls experiential; Bowles (1981) sees a relationship between feminist scholarship and hermeneutics; Anderson, Armitage, Jack, and Wittner (1990) present oral history as an opportunity for women to speak for themselves; Armstrong and Armstrong (1987) advise researchers to supplement numbers with qualitative data.

But Jayaratne (1981) and Scott (1985) caution feminists not to dismiss quantitative approaches. They recommend choosing methods appropriate to the question being asked. Kelly (1978) and Eichler (1987) argue that in the right hands any method can be feminist. As passionate and heretical as feminist scholarship might be, Du Bois (1981) opposes its association with any particular method and Harding (1987) calls the search for a "distinctive feminist method of inquiry" a fruitless one. She defines method as techniques for gathering evidence and acknowledges that feminists have carried out "evidence-gathering" in ways different from traditional ones. But the most powerful feminist studies are not distinguished by the research methods they use.

The most powerful studies, according to Harding, take class, race, and cultural differences into account, use women's experiences as resources for social analysis, design methods and analyses consistent with the origins of the research problem, and incorporate the researchers' beliefs and behaviors into the evidence for or against the claims advanced in the research results. She challenges feminist epistemology to explain why this openly political and value-laden research produces more complete and less distorted social analyses than its purportedly objective traditional counterpart.

Feminists' struggle to accomplish what Eichler (1987) calls the "urgent task" of making feminist research unnecessary by replacing an overall sexist approach with a non-sexist one has resembled an archeological dig. With the new insights offered at each layer of exploration have come new questions and challenges. At the first layer, feminists began identifying gaps in the disciplines and filling them with information about women. Forced to explain the gaps, feminists moved to the next layer, where they began examining theories, methods, and paradigms for misogynist biases. Challenged with correcting the biases, they went yet a layer further and began exploring and describing female experience (Laws, 1978).

Patai (1983) reminds feminist researchers, whether they are blazing new paradigms, inventing new research methods, or simply presenting a more accurate picture of scholarship and of the world, that feminism is a utopian project aimed at a different and better society. The power of the feminist vision of research is its potential to "defamiliarize," its ability to move people to new levels of awareness.

ANNOTATIONS

001. Acker, Joan, Kate Barry, and Joke Esseveld. "Objectivity and Truth: Problems in Doing Feminist Research." Women's Studies International Forum 6(4):423-435 (1983).

> Acker, Barry, and Esseveld list the following principles of feminist research: 1) to contribute to women's liberation by producing knowledge useful to women; 2) to gain knowledge using methods that are not oppressive; and 3) to develop a perspective that questions dominant intellectual traditions and reflects on itself. In response to conducting research according to these principles, they identify the following problems: 1) no research process completely erases the contradictions in the relationship between the researcher and researched; 2) it is difficult to analyze change as a process; and 3) it is difficult to organize data and to present the totality of women's lives. The adequacy of interpretation can be determined by asking if the active voice of the subject can be heard; if the theoretical construction accounts for the investigator as well as those investigated; and if the reconstruction reveals "the underlying social relations that eventuate in the daily lives" being studied.

002. Alcoff, Linda. "Justifying Feminist Social Science." Hypatia 2(3):107-127 (1987).

> Alcoff encourages feminist social scientists to explain and justify their methods of theory-choice. Theories in feminist social science have "emancipatory implications for women's position in society." She examines two existing models of theory-choice, the Holistic and the Constructivist, to see if they solve the problem of feminist social science. Neither model, she concludes, solves the problem. Alcoff challenges feminists to develop epistemology and "a model of theory-choice consistent with...new conception[s] of the process of gaining knowledge without sacrificing its ability to explain and justify its existence as a reliable, though not foolproof, process."

003. Anderson, Kathryn, Susan Armitage, Dana Jack, and Judith Wittner. "Beginning Where We Are: Feminist Methodology in Oral History." In Feminist Research Methods: Exemplary Readings in the Social Sciences, edited by Joyce McCarl Nielsen, pp. 94-112 (Boulder, Colorado: Westview Press, 1990).

> Oral history offers the opportunity for women, whose experiences have often been overlooked, to speak for themselves. When an interviewer uses appropriate techniques, women can be encouraged to "say the unsaid." Anderson, Armitage, Jack, and Wittner draw on the perspectives of Marcia Westkott (see annotation in this chapter) and Dorothy Smith (see annotations in the Sociology chapter) to develop their approach to oral history. From Westkott, they learned that traditional social science assumes that people are free to act according to how they feel and think. In patriarchal society, however, only males of certain classes and races may act freely and women's behavior may not always reflect their thoughts. From Smith, they learned to begin with women's actual daily lives and move from there to understand their activities in the context of organizational processes. Anderson urges oral historians to explore emotional and subjective experience as well as facts and activities. Jack advocates listening in a new way and examining the words women use to describe their lives. Wittner advises feminists to become familiar with symbolic interactionism, an approach which emphasizes process more than structure and rejects the idea of the neutral, objective researcher. Armitage stresses the need to make women subjects rather than objects of study.

004. Armstrong, Pat and Hugh Armstrong. "Beyond Numbers: Problems with Quantitative Data." In Women and Men: Interdisciplinary Readings on Gender, edited by Greta Hofmann Nemiroff, pp 54-79 (Markham, Ontario: Fitzhenry & Whiteside, 1987).

Armstrong and Armstrong argue that numbers and number gathering methodology cannot be separated from social context or the ideas that lead to their selection. They also argue against numbers as the most accurate or relevant kind of fact. To develop a complete view of women at work, qualitative as well as quantitative data must be collected. Qualitative data check facts, expose holes, and add context to quantitative data. As Armstrong and Armstrong conclude, "theory, statistics, and qualitative data are all necessary for rigorous research."

005. Bowles, Gloria. "The Uses of Hermeneutics for Feminist Scholarship." Women's Studies International Forum 7(3):185-188 (1984).

Bowles discusses similarities between feminist scholarship and the hermeneutical approach, which rejects the idea of a detached, neutral, or objective position for a researcher. She suggests that feminists use hermeneutics, "since for scholars presently outside [feminist] circles these critiques could be a prelude to an understanding of feminist thought." What feminist women scholars offer that male hermeneutic scholars lack is the ability to "stand removed enough from the tradition to see things differently." Because of this removed stance, feminists will propose alternatives to the white Western tradition of thought.

006. Bowles, Gloria and Renate Duelli-Klein. "Introduction: Trying to Find Out How to Find Out What We Know." In Theories of Women's Studies II, edited by Gloria Bowles and Renate Duelli-Klein, pp. 1-10 (Berkeley, California: University of California, Women's Studies Department, 1981).

In this introductory essay to a collection of papers, Bowles and Duelli-Klein suggest that feminist research approaches are so different from traditional approaches that the term "social sciences" cannot apply comfortably to both. "At the heart" of what makes feminist approaches unique is an emphasis on research for women rather than for the academy or for the career of the researcher, research that will improve "the daily life and the general lot of a diversity of women." The experience all women share — oppression — offers a common ground on which researchers and the researched come together. "Women researchers, then, must begin with [their] own experience."

007. Bristow, Ann R. and Jody A. Esper. "A Feminist Research Ethos." Humanity and Society 8(4):489-496 (1984).

Bristow and Esper use the example of their research on rape to demonstrate the use of consciousness raising in the research process. Two critical assumptions give their work its feminist emphasis: 1) research participants are experts in their own right; and 2) the subject of their research is a social not an individual phenomenon, i.e., rape is a product of sexism and social sanctioning of violence not the action of sick individuals. Their research involved interviews with women, but these interviews were conducted as consciousness raising dialogues rather than as interrogations in which the researcher as expert reveals nothing about herself but objectively listens to the participant. Bristow and Esper stress the importance of three different dialogues which inform the research process. The researchers' internal dialogue involves the researcher examining her own values and experiences in light of the effect these may have on the research. The participant-researcher dialogue is a mutual exchange in which the participants' experiences are validated and the researcher is changed. The researcher-society dialogue increases the researcher's awareness of the social context in which the subject of the research occurs. Results of feminist research, say Bristow and Esper, must be disseminated not just professionally but also to women who might benefit from the results and into areas where they might affect social policy and treatment.

008. Code, Lorraine. "Credibility: A Double Standard." In Feminist Perspectives: Philosophical Essays on Method and Morals, edited by Lorraine Code, Sheila Mullett, and Christine Overall, pp. 64-87 (Toronto, Ontario: University of Toronto Press, 1988).

Women are associated with experience. Knowledge, because it is experimental and objective, is defined as superior to experience. Code suggests that knowledge is "impoverished" because it has excluded experience, emotion, and practical and subjective elements. But she rejects the idea of pasting feminine values on to "already existing assumptions about good scientific practice, in order to arrive at an androgynous amalgam." Code recommends that thinking in terms of dichotomies be replaced by thinking in terms of differences, that bipolar opposites be replaced by gradations. She also distinguishes between scientific results that increase people's understanding about themselves and the world and results that improve scientific techniques. Code advocates "epistemic responsibility" to "regulate cognitive activity in much the way that virtues, such as kindness or justice, regulate moral activity...."

009. Cook, Judith A. "An Interdisciplinary Look at Feminist Methodology: Ideas and Practice in Sociology, History, and Anthropology." Humboldt Journal of Social Relations 10(2):127-152 (1983).

Cook outlines four "epistemological ideas" that are consistent in feminist research as it is practiced in sociology, history, and anthropology: 1) there is a lack of information about women; 2) there is a bias in the lack of women researchers; 3) previously investigated phenomena need to be reconceptualized to include women's experiences; and 4) the kinds of research questions asked determine the results obtained and have implications for actions that can be taken. To describe feminist methodology, Cook examines the practice of feminist research in the three disciplines she is examining. Feminist sociologists are moving away from quantitative research and toward qualitative research that takes the respondent's frame of reference into account. They are also applying triangulation, that is, the use of more than one research technique (usually one qualitative and one quantitative) simultaneously, so that findings complement each other. Feminist historians are moving away from "oppression" models that emphasize women's subjugation and from "compensatory" models that focus on exceptional women and toward an examination of ordinary women as they live their lives. Relational analysis has been used to understand women's position relative to men's. Women are being studied in and of themselves through an examination of letters, diaries, and memoirs, and in relation to the dominant culture. In addition, feminist historians are concentrating on developing quantitative data on women's experiences that has previously been lacking. Feminist anthropologists are trying to overcome the double male bias, which occurs when male anthropologists obtain data about women from males in the culture being studied, by replicating research and comparing the results. Comparative studies are being done both cross-culturally and within a culture. In all three disciplines, feminist methodology attempts to move beyond present research frameworks and to "unveil the distortions of a sexist society while working toward a transformation of the future."

010. Currie, Dawn and Hamida Kazi. "Academic Feminism and the Process of De-radicalization: Re-examining the Issues." Feminist Review 25: 77-98 (1987).

Currie and Kazi ask if "academic feminism is the graveyard of radical ideas." They point to the method of doing feminist research as one possible source of the de-radicalization of feminist ideas. They emphasize the development of research for women, research that provides understanding of oppression and results in change. To achieve a unity of theory and practice, this research must relate the personal to the social. The development of feminist methods does not mean the exclusion of other research methods. Feminists must use all available techniques and technologies to draw women together towards a "new social transformation" and to achieve a "global vision."

011. Du Bois, Barbara. "Passionate Scholarship: Notes on Values, Knowing and Method in Feminist Social Science." In Theories of Women's Studies II, edited by Gloria Bowles and Renate Duelli-Klein, pp. 11-24 (Berkeley, California: University of California, Women's Studies Department, 1981).

While committed to the idea that feminist scholarship represents "necessary, vital, and vitalizing departures" from the scientific and political norms and functions of androcentric social science, Du Bois opposes the idea of a "distinctively feminist scientific method." The first step for feminist researchers is to learn to see, and to generate words and concepts "grounded in the actual experiencing of women." To avoid mystifying or rigidifying their "science-making," feminists must validate, encourage, and support one another. Complexity and seeing things in context are preferable to "dichotomy, duality, linearity, and fixity." Du Bois describes the passionate nature of feminist scholarship as "necessary heresy."

012. Duelli-Klein, Renate. "How To Do What We Want To Do: Thoughts About Feminist Methodology." In Theories of Women's Studies, edited by Gloria Bowles and Renate Duelli-Klein, pp. 48-64 (Berkeley, California: University of California, Women's Studies Department, 1980).

Duelli-Klein says methods link theory and practice, translate theory into action. She ties feminist methodology with "transdisciplinary" research that goes beyond the scope of any single discipline. Research on women differs from research for women. The latter is feminist scholarship because it investigates "the reality of women's experiences with the ultimate goal of changing women's status and position for the better." Traditional scientific methods rely on isolating variables and investigating them in a linear, additive fashion. Such "context-stripping" approaches or approaches hampered by sexist gender stereotypes "are not suited to research on how women in today's society come into being...."

013. Duffy, Mary E. "A Critique of Research: A Feminist Perspective." Health Care for Women International 6(5-6):341-352 (1985).

Duffy says that "the feminist critique is not an alternative paradigm." It is, rather, a challenge to male bias that can be used as a guideline to review existing and develop new research. Essential to the guideline are: 1) feminist consciousness in the researcher; 2) research questions emerging from the concerns of women; 3) openly worded research questions that identify, label, and seek to change oppression; 4) methodology that validates women's experiences, ideas, and needs; 5) an acceptance by the researcher of multiple truths and of her own influence on the research results; and 6) research for women with the primary goal of social change.

014. Eichler, Margrit. The Double Standard: A Feminist Critique of Feminist Social Science. New York: St. Martin's Press, 1979.

Eichler uses the concept of the double standard as a criterion to determine the existence of a difference that can be attributed to sex. By double standard she means that two things which are the same are measured or evaluated by different standards. According to Eichler, sexist science is dominated by a double standard that allows identical behaviors by men and women to be described and analyzed differently. Sexist science ignores women and yet applies conclusions and theories based on male samples to them; sexist science considers women only in relation to men; sexist science takes the male as the norm and the female as a deviation from the norm; and, sexist science uses sexist language to communicate its findings. Sexist science, through the double standard by which it interprets results, maintains the sex structure from which it arose and in which it is grounded. Eichler sees the two tasks of feminist science as first, to point out the various ways in which accepted scientific methods are sexist and distorting, and second, to devise new methods and theories that will not have the weaknesses that sexist science has. Feminist science should account for the behavior of all human beings. Feminist science must use non-sexist language, not because it solves the problem of the exclusion of women, but rather because it helps researchers recognize when women are being excluded. Feminist science must stop using methodologies that focus on differentiating the sexes and treat qualities of actions (for example, rationality and emotionality) as mutually exclusive. Feminist science must never treat sex as an explanative variable. Both sex differences and similarities must be charted and described and attempts must be made to explain observed sex differences in non-sexual, social manners. Feminist science must understand sex roles as the systematic form of crippling that they are and feminist science must seek to abolish the sexual double standard.

015. Eichler, Margrit. "The Relationship Between Sexist, Non-sexist, Woman-centered, and Feminist Research in the Social Sciences." In Women and Men: Interdisciplinary Readings on Gender, edited by Greta

Hofmann Nemiroff, pp. 21-53 (Markham, Ontario: Fitzhenry & Whiteside, 1987).

Eichler argues that any method can be used in a sexist manner or in a non-sexist manner. Methods are sexist when: 1) one sex is asked about the other and the answers are assumed to represent reality for the other; 2) questions asked do not reflect the spectrum of female-male behaviors, attitudes, etc.; 3) sex of participants is not properly taken into account; 4) any sexually identified objects or persons are not controlled for; 5) research instruments are validated on one sex but used with both; and 6) data collected on both sexes are not analyzed by sex. It is not possible to go directly from sexist to non-sexist research. Two intervening steps are necessary: the realization that traditional research is sexist and a woman-centered examination of the issues. "The most urgent task of feminist research is to make itself unnecessary by replacing the overall sexist paradigm with a non-sexist one."

016. Freeman, Jo. "The Feminist Scholar." Quest 5:26-36 (1979).

Freeman finds no contradiction in being a feminist scholar even though feminist clearly implies advocacy for a particular viewpoint: "that women and men have the same potential for individual development [but] social institutions create differences [and] there is [no] meaningful choice for members of either sex as long as there are socially prescribed sex roles and social penalties for those who deviate from them." All scholars come to their research with a political perspective. The primary responsibility is not to be objective but rather to reexamine constantly one's perceptions. Only those out of power can allow themselves to be single-minded; power comes with the responsibility of critical reflection. Freeman sees feminism as compatible with scholarship but incompatible with the prestige-based system of academia.

017. Gergen, Mary M. "Toward a Feminist Metatheory and Methodology in the Social Sciences." In Feminist Thought and the Structure of Knowledge, edited by Mary M. Gergen, pp. 87-104 (New York: New York University Press, 1988).

According to Gergen, feminist thinkers reject the following "traditional empiricist methodological principles: 1) independence of scientist and subject; 2) dealing with the subject outside of the physical and historical contexts in which it usually exists; 3) value-neutral theory and practice; 4) independence of the scientist and the facts; and 5) the superiority of the scientist over other people. "Feminist-inspired" research treats scientists as participants in the research project, interconnected to the subjects and the facts, and prone to personal interpretations and linguistic constraints.

018. Gorelick, Sherry. 'Giving Voice', Giving Vision: Theory, Process, and Standpoint in Feminist and Marxist Methodology. Presentation at a meeting of the American Sociological Association, pp. 1-16 (1988) (Paper available from Sociological Abstracts Reproduction Service, .25 per page and $1.50 search and postage).

Gorelick says that feminist methodological critiques have been made on three levels: 1) the philosophical level, which exposes the pretence of value-free science and objectivity; 2) the moral level, which exposes the objectification and exploitation of subjects; and 3) the practical level, which points out that the power imbalance between researchers and the researched leads to "distortions, lying, even farcical results." Feminists must uncover different experiences of diverse groups of women and the processes that created these differences. "The practice of methodology must change not only theory and society, but all of us who live in it, what we do and how we think."

019. Harding, Sandra. "Introduction: Is There a Feminist Method?" and "Conclusion: Epistemological Questions." In Feminism and Methodology: Social Science Issues, edited by Sandra Harding, pp. 1-12, 181-190 (Bloomington, Indiana: Indiana University Press, 1987).

Harding distinguishes method — techniques for gathering evidence — from methodology — a theory and analysis of how research should proceed — and from epistemology — issues about an adequate theory of knowledge or justificatory strategy. Feminists have carried out methods of evidence-gathering in ways different from the ways used by traditional androcentric researchers; feminists have argued that traditional theories have been applied in ways that make it difficult to understand women, or men, as gendered; feminists have objected to the exclusion of women as knowers or agents of knowledge. But, Harding argues, "it is not by looking at research methods that one will be able to identify the distinctive features of the best of feminist research." She identifies three features which account for the "distinctive power of feminist research:" 1) using women's experiences, taking into account the differences across classes, races, and cultures, as resources for social analysis; 2) designing research for women, i.e., the purposes of research and analysis are not separable from the origins of research problems; and 3) incorporating the beliefs and behaviors of the researcher as part of the empirical evidence for (or against) the claims advanced in the results of the research. While not related to a feminist method per se, these features "show us how to apply the general structure of scientific theory to research on women and gender." Two epistemologies try to account for the fact that "politically value-laden research processes...are producing... more complete and less distorted social analyses." One epistemology, feminist empiricism argues that sexist and androcentric science is bad science, and that the faults of such science can be eliminated by stricter adherence to standard empiricist rules. Feminist empiricists believe that women are more likely than men to produce claims unbiased by androcentrism, that the scientific method has not been effective at eliminating wide-spread biases like androcentrism, and alternative approaches may be required to deal with the "profound questions [concerning women's world's and the social relations between the sexes] which are no longer marginalized as deviant." The second epistemology, the feminist standpoint, believes that knowledge is based on experience and that women's experiences, through struggles against male domination, "provide potential grounding for more complete and less distorted knowledge claims than do men's." Harding emphasizes that feminist researchers never defend relativism, i.e., propose that men's and women's experiences provide equal grounds for reliable knowledge claims. She does, however, propose that men can do feminist research if it satisfies the three criteria listed above. Harding concludes with a caution by describing critiques some groups of feminists have made of the belief that "there can be a kind of feminist author of a new 'master story...,'" one true story about the world. Reality can only be governed by one set of rules when one person or group dominates the whole, these critics say. Women must be united in their opposition to any kind of domination.

020. Harding, Sandra. "The Method Question." Hypatia 2(3):19-35 (1987).

Harding argues against "the idea of a distinctive feminist method of research." She differentiates method, methodology, and epistemology: a research method is a technique for gathering evidence; a methodology is "a theory and analysis of 'the special ways in which the general structure of a theory finds its application in particular scientific disciplines';" and epistemology is a theory of the nature, scope, and reliability of knowledge. Feminist epistemologies have arisen in response to three problems with traditional research: 1) if scientific method is supposed to be so objective, why have sexist and androcentric biases gone undetected? 2) since knowledge is supposed to be based on experience and male experience has been defined as more fruitful ground for the generation of scientific hypotheses, is the idea of woman as knower a contradiction? and 3) research processes guided by the politics of the women's movement have produced more objective research but how can infusing science with politics improve the empirical quality of the results? The characteristics of the "most illuminating examples of feminist research" include: 1) the discovery of gender and its consequences; 2) the use of women's experiences as scientific resources; and 3) scrutiny of the class, race, culture, and gender assumptions, beliefs, and behaviors of the researcher as part of the research process. Harding concludes that the "search for a distinctive feminist method of inquiry is not a fruitful one." No simple recipe for research exists that can allow feminists to bypass "the difficult and sometimes painful...processes of learning how to see and create ourselves and the world in the radically new forms demanded by our feminist theories and practices."

021. Howard, Judith A. "Dilemmas in Feminist Theorizing: Politics and the Academy." Current Perspectives in Social Theory 8:279-312 (1987).

Howard links the "dominant ontological and epistemological positions" of disciplines to the possibility for feminist scholarship. Ontology addresses what is true and, therefore, worth studying. Epistemology addresses how we can know. In the social sciences, the most significant ontological decision is between the public (government, production, economic exchange) and private (family, reproduction) domains. Feminist theory is less likely to develop in disciplines that emphasize the public domain or that maintain a rigid division between the public and private domains. Positivist and functionalist epistemologies, which emphasize quantitative methodologies, order, consensus, and stability, discourage the development of feminist theory.

022. Jayaratne, Toby Epstein. "The Value of Quantitative Methodology for Feminist Research." In Theories of Women's Studies II, edited by Gloria Bowles and Renate Duelli-Klein, pp. 140-161 (Berkeley, California: University of California, Women's Studies Department, 1981).

Jayaratne believes that the use of both quantitative and qualitative methods in the social sciences "can help the feminist community in achieving its goals more effectively." While it is more superficial than qualitative research, quantitative research appears more objective and can often be effective in changing public opinion. Jayaratne recommends that feminists value quantitative research for its benefits and "work to change those elements which are antithetical to feminist ideas."

023. Kelly, Alison. "Feminism and Research." Women's Studies International Quarterly 1:225-232 (1978).

Kelly answers the question, "what is feminist research?" by saying that research is feminist if the reasons for undertaking it are feminist. She divides the research process into three stages: 1) choosing the topic and formulating the hypothesis; 2) carrying out the research and obtaining results; and 3) interpreting the results. Kelly believes that feminism determines the first stage and often leads to new questions, but not always. She also believes that a feminist analysis must be brought to bear on interpreting research results. For example, with regard to biologically-based sex differences, researchers must ask what is important about the trait? why is it considered desirable? what compensating virtues are possessed by the opposite sex? Kelly is adamant "that feminism has little place in determining the research methods used or the results obtained." Any method can be feminist, she asserts, in the right hands.

024. Lather, Patti. Feminist Perspectives on Empowering Research. ERIC Document #ED 283 858 (1987).

Lather defines feminist research as putting "the social construction of gender at the center of one's inquiry." While she acknowledges the "multi-paradigmatic" nature of feminist empirical work, Lather favors the approach of those who "maximize the research process as a change-enhancing, reciprocally educative encounter." This praxis-oriented inquiry involves a relationship between researchers and the researched, in which both receive an education and both participate in transformative social action. "Through dialogue and reflexivity," claims Lather, "design, data and theory emerge, with data being recognized as generated from people in a relationship."

025. Laws, Judith Long. Feminism and Patriarchy: Competing Ways of Doing Social Science. ERIC document # ED 166 081 (1978).

Laws reviews the history of feminist scholarship. She lists three distinct foci: 1) the earliest feminist research filled in gaps within disciplines but didn't challenge existing paradigms or cross disciplinary lines; 2) as feminist scholars encountered misogynist biases, they began to protest against existing paradigms; and 3) feminist scholars began to explore female experience. Feminist researchers have sought out innovative methodologies because they reject the subject/object assumptions of positivism, because they need to accommodate data previously not part of the canon and because the questions they are asking require a larger scope than traditional methodologies can handle. Feminist scholarship centers around women, studies experience which is uniquely female or studies universal experiences from a female perspective, is concerned with the social uses of knowledge about women, and is interdisciplinary.

026. Light, Linda. "The Influence of Feminism and Collectivity on the Research Process: The Vancouver Women's Health Collective." Atlantis 4(2):108-20 (1979).

Light advocates the interactive method of research based on "the assumption that researchers and those who are being researched are equals." The interactive method places the value of the research for the subjects on an equal level with its value for the researchers and for funding sources. People being researched, according to the interactive model, have as much right as researchers to determine what is researched, how the research is done, and what is done with the results. Light describes the integrated approach as "the bringing together of the various threads of...personal, political, and professional lives into an integrated whole."

027. Lorde, Audre. "The Master's Tools Will Never Dismantle the Master's House." In This Bridge Called My Back: Writing By Radical Women of Color, edited by C. Moraga and G. Anzaldua, pp. 98-101 (Watertown: Persephone, 1981).

Lorde calls any discussion of feminist theory that doesn't involve the perspectives of women of color, poor women, and lesbians "a particular academic arrogance." She claims difference is not something to be tolerated. Instead, it is "a fund of necessary polarities between which our creativity can spark like a dialectic." The personal as the political will only illuminate all our choices when each woman reaches inside herself and touches "that terror and loathing of any difference that lives there."

028. Maguire, Patricia. Doing Participatory Research: A Feminist Approach. Amherst, Massachusetts: The Center for International Educational, School of Education, University of Massachusetts, 1987.

Participatory research critiques positivism but, unless researchers are sensitive to male biases, it will not critique a. Feminism can expand participatory research to provide a "broader, more inclusive analysis of all forms of oppression." Feminist participatory research simultaneously recognizes gender, class, and race or culture, taking the commonalities and diversities of people's experiences into account. Such research benefits both women and men and challenges patriarchy when it pays attention to the differences in male and female perceptions. Maguire recommends that participatory researchers familiarize themselves with feminist theories and practices, debate their findings with a wide circle of colleagues, and take a feminist approach to planning, implementing, and evaluating their projects.

029. McCormack, Thelma. "Good Theory or Just Theory? Toward a Feminist Philosophy of Social Science." Women's Studies International Quarterly 4(1):1-12 (1981).

McCormack argues for the use of simulation as the methodology best suited to feminist research. She believes that simulation is androgynous in terms of intellectual skills required and that it lends itself to transcending history. Feminist research, which is humanistic and value-oriented like other just research (for example, Myrdal's research on racial equality, or peace research), is ideally suited to the use of simulation methods. McCormack provides an example of her own research using simulation. As a way of studying husband-wife interaction and influence in voting, she has couples discuss two political candidates. The candidates, however, are women with feminist orientations and the legislature in which the elected woman will serve is numerically dominated by women. The participating couples are real, the electoral process is the familiar one, the issues the candidates are debating and the candidates' profiles are taken from campaign literature. What is hypothetical, futuristic, unreal is the feminist political culture.

030. Mies, Maria. "Towards a Methodology for Feminist Research." In Theories of Women's Studies II, edited by Gloria Bowles and Renate Duelli-Klein, pp. 25-46 (Berkeley, California: University of California, Women's Studies Department, 1981).

Mies begins with the assumption that "there is a contradiction between the prevalent theories of social science and methodology and the political aims of the women's movement." If women's studies uses traditional methods, it will become an instrument of repression. Mies encourages feminist scholars to use their "double consciousness" — women's simultaneous view of their own repressed subjectivity and the objective world of research — as a methodological and political opportunity. She offers these guidelines for feminist research: 1) the replacement of value-free research with partiality, achieved through partial identification with the research objects; 2) the replacement of the vertical relationship between researcher and researched with the "view from below;" 3) the replacement of uninvolved spectator knowledge with active participation in women's liberation; 4) using change of the status quo as the starting point for research; 5) making the research process a process of conscientization, or perception of the "social, political, economic contradictions and...action against the oppressive elements of reality;" 6) studying women's individual and social history; and 7) replacing individualism, competition, and careerism with the a sense of the collectivity of women's experiences.

031. Minnich, Elizabeth K. "A Devastating Conceptual Error: How Can We Not Be Feminist Scholars?" Change 14:7-9 (1982)..

Feminist scholarship, says Minnich, "is based on the belief that theories and terms claiming to be general should indeed be general." This belief is radical because tradition is built around the partial terms, "man" and "mankind." Minnich advises scholars to stop treating women and other excluded groups as minorities who can be kept on the fringes of the curriculum.

032. Nielsen, Joyce McCarl. "Introduction." In Feminist Research Methods: Exemplary Readings in the Social Sciences, edited by Joyce McCarl Nielsen, pp. 1-37 (Boulder, Colorado: Westview Press, 1990).

Nielsen argues that, although there are many feminist methods, a distinctive feminist approach to research exists. The "irreducible element" is a focus on women's experiences. This focus leads to reinterpretations, reconstructions, and reanalyses of existing data, and constitutes a paradigm shift in the Kuhnian sense.

033. Patai, Daphne. "Beyond Defensiveness: Feminist Research Strategies." Women's Studies International Forum 6(2):177-189 (1983).

Patai describes feminist research strategies that have evolved from her research on utopian fiction by women. By strategy, she means "a pattern of decisions that is designed to attain certain objectives." In its advocacy for a different and better society, feminism is a utopian project. The power of a utopian vision lies with its potential to defamiliarize, that is, to move a person to a new level of awareness. Patai's two strategies include: 1) acting as if subjects are of general interest and that women constitute the human norm; and 2) treat the areas of research that involve men in terms of men's gender identity (that is, withdraw from men the assumption that they represent the generally human). Until the rules of relevance and irrelevance are questioned and overturned, "we will all be trapped by the world that these rules create and that our language constantly reproduces."

034. Reinharz, Shulamit. Dimensions of the Feminist Research Methodology Debate: Impetus, Definitions, Dilemmas & Stances. ERIC Document # ED 209 297 (1981).

Reinharz begins with definitions. Method refers to procedures or techniques used for a research project; methodology refers to assumptions inherent in the methods or procedures. Feminist can refer to a person or to an ideology. Feminist methodological criticism attacks both technique and values. According to Reinharz, feminists have taken three different methodological positions: 1) since science is inherently patriarchal, feminists must change the assumptions about how knowledge is produced; 2) thinking that science is patriarchal is a patriarchal trap so women should work to change science from the inside by attaining positions of power and serving as role models; and 3) don't worry if science is patriarchal or not, just use whatever methods and resources you can to do research helpful to women. Reinharz believes that the "dialectic energy" generated by the debate among proponents of these three positions is the "most significant element of feminist methodology."

035. Reinharz, Shulamit. "Experiential Analysis: A Contribution to Feminist Research Methodology." In Theories of Women's Studies II, edited by Gloria Bowles and Renate Duelli-Klein, pp. 68-97 (Berkeley, California: University of California, Women's Studies Department, 1981).

The first step in developing a new research method, says Reinharz, is to believe that personal dissatisfaction with traditional methods derives from "structural inconsistencies and skewed assumptions underpinning the methods themselves." The second step is to specify the assumptions being challenged. The third step is to connect assumptions with research methods. Reinharz outlines a method she developed called "experiential analysis" that produces growth and understanding in the areas of the problem investigated, the persons doing the investigation, and the method used. Experiential analysis assumes that researchers will draw on many disciplines and that "people are intentional beings who create and discover meaning." Reinharz suggests that experiential researchers gather data in natural settings and approximate the lived realities of their subjects, attempt to be part of the environment rather than manipulators of it, include actions as well as words in the data, and collaborate with subjects to analyze and publish the results.

036. Reinharz, Shulamit, Marti Bombyk, and Janet Wright. "Methodological Issues in Feminist Research: A Bibliography of Literature in Women's Studies, Sociology, and Psychology." Women's Studies International Forum 6(4):437-454 (1983).

The purpose of the bibliography is to gather the literature that had been published up to 1983 on "feminist concerns with the conduct of academic research." The bibliography is divided into ten sections: 1) frameworks (references which help put the whole question of feminism and research and the relationship between them into perspective); 2) who has access to doing and publishing research; 3) uncovering ignored topics and data concerning women; 4) biases in research which can inform the understanding of gender bias: racism, heterosexism, and ageism; 5) sexist bias in research; 6) critiques of conventional methods from a feminist perspective; 7) feminist research alternatives; 8) cognitive style differences between women and men and their relevance for research orientations; 9) discussions by women of their experiences as researchers; and 10) bibliographies and additional resources. Most of the references come from sociological and psychological literature although some are drawn from other disciplines. The emphasis is on United States materials.

037. Reuben, Elaine. "In Defiance of the Evidence: Notes on Feminist Scholarship." Women's Studies International Quarterly 1:215-218 (1978).

Reuben distinguishes research by and about women from feminist scholarship, pointing out that they are not always the same thing. While feminist scholarship may have started out by filling in the blanks in many disciplines, its result has been to demonstrate needed revisions in the canon, and in concepts of genre and periodicity. Feminist scholars must maintain a consciousness of their own research processes and epistemologies. Their focus on problems generates the need to cross the boundaries between disciplines. Feminist scholars must be able to tolerate anxiety because no "sure and certain prescription" defining topic, method, or audience exists. Feminism challenges scholarship as it has been institutionalized and extends beyond the academy.

038. Rich, Andrienne. "Women's Studies - Renaissance or Revolution?" Women's Studies 3:121-126 (1976).

Rich begins by rejecting the either/or dichotomy proposed in her title and the terms "renaissance" and "revolution" as "labelling inherited from patriarchal history." She views women's studies as "a pledge of resistance: Man shall no longer make the world in his image." She encourages the development of women's studies beyond the university, in rape crisis centers, divorce clinics, health collectives, press collectives, and other types of action. Feminist scholars must avoid writing and thinking as if androcentric thought were the mainstream. To end patriarchy, feminists must "remake, not just the content, but the forms of knowing and acting."

039. Ring, Jennifer. "Toward a Feminist Epistemology." American Journal of Political Science 31:753-772 (1987).

Ring says that feminists, such as Catharine MacKinnon (see Political Science chapter), who reject a dichotomy between the mind and the world, relinquish several thousand years of philosophical history. She describes such self-isolation as "tantamount to accepting the destructive equation of 'man' with 'human'." Ring suggests that dialectics offers feminists a way to address the question of how anybody knows anything without forcing them to accept the destructiveness of male objectivity. Dialectical theory sees subject and object as methodologically interpenetrable. This prohibits the objectification of women and their association with nature, and forces human beings to be aware of the extent to which they are shaped by the empirical world.

040. Roberts, Joan I. "Beyond Intellectual Sexism." In Issues in Feminism: A First Course in Women's Studies, edited by Sheila Ruth, pp. 21-26 (Boston: Houghton Mifflin Company, 1980).

When Roberts first began studying women, she saw her task as discovering and presenting the facts of sex discrimination and adding new knowledge that would reduce inequities and expand roles for both women and men. The more she studied, however, the more she realized that her task was, in fact, "a daring and difficult reassessment of social reality" that would confront major paradigms in several disciplines. Facts and concepts about women often don't exist; conclusions about both sexes are based on studies of only males; conclusions about females are based on opinion rather than fact. Existing theories and models cannot be adopted without questioning their origins. The objectivity of science sustains the subjective bias that women are inferior. The ultimate goal of the study of women is the "creation of new social being."

041. Saarinen, Aino. "Feminist Research: In Search of a New Paradigm." Acta Sociologica 31(1):35-51 (1988).

Saarinen relates feminist research to the feminist movement by describing the way in which both aim toward a new world-view. Two projects are essential to the development of this world-view: deconstruction and reconstruction. Deconstruction asks why and to what extent scientific thought is a, why has knowledge concerning women been passed through an "ideological filter," why has male experience been viewed as the standard model for human life. Reconstruction attempts not to find new answers to old questions but rather to formulate new questions concerning women's own experiences from women's points of view. It involves four interwoven, overlapping steps. Compensatory research is research based on male or mainstream values which takes an interest in women. It is the "exceptional woman" or equal opportunity type of research which looks for women who have achieved in similar ways to men. Contribution research examines women in their own spheres but doesn't take issue with their role as supporters or maintainers of the "front stage" role of men. Transitional research, or "strength and dignity" research, views ordinary women as subjects rather than as objects and sees their sphere of activity — the private sphere of reproduction, family life, sexuality — as the"front stage." Theories, concepts, and methods developed for understanding men's experiences are not adequate to describe and analyze the experiences of women, and gender is seen to be a dimension of social reality rather than a natural fact. The last step, integrative research, involves a synthesis in which society is studied as a sex/gender system, a relationship between female and male cultures where gender "is the object and result of a continuous practical and ideological struggle." The goal of integrative research is to "articulate a new scientific paradigm, a paradigm where the category of gender and the sex/gender system represent integral parts of scientific research into human society and its reality." Feminist scholars examine the sources of the mainstream to determine what they omitted to say and also develop new research techniques for uncovering genuine female experience including an examination of different products (for example, crafts as well as publications) and a different interaction between researcher and researched (i.e., more interactive). The paradigmatic challenge of feminist research is to develop a scientific institution that views gender as not only a social category but also as a category of the theory of science.

042. Scott, Patricia Bell. "Debunking Sapphire: Toward a Non-Racist and Non-Sexist Social Science." In All the Women Are White, All the Blacks Are Men, But Some of Us Are Brave: Black Women's Studies, edited by Gloria T. Hull, Patricia Bell Scott, and Barbara Smith, pp. 85-92 (Old Westbury, New York: Feminist Press, 1982).

> Scott calls for an eradication of "isms" from American institutions — racism, sexism, classism — and the movement toward a more humanistic and realistic philosophy of the social sciences. She lists three "action-oriented strategies" for encouraging research into the Black female experience: 1) making people aware of overt, covert, and institutional racism and sexism; 2) bringing a different perspective into academia by hiring more Black and women scholars; and 3) engaging wide audiences of people in discussions related to the media images of Black women. She closes by challenging readers to assist her "in debunking Sapphire!"

043. Scott, Sue. "Feminist Research and Qualitative Methods: A Discussion of Some of the Issues." In Issues in Educational Research: Qualitative Methods, edited by Robert G. Burgess, pp. 67-85 (Philadelphia, Pennsylvania: Falmer Press, 1985).

> Scott questions two common assumptions about feminist research: that it must be done by women about women and that it must use qualitative methods. To be feminist, research, regardless of the method used, "must take women's oppression as one of its basic assumptions" and must include the researchers' experiences as data. Just as race research must study white racism, feminist research must study male sexism. Men can do research that "challenges sexist assumptions" but only women, who have knowledge and experience of oppression, can do research that is actually feminist. Scott recommends that feminist researchers use methods appropriate to the questions they are asking and warns against linking feminism with any particular methodology.

044. Sherwin, Susan. "Philosophical Methodology and Feminist Methodology: Are They Compatible?" In Feminist Perspectives: Philosophical Essays on Method and Morals, edited by Lorraine Code, Sheila Mullett, and Christine Overall, pp. 13-28 (Toronto: University of Toronto Press, 1988).

> In answering the question she poses in the title of her essay, Sherwin is careful to avoid dichotomous thinking, a characteristic of traditional methodologies that feminists have criticized. While she finds many differences between philosophical methodology and feminist methodology, she takes "care not to define philosophical

methodology as inherently opposed to feminist thought or to imagine the differences in approach to involve a schism that cannot be crossed." The differences between the two methodologies identified by Sherwin include: 1) a feminist emphasis on the personal, the subjective, emotion and feeling, and a range of related experiences contrasted with a philosophical emphasis on objectivity, abstraction, generalization, and universality; 2) a feminist emphasis on interdisciplinary scholarship, eclectic methodology, and cross-disciplinary thought contrasted with a philosophical emphasis on criticizing rather than adopting the methods of disciplines it examines; 3) a feminist emphasis on the use of theory for social action contrasted with a philosophical emphasis on value-free reasoning; and, 4) a feminist emphasis on cooperative, collective progress toward overall goals contrasted with the philosophical emphasis on the adversary method in which researchers aim aggressively to demolish each other's work. There are some shared methodological approaches, however, that lead Sherwin to conclude that feminism and philosophy are not incompatible and that "significant effort from each end" can bring the two together, at least to some extent. Both are skeptical of authoritative pronouncements of truth and both reject the notion of one "authorized method." Each would violate its own principles by rejecting the methods of the other.

045. Stanley, Liz and Sue Wise. "Feminist Research, Feminist Consciousness and Experiences of Sexism." Women's Studies International Quarterly 2:359-374 (1979).

Stanley and Wise received obscene phone calls because their number was listed as the contact number for lesbians. For seven weeks they recorded verbatim all the obscene calls. Of the 286 total calls received, 105 were obscene. On the basis of their research related to the phone calls, Stanley and Wise emphasize that all research involves an interaction between researcher and researched, even when the researched are secondary sources or other objects. Feminist research should be concerned with all aspects of reality and all participants in it, including the part played by men in interactions between women and men. "Feminism directly confronts the idea that one person or set of people have the right to impose definitions of reality on others. Feminist research and researchers should attempt to avoid doing the same thing in research situations."

046. Stimpson, Catharine R. "Our Search and Research: The Study of Women Since 1969." Comment on Conferences and Research About Women 14:1-2 (1983).

> In seeking to reconceptualize reality, feminists have expressed "four overarching theories:" 1) the study of women and the differences among them is important and exposes sex/gender arrangements; 2) sexism, institutionalized discrimination against women, exists; 3) the world actually consists of two worlds, the public world of male culture and the private world of female culture; and 4) the nature, cause, and meaning of sexual difference must be understood. As these overarching concepts have developed, says Stimpson, the picture of women has shifted from one of victims to one of resistors. Feminist research aims not only to be intellectual but also "to change women's and men's lives, institutions, and moral values."

047. Vickers, Jill McCalla. "Memoirs of an Ontological Exile: The Methodological Rebellions of Feminist Research." In Feminism in Canada: From Pressure to Politics, edited by Angela R. Miles and Geraldine Finn, pp. 27-46 (Montreal: Black Rose Books, 1982).

> Vickers borrows from Mary Daly when she says that feminist theorists ask "non-questions." Non-questions challenge patriarchy so completely that those "who work entirely from within [the] established tradition of thought" cannot even recognize them as questions. Feminism's methodological "violations" have occurred in phases: 1) the first phase involved studies of women "within the framework of male-stream thought" when feminists began to identify with the the subjects of the research; 2) the second phase occurred when disciplinary knowledge about women conflicted with the feminist researchers' experiences and intuitions; and 3) the third phase occurred when feminist researchers realized that traditional research methods hide the things they need to reveal. Feminist research rebels in five ways: 1) against decontextualization; 2) for restoring a clear link between actors and the consequences of their actions (agency); 3) against attributing customs or rites to the female victims they harm; 4) against objectivity; and 5) against linearity, inevitability, and laws. Vickers claims that feminists' attempts to "understand and explain the nature of female experience reveals a praxis" for deciding what to discard and what to save from "male-stream thought."

048. Westkott, Marcia. "Feminist Criticism of the Social Sciences." Harvard Educational Review 49:422-430 (1979).

Westkott examines feminist criticism of and implied alternatives to the content and the purpose of social knowledge of women as well as the methods used to gain that knowledge. She claims that most criticisms of method are derived from criticisms of content. Bias is reflected in the way that questions about women are asked and in "the absence of concepts that tap women's experience." As of 1979 when Westkott wrote her article, she could turn only to Dorothy Smith (see entries in the Sociology chapter) for feminist challenges to the "epistemological basis of mainstream social science." Smith, she says, argues against the norm of objectivity that separates the subject of research from its object. In this criticism, feminism resembles and draws on the Marxist and the interpretive traditions when it sees research questions as a product of the researcher's concerns and experiences. Westkott cautions against a social science about women and proposes, instead, a social science for women that "informs the knowledge it seeks with an intention for the future rather than a resignation to the present." The feminist critique of social science emphasizes, Westkott concludes, "a dialectical approach to social knowledge" by which she seems to mean an open, interactive, and "humanly-compelling" approach.

049. Wylie, Alison, Kathleen Okruhlik, Leslie Thielen-Wilson, and Sandra Morton. "Feminist Critiques of Science: The Epistemological and Methodological Literature." Women's Studies International Forum 12(3):379-388 (1989).

Wylie, Okruhlik, Thielen-Wilson, and Morton provide a bibliography of sources in which feminists critique science in general (including social science) and biology in particular. In the introduction preceding their listing of sources, they summarize the content of the critiques. As the sources of inspiration for the feminist critiques of science, the authors list androcentric scientific practices, which have ignored women or justified their subordination, and patriarchal power structures, which have excluded women from participation as knowers. Feminists have identified science as a social, political, and gendered institution. The authors caution feminists on the epistemological and practical levels. As they demonstrate the role values have played in scientific inquiry, feminists may also be denying the "emancipatory potential of feminism." They must be able to articulate models that show how science will be reformulated once it incorporates feminist values.

3

SOCIOLOGY

INTRODUCTION

Sociology, anchored in positivist epistemology, has resisted and will continue to resist feminist influence, say Stacey and Thorne (1985). They contrast sociology with history and literature, the interpretive disciplines, and with anthropology, which has made gender central. While Stacey and Thorne acknowledge that feminists have identified and filled gaps in sociological research, they complain that dominant paradigms remain unchanged and co-opted feminist methodologies remain isolated outside of the mainstream.

Ward and Grant's (1985) analysis of all full-length articles published in all issues of ten major sociological journals for the years 1974-1983 confirms Stacey and Thorne's beliefs. Feminism has brought previously ignored areas of women's experience to the forefront. Many researchers now use non-sexist language and data collection and analysis techniques. But, mainstream researchers avoid citing radical articles, confining radical sociologists to what Ward and Grant describe as a research "ghetto." Major journals still publish a disturbingly high percentage of studies that draw conclusions about all people after examining only one gender. Women's participation in editing and gatekeeping determines the quantity and character of gender-related articles a journal publishes.

The politics of research and publication hinders change. Feminists attempting to redefine a social situation (sexual harassment, for example) to reflect women's experiences encounter, say Gillespie and Leffler (1987), the "political undertones" of scientific methodology. To receive funding or recognition, feminists must use sampling strategies, operational definitions, and data analysis techniques respected by conventional science. Such conventions compromise or prevent redefinition.

Feminism's critique of sociology has precursors (Farganis, 1986). Proponents of Marxism, ethnomethodology, and naturalistic inquiry share many of feminism's disatisfactions and offer similar suggestions for methodological improvement. Among themselves, feminists vary on how to approach research. Graham (1983), for example, opposes survey methodology because it produces gender bias by obscuring "the self understanding of the female subject." Clegg (1975), on the other hand, warns feminists against proscribing any particular methods; an intolerance for variety is precisely what has weakened traditional research. Any qualitative or quantitative method can exhibit sensitivity to gender and a self-reflecting approach. Sprague and Zimmerman (1989) suggest that feminist sociologists' rejection of quantitative methods isolates them at the periphery of their discipline.

Osmond (1984) objects to Walker and Thompson's duality (1984) between feminist research and scientific methods. Feminist researchers, she claims, should rely on traditional methods when these methods do not "invoke sexist assumptions." Feminists contribute, according to Osmond, by refusing to treat appearances as if they were truth or reality.

Smith questions sociology's fundamental principles when she rejects objectivity, which justifies the separation of a researcher from the experiences of daily life (1974), and when she looks to the "everyday world as problematic" (1979). Andersen (1983), however, defends the sociological canon: asking the question "what is life like for women?" renders even classical theory reliable.

Many feminists would agree with Stacey's (1988) definition of feminist research as "on, by, and especially for women...." To gain an understanding of the mechanisms by which the powerful operate, however, Smart (1984) encourages feminists to study not only women but also men in positions of power. Chafetz (1988) objects to extreme activist definitions of sociological research resembling the Nebraska Sociological Feminist Collective's (Hartung, Ollenburger, Moore, and Deegan., 1988). The Collective claims that research should not be conducted unless it empowers "wimmin outside of the academy." Chafetz separates the activist and intellectual enterprises. Theories which can be used to change situations disadvantageous to women pass her "acid test."

Even though they have percursors and partly because of their differences, feminists have added to our understanding of methodology in terms of approach, purpose, objectivity, the omission of women, and gender.

Approach

Approach focuses on the process of research. Stanley and Wise (1981) insist that researchers explain "how/why [they] came to know what they know...[and what] the research procedures [are] which underlie the knowledge they produce." Such explanation and sharing takes the mystery out of research and exposes the researcher's vulnerability. The Committee on the Status of Women in Sociology of the American Sociological Association (1980) lists five places in the research process where sexist bias occurs: problem selection and formulation, review of previous research, sample or population selection, validity issues, and interpretation of results. Oakley and Oakley (1979) describe five parallel ways sexism enters the process of gathering and using statistics: in the areas chosen for statistical analysis, in the concepts used to organize and present the statistics, in the collection of data, in the processing of the statistics, and in their presentation.

Osmond (1984) recognizes as feminist research that does not limit our understanding of women's experiences but that does change the awareness of as many of those concerned with the research as possible. Feminists replace a controlling, manipulative process with a communal, participatory one (Bernard, 1973; Millman and Kanter , 1975). McNamee's (1987) comparisons between the systemic family therapy model and feminist research emphasize intervention rather than control, and an encouragement of, rather than simply an accounting for, change.

Purpose

Feminist sociologists object to research performed only for the benefit of the researcher. Research must achieve social change by empowering, improving, and transforming women's lives (Nebraska Sociological Feminist Collective, 1983; Walker and Thompson, 1984; Cook and Fonow, 1986). If it begins from subjective experience, research will help all participants understand the structure and organization of their worlds (Smith, 1974). Respondents, as well as researchers, must determine study execution and design (Col, 1982; Cook and Fonow, 1986). By reducing the separation between themselves as researchers and their respondents, feminists intend protection and support. Through experience, however, Stacey (1988) learned that the more personal the research relationship, the more the respondents risk exploitation, manipulation, betrayal, and desertion. With subjectivity comes increased responsibility. Epstein (1974) says that, in addition to promoting social change, research must uncover gaps in knowledge about groups other than the dominant one.

Objectivity

Objectivity in research masks the objectification of women and minorities says the Nebraska Sociological Feminist Collective (Hartung, Ollenburger, Moore and Deegan, 1988). Feminist researchers claim no objectivity and encourage all researchers to acknowledge and analyze their ideological positions (Cook and Fonow, 1986). The objective goal of a separation between the researcher and the respondents serves the former's purpose and exploits the latter. As Oakley (1981) puts it, "no intimacy without reciprocity." Researchers traditionally use the passive voice, an indirect form of expression which exempts them from ethical responsibility (Hartung, et al., 1988). Smith (1974) also relates objectivity to exploitation. Researchers separate themselves, she says, not only from respondents but also from all subjectively lived experiences. Such separation requires that someone (women) take care of the (male) researcher's "concrete and particular" daily needs to enable his scientific pursuits. Objectivity, taken to its full extent, "discredits and deprives of the authority to speak those who know society differently."

Omission of Women

Sociology has asked the questions to which men have wanted answers (Bernard, 1973). As a result, sociology typifies society only if women and minorities are excluded (Snyder, 1979). Systematic inattention to the place and participation of women in social life (Epstein, 1974) has led to single-gender studies and the use of male experience as the norm (Andersen, 1983; Ward and Grant, 1985). It has also resulted in the creation by men of a discourse within which women sociologists must function - a discourse "which is not [women's] own and which describes a landscape in which they are alienated" (Smith, 1978). The use of this discourse disenfranchises women researchers from their own experience (Roberts, 1981). To decide if research and statistics include women, Oakley and Oakley (1979) ask the following questions: to what extent are women represented, how does this representation match their actual life roles, and how does it make sense in terms of women's actual life situations.

Gender

If feminist research can be identified by any one feature, that feature is its sensitivity to gender. Having a sensitivity to gender means acknowledging its pervasive influence by putting women at the focus of the analysis, recognizing the prevalence of male-centered bias, and taking the researcher's gender into account (Cook and Fonow, 1986). In good feminist methodology, gender occupies a central place in the research design, analysis, and discussion (Osmond, 1984). Sexist research ignores sex even when it is the most important variable (Smart, 1977; Graham, 1983). Because of its failure to recognize that sex determines one's standing in the social structure, social stratification research has presented a distorted picture of society (Acker, 1972-73). The relationship between gender and class (Daniels, 1975) suggests that socialization rather than biology determines sex differences (Stacey and Thorne, 1985).

The gender dichotomy has misled feminist researchers just as it has misled traditional researchers. Matthews (1982) urges feminists to remain "ideologically committed to seeing two genders at the same time... and to reduc[ing] the degree to which society is overall a gender conscious society." Levy (1988) cautions that introducing an "estrocentric bias" will repeat instead of solve the problems caused by an androcentric science.

Gender is central in feminist research but black feminists such as Brewer (1989) insist that gender alone is not enough: "the simultaneity of racism, sexism, and classism is a reflection of the power of white male patriarchy in the subjugation and oppression of women of color."

ANNOTATIONS

050. Acker, Joan. "Women and Social Stratification: A Case of Intellectual Sexism." American Journal of Sociology 78 (4): 936-945 (1972-1973).

> Acker lists six assumptions made explicitly or implicitly about the social position of women in the social stratification literature: 1) the family, rather than the individual, is the unit; 2) the social position of the family is determined by the status of the male head of the household; 3) females live in families and their status is therefore determined by the males to whom they are attached; 4) the female's status is equal to that of her man's; 5) women determine their own social status only when they are not attached to a man; and 6) women are unequal to men in many ways but this is irrelevant to the structure of stratification systems. These assumptions result in a distorted picture of society which could be corrected if the "insight that sex does affect standing in the social structure" were incorporated into sociology.

051. American Sociological Association, Committee on the Status of Women in Sociology. "Sexist Biases in Sociological Research: Problems and Issues." ASA Footnotes (January, 1980): 8-9.

> The Committee on the Status of Women in Sociology lays out, in chart form, five aspects of the research process where sexist bias frequently occurs. Under each of the five aspects, the chart lists problems and then provides an example of each problem. The five aspects and their associated problems include: 1) research problem selection and formulation (gender-blind social theory, significant topics ignored, selective treatment of topics, a research problem formulated for men or women only, a research model thought to apply to men or women only, inadequate exploration of topics which transcend sex-stereotyped divisions, pejorative labeling or conceptualization); 2) review of previous research (failure to mention that samples are single-sex or have highly imbalanced sex ratios, failure to observe methodological weaknesses of previous research); 3) selection of population and sample (women or men are arbitrarily excluded from sample, inadequate justification for exclusion of men or women from

sample); 4) validity issues (biased question wording in surveys, scales validated on a single sex, cross-sex interviewing); and 5) interpretation of research results (over-generalization of single-sex studies, improper titles which don't reveal single-sex nature of research, inferences unwarranted by data). The Committee states that many of the issues they have identified as sexist problems in sociological research could also be generalized to race and class.

052. Andersen, Margaret L. Thinking About Women and Rethinking Sociology. ERIC document #ED 244 891 (1983).

Andersen believes that the fundamental assumptions of sociology are consistent with a feminist perspective and methodology. These fundamental assumptions include: 1) that sociology is an empirical discipline whose intention is to provide accurate accounts of social realities; 2) that nothing is void of social context; 3) that reality is socially contructed rather than predetermined and that human beings shape social behavior through a process of interpretation; 4) that a human consciousness and social structure shape one another so that the personal is the political; 5) that behavior is learned rather than innate so behavior can change; and 6) that sociology thrives on variations in human behavior in terms of gender, race, class, culture, and historical experience. In spite of this consistency, feminism has raised some valid criticisms of sociological research: it has largely omitted women and distorted reality by making generalizations based on the dominant groups' behavior and values and it has failed to adapt concepts and theories to changes in observations. Andersen discusses Marcia Westkott's (see annotation in the "General" chapter) and Dorothy Smith's (see annotations below) approaches to feminist social science, describing Westkott's view of women as outsiders and insiders in terms of sociology and Smith's belief that the alienation between subjects and objects in research should be broken down. The sociological canon does not have to be discarded, says Andersen, if researchers approach classical sociological theory with Andrienne Rich's question in mind: "What is life like for women?"

053. Bernard, Jessie. "My Four Revolutions: An Autobiographical History of the ASA." In Changing Women in a Changing Society, edited by J. Huber, pp. 11-29 (Chicago: University of Chicago Press, 1973).

In her classic article on the effects of feminism on sociological research, Bernard describes four revolutions in which she has participated: the official recognition, in the 1920s, that empirical research was as important as grand conceptualizing; the emanicipation in the 1930s of the American Sociological Association

(ASA) from the University of Chicago; the formation in the 1950s of the Society for the Study of Social Problems as a protest against the ASA's neglect of social problems, its "uncritical placing of sociological know-how at the disposal of industry," and as a protection against McCarthyism; and the feminist revolution of the late 1960s that insisted on fighting discrimination within the profession and within society at large and on counteracting the sexist bias in the discipline. Women critics of sociology have modified, corrected, and refined the classic paradigms like functionalism, interactionism, and socialization. They have also criticized the substantive questions raised by sociology and the research methods used to answer these questions. The questions asked have been the questions to which men want answers; women are asking questions that take women as a collective entity into account. The methods available - agentic methods based on variables that generate "hard" data - determine the acceptable questions. Women are using communion research based on human beings that generates soft data and thus are expanding the questions that can be asked. Bernard concludes her article by asking whether or not reorienting paradigms to actually take account of women will, in the end, be successful. Fifteen years after her article appeared in this collection, we still need to ask ourselves the same question.

054. Bernard, Jessie. "Re-Viewing the Impact of Women's Studies on Sociology." In The Impact of Feminist Research in the Academy, edited by Christie Farnham, pp. 193-216 (Bloomington, Indiana: Indiana University Press, 1987).

Bernard re-views the historical connections between sociology as a discipline and women's studies and feminism. Sociology's own struggle for academic acceptance and respectability, particularly in the first two or three decades of the century, "led it to dissociate itself...from feminist thinking and the activism of women, which was considered status-reducing at that time." She believes that feminism is calling for a paradigm shift akin to the one Galileo introduced. Just as pre-Galilean astronomers viewed the universe from the earth's point of view, pre-feminist sociologists have viewed society from the part of it they experience. Non-males and non-male experiences have been seen, "in effect, [as male sociologists'] satellites." Keeping the female world all but invisible has allowed sociologists to escape from viewing themselves as "part of the oppression of the underdog," to avoid meeting "the enemy and discovering it was them." Bernard believes it is only a matter of time until feminist paradigms will "overtake, if not replace, the conventional ones of the received sociological canon."

055. Brewer, Rose M. "Black Women and Feminist Sociology: The Emerging Perspective." American Sociologist 20(1): 57-70 (1989).

Black feminists are making what Brewer calls the fourth critique of "the subject matter, methods, and social control functions of sociology." The three precursor critiques to emergent black feminist theory are the radical critique, the black struggle for liberation, and the feminist critique. The core of black feminist theory is an examination of the theoretically and empirically important ways in which racism, sexism, and classism cohere. An essential reality is missed when these social forces are examined separately: "the simultaneity of racism, sexism and classism is a reflection of the power of white male patriarchy in the subjugation and oppression of women of color." Black women need to begin to explain to themselves, for themselves, and for others what their experiences mean. Things presumed to be unproblematic — training to become a sociologist, for example — are problems for minority women, who comprise only 1.9 percent of sociology faculty members. The challenge facing this small number of scholars is to revise existing theories through "black women's experiences, historical positioning, cultural perceptions, and social constructions" so that "theoretical tools forged without a group in mind" can be useful.

056. Chafetz, Janet Saltzman. Feminist Sociology: An Overview of Contemporary Theories. Itasca, Illinois: F. E. Peacock Publishers, 1988.

Chafetz presents an overview of "the major types of feminist theory in sociology or directly useful to sociologists that have emerged since about 1970." Her book is organized into chapters, each of which focuses on one of four broad issues: the causes of gender inequality, mechanisms that maintain systems of gender inequality, the consequences of systems of gender inequality, and the processes of change in these systems. Chafetz defines theory as "any systematic attempt to understand or explain...that is amenable to empirical testing and potential falsification." Theory is integrally related to research in that both attempt to explain what we know or can know empirically about the social world. The "acid test of whether a theory is feminist rests with whether it can be used (regardless of by whom) to challenge, counteract, or change a status quo that disadvantages or devalues women." In addition, feminst theories have three other characteristics: 1) a focus on gender; 2) a view of gender relations as problematic; and 3) a view of gender relations as neither natural nor immutable. The fact that feminist theories tend to be political and tend to advocate social change doesn't imply that they are intrusive or biased. It simply means they are self-conscious and explicit.

057. Clegg, Sue. "Feminist Methodology - Fact or Fiction?" Quality and Quantity 19: 83-97 (1975).

Clegg argues against "the formulation of a specific feminist methodology, in the sense of a set of defined epistemological and/or methodological reconstructions." Prescriptions for method would be no more beneficial in terms of feminism than they have been for traditional research approaches. Quantitative or qualitative research, interviews or surveys can all be feminist depending on the questions the research starts with and the intepretation the results are given. Feminists' primary contributions to research are a commitment to "reflexivity," by which Clegg appears to mean reflecting on and examining one's own research choices, and the ability to raise questions about research encounters that evolve from a sensitivity to gender.

058. Col, Jeanne-Marie. Interviewing Women in Groups: A Liberating Methodology. ERIC Document #ED 249 160 (1982).

A liberating method of interviewing is nonexploitative, requires the interviewer to give as well as receive in the process, allows the respondents some control over the situation, encourages two-way communication between the researcher and the respondents, involves research questions that have as much meaning to the respondents as they do to the researchers, strives for complexity and diversity of viewpoints, and deals with the respondents within the context of their ordinary life situations. Col's group interviews with Ugandan students 1) allowed the researchers to hear explanation as well as description; 2) gave the researchers faith in the external validity of their discoveries because these discoveries were developed through lively group interaction; 3) produced intersubjectivity, or the connection between objectivity and subjectivity, as individuals' perceptions were revised and incorporated into one or more group perspectives; 4) allowed the respondents to be more creative and active because they had control and could participate in the directions the interviews took; 6) encouraged the use of inductive logic as the groups drew from particular instances and experiences to create a consensus; and 7) allowed the respondents to grow as individuals through problem sharing.

059. Cook, Judith A. and Mary M. Fonow. "Knowledge and Women's Interests: Issues of Epistemology and Methodology in Feminist Sociological Research." Sociological Inquiry 56 (1): 2-29 (1986).

Cook and Fonow's article is actually a useful literature review, covering 1977 through 1985, that describes sociological studies in which feminist methodology has been used and literature which explores what a feminist research methodology could and should be. As research strategies that have been employed in feminist research studies, they list visual techniques, such as photography and videotaping; triangulation, which involves the use of more than one research technique at a time; linguistic techniques, based on conversational analysis; textual analysis, or the study of written texts; refined quantitative approaches, which take context into account; collaborative strategies, which involve conducting and reporting the results of research collectively; and "use of the situation-at-hand," in which data are collected and analyzed with regard to existing circumstances (for example, obscene phone calls from men to a lesbian contact phone number). As basic epistemological principles that apply to feminist research methodology, Cook and Fonow list: 1) acknowledging the prevasive influence of gender by defining women as the focus of analysis, recognizing the male-centered bias present in most sociological research, and taking the researcher as a gendered being into account; 2) focusing on consciousness-raising by using consciousness-raising techniques to gather data, acknowledging a researcher's feminist consciousness and its influence on the research, and including social change as one of the goals of the research process; 3) rejecting the subject/object separation by examining ways women participants have been subordinated as researchers, assistants, and respondents and challenging the assumptions that quantification and a strict separation between the researcher and the respondent necessarily imply objective truth; 4) examining ethical concerns by anticipating the consequences of research for respondents and ensuring that respondents receive the information they need, by evaluating the use of language as a means of subordination, and by questioning the fairness of gatekeeping practices; and, 5) emphasizing empowerment and transformation by achieving research results that can help women change the oppressive and exploitative aspects in their lives and by involving the potential target group in the design and execution of the study.

060. Daniels, Arlene Kaplan. "Feminist Perspectives in Sociological Research." In Another Voice: Feminist Perspectives on Social Life and Social Science, edited by Marcia Millman and Rosabeth Moss Kanter, pp. 340-380 (Garden City, New York: Anchor Books, 1975).

While Daniels' chapter focuses primarily on research questions within three broad categories (distribution of economic and occupational opportunities, socialization, and quality of life and life styles) that a feminist perspective will cause sociology to raise, it does point to some methodological consequences of a feminist approach as well. Sociological research must be designed to examine women as a class (a perspective Daniels traces to Kate Millet) and to value interpersonal and feeling structures as well as institutional structures (a perspective Daniels traces to Dorothy Smith). The fact that Daniels' conclusions about feminism and sociology grew out of interviews she conducted with about a hundred researchers offers an interesting methodological example in itself.

061. Eichler, Margrit. "And the Work Never Ends: Feminist Contributions." Canadian Review of Sociology and Anthropology 22(5): 619-644 (1985).

Margrit identifies four stages of development in the feminist critique of sociology: 1) focus on women; 2) focus on sex roles; 3) the development of a feminist approach; and 4) a focus on epistemological concerns. All stages have demonstrated efforts to expose and change sociological sexism and to collect new data. Feminist scholarship, "committed to understanding the situation of women," assumes the all research is value-oriented. The new epistemology it seeks will allow for adequate understanding of both males and females. Four central feminist propositions include: 1) knowledge has been constructed by men for the benefit of men; 2) the dominant approaches to sociology support and maintain patriarchy; 3) social science has been the handmaiden of sexism; and 4) men and women's different positions in society have resulted in different perspectives that will remain as long the current sex structure is in place.

062. Epstein, Cynthia Fuchs. "A Different Angle of Vision: Notes on the Selective Eye of Sociology." Social Science Quarterly 55 (3): 645-656 (1974).

Epstein discusses the "incomplete and probably distorted view of reality" sociology has given "because of its systematic inattention to the place and participation of women in social life." She dismisses the existence of different male and female perspectives and asserts that sociological methods "have not been specifically deficient with regard to women." They have been deficient, however, in failing to point out gaps in knowledge about any group other than the dominant one. The major problem in sociology stems from the failure of most social scientists to consider women to be interesting or important topics. It is primarily women sociologists who have studied women and these sociologists have had less access to influential mentors and tend to be read and cited less than male sociologists. Epstein demonstrates how models can distort perceptions and limit vision and understanding. The early socialization model, for example, which assumes that personality is formed early and changes little, fails to recognize "the striking changes in self-image, self confidence, aspiration, and motivation which seem to result when women experience professional success." Epstein concludes by reconceptualizing the work of selected sociologists that have provided "theoretical rationalizations for a perpetuation of male domination." Talcott Parsons' interpretation of the family as a "pattern maintenance" institution separate from the instrumental arenas of economy and politics, for example, is no more valid than an interpretation of the family as an instrumental institution where the education and training of youth for participate in the culture occurs.

063. Epstein, Cynthia Fuchs. "Women in Sociological Analysis: New Scholarship Versus Old Paradigms." Soundings 64: 149-162 (1981).

Epstein criticizes the theoretical models that have shaped sociology for the last decade for their failures to deal meaningfully with the place of women in society and their production of an image of society quite distant from reality. Sociological methods, she claims, are generally deficient for failing to question gaps in knowledge about any group except the dominant one. She points to socialization theory, political sociology, and stratification theory to illuminate specific examples of the consequences of the omission of women.

064. Farganis, Sondra. "Social Theory and Feminist Theory: The Need for a Dialogue." Sociological Inquiry 56(1): 50-68 (1986).

Farganis argues that the feminist critique of positivism has disregarded, to its disadvantage, the "social and political implications of certain [other] methodological positions, for example, Critical Theory, the Frankfurt School, and the writings of Habermas. Such disregard has resulted in "a dangerous trivialization of hermeneutics, redefining verstehen as simply intuitive understanding," and the tendency to imply that women are biologically more suited to achieving this understanding. Farganis calls for a "reasoned discourse" between feminist and social theory.

065. Gillespie, Dair L. and Ann Leffler. "The Politics of Research Methodology in Claims-Making Activities: Social Science and Sexual Harassment." Social Problems 34(5): 490-501 (1987).

Using sexual harassment as an example, Gillespie and Leffler demonstrate that scientific "methodology always has political undertones, although the presence of 'scientific standards' may obscure them." The process of changing the definition of the personal office romance to organizational sexual harassment constitutes a definitional claim. Advocates of redefinition must validate their claims according to the sampling strategies, operational definitions, measurement instruments, and data analysis techniques of conventional science in order to show that incidence of the problem is widespread rather than rare or isolated, that victims are suffering genuine harm, that the problem is the result of social factors, and that institutional solutions are required. Until claims-makers establish "adequate empirical documentation to support their new definition..., the status quo definition will continue to dominate."

066. Graham, Hilary. "Do Her Answers Fit His Questions? Women and the Survey Method." In The Public and the Private, edited by Eva Garmarnikow, David Morgan, June Purvis, and Daphne Taylorson, pp. 132-146 (London: Heinemann, 1983).

While Graham acknowledges that survey research has been effective in raising social consciousness, she believes that surveys obscure "the self understanding of the female subject." The four principles of the survey method and the problems they create in terms of women respondents are: 1) surveys deal with social units: families or individuals as units lose their social contexts and become excessively individualized by surveys; class, race, or gender become properties of individuals rather than dimensions of social structure; nature and patterns of power relevant to social relationships are masked; 2) individuals can be treated as equivalent units: surveys obscure the fact that individuals and groups of individuals occupy different and unequal positions; the effects of social inequality can be measured through surveys but the method provides no means of understanding causes as well as consequences; 3) units and their outputs have an object form: this principle implies that experiences have existence outside of the individuals who have them and that they can be verbalized; for much of women's experience, however, an adequate language for expression has not existed; and 4) units and their outputs can be measured; the ability to measure is based on "common-sense assumptions" made about everyday lives; since the assumptions tend to arise out of male perspectives that dominate social sciences, measurement may capture the activities and social relationships of men but distort those of women, whose lives have been "hidden from history." Graham warns that the survey method itself may well be a significant source of gender bias.

067. Grant, Linda, Kathryn B. Ward, and Xue Lan Rong. "Is There an Association Between Gender and Methods in Sociological Research?" American Sociological Review 52 (6): 856-862 (1987).

Grant, Ward, and Rong empirically test the assumptions about gender and methods: that female researchers prefer qualitative methods and that qualitative methods are more appropriate than quantitative when gender and women's issues are the subjects of inquiry. They took as their hypotheses: 1) that women scholars are less likely than male scholars to use quantitative methods; 2) that works focusing on gender or women's experiences are less likely than other research to use quantitative methods; and 3) that works focusing on gender written by women are less likely than other works to use quantitative methods. Based on a stratified random sample from a population of 3674 full length articles published in ten major sociological journals between 1974 and 1983, Grant, Ward, and Rong obtained the following results: 1) women were less likely than men, regardless of article topic, to use quantitative methods; 2) the majority of all papers on all topics used quantitative methods; 3) gender articles written by men or by women were more likely to use quantitative than qualitative methods; and 4) author gender and topic have significant effects on the probability that a published article used quantitative methods. Either feminist researchers have been wrong in their assumptions that qualitative methods were more suited to studying gender and women's experiences or research on gender is made more palatable to editors and reviewers when it is conducted using the dominant (quantitative) methodology.

068. Hall, M. Ann. "Knowledge and Gender: Epistemological Questions in the Social Analysis of Sport." In Women and Men: Interdisciplinary Readings on Gender, edited by Greta Hofmann Nemiroff, pp. 80-101 (Markham, Ontario: Fitzhenry & Whiteside, 1987).

Hall says that "the notion of an epistemological standpoint of women" involves abolishing the vertical relationship between researcher and researched. This process of "conscientisation" replaces the view from above by the view from below because the objects of oppression provide the perspective on an oppressive reality. Consciousness raising will be a product of the research process. "Meaningful change for women in sport will come only through a collective feminist consciousness that comprehends the dialectical relationship between knowledge and action."

069. Hall, M. Ann. Sport and Gender: A Feminist Perspective on the Sociology of Sport. Ottawa, Ontaria: Canadian Association for Health, Physical Education and Recreation, 1981.

The entire field of sport sociology is relatively new and of relatively low status within the profession of sociology as a whole, and most of the sport sociologists have been men. Empirical evidence suggests that no conscious effort has been made to discriminate against the study of gender or women in the whole area of sport sociology. It is clear, however, from the existing literature, that the significance and meaning of gender have not been adequately taken into account. Implicit assumptions about how women do and should behave color the research topics and results.

070. Hartung, Beth, Jane C. Ollenburger, Helen A. Moore, and Mary Jo Deegan. "Empowering a Feminist Ethic for Social Science Research: Nebraska Sociological Feminist Collective." In A Feminist Ethic for Social Science Research, edited by the Nebraska Sociological Feminist Collective, pp. 1-22 (Lewiston, New York: Edwin Mellen Press, 1988).

This annotation includes information from the essay cited in entry 70 and from an article by the Nebraska Sociological Feminist Collective ("A Feminist Ethic for Social Science Research," Women's Studies International Forum 6(5): 535-543 (1983)) from which parts of the essay are derived. The Nebraska Sociological Feminist Collective, a group of women concerned with racism, sexism, classism, and heterosexism within sociology, focuses on four issues central to the development of a feminist ethic: 1) wimmin as research objects; 2) research by, for, and about wimmin; 3) language as used and abused in sociology; and 4) the gatekeeping process in employment, funding, and research. Objectivity, says the Collective, "simply masks the objectification of wimmin and all minorities." All research must lead to the empowerment of wimmin outside of the academy or it should not be conducted. "We must not undertake research until and unless we can make guarantees to our informants." Offensive language determines and is determined by offensive theory and research. The language of sociology omits misogyny "as a meaningful sociological concept because it is an intergral part of the sociological paradigm." Use of the passive voice is a way of abdicating responsibility for the ethical concerns of "subjects" and for the ethical underpinning of ideas themselves. Feminists have difficulty passing or becoming the gatekeepers because feminism is viewed as an ideology and therefore not objective. Feminist sociologists must figure out how to bypass gatekeepers, become gatekeepers without becoming oppressive, and design alternatives to the present academic system of power and information control. The article and essay end with specific recommendations for putting a feminist ethic into practice. Unlike traditional social scientists, who "seek knowledge for the advancement and enlightenment of the discipline itself" and who are accountable only to the profession, feminist researchers "analyze social oppression to empower wimmin and minorities...and are accountable to...peers, the wimmin's movement, a feminist ethic, wimmin, and oppressed people."

071. Levy, Judith A. "Gender Bias as a Threat to Construct Validity in Research Design." In A Feminist Ethic for Social Science Research, edited by the Nebraska Sociological Feminist Collective, pp. 139-157 (Lewiston, NY: Edwin Mellen Press, 1988).

Construct validity is the approximate validity with which one can generalize about higher order constructs from research operations. Constructs themselves have no actual existence "except within the theory and imagination of their producers." The terms validity, feminine, and gender are all examples of constructs. Levy believes that gender bias enters into the development of constructs at three points: 1) when specifying the variables that form a construct (for example, Gross National Product excludes household as a measure of a country's productivity); 2) when developing the language used to establish functional relationships (for example, language which "animates" men and "deanimates" women); and 3) during research operations (for example, due to androcentric "experimenter expectancy"). The solution to the male bias in science does not lie in "introducing new constructs which unfairly disadvantage males or contribute to an estrocentric bias." New constructs must be developed with better explanatory and predictive power that incorporate both feminist consciousness and what have been "valuable and valid elements of traditional science."

072. Malseed, Joanna. "Straw Men: A Note on Ann Oakley's Treatment of Textbook Prescriptions for Interviewing." Sociology 21(4): 629-631 (1987).

Malseed quotes from the textbooks criticized by Oakley in her article, "Interviewing Women: A Contradiction in Terms" (see annotation below), to demonstrate that "Oakley's confrontation with the textbooks' prescriptions for interview techniques stems less from the inadequacies of a masculine paradigm of society and more from her inadequate characterisation of the texts." The textbooks describe informal interviewing, which involves a more conversational, less hierarchical, and less pre-determined approach, as appropriate for research into complex, subjective phenomena. Malseed suggests that Oakley's own interviewing techniques fall into the informal category already allowed for by traditional social research textbooks and methodologies.

073. Matthews, Sarah H. "Rethinking Sociology Through a Feminist Perspective." American Sociologist 17(1): 29-35 (1982).

Matthews criticizes feminist critiques of sociological research because they "are rooted in and reinforce the supposed importance of the gender dichotomy." She believes the value of a feminist approach to sociological research lies with the "accumulating evidence that gender is not a good index to understanding the social world." Matthews uses examples to demonstrate the extent to which feminist researchers remain trapped in the notion of gender as fact rather than as social construction. Gender as fact blinds sociologists to non-sexual explanations of behavior and to the lack of relationship between behavior and gender. According to Matthews, for example, single parenthood is a situation that may be descriptive of more women than men but does not belong exclusively to women. Feminism as a political philosophy, she urges, is "ideologically committed to seeing two genders at the same time...and seeks to reduce the degree to which society is overall a gender conscious society." This must be reflected in feminist critiques of sociological research.

074. McNamee, Sheila. Breaking the Patriarchal Vision of Social Science: Lessons from a Family Therapy Model. ERIC Document #ED 292 155 (1987).

McNamee describes the Milan model of systemic family therapy which she believes can be translated into a feminist method for doing research. Using a clinical model for research emphasizes that the distinction between social control and social intervention is arbitrary and, sometimes, counterproductive. The Milan systemic model of family therapy, which is based on the work of Gregory Bateson, focuses on hypothesizing, circular questioning, and neutrality. Hypothesizing relies on pragmatic truth — the belief in selective truths or hypotheses dependent on perspective — instead of classical truth — the belief in one correct story. Circular questioning, also called "gossiping in the presence," involves asking questions that "address a difference or define a relationship as opposed to questions of facts and feelings that require a judgment of difference by (digital) distinction." Answers to circular questions reveal how actions and behaviors are interpreted. Neutrality is the ability to accept everything at face value but reject anything as classical truth. It involves avoiding moral judgment and remaining curious about all views and behaviors. If researchers carry hypothesizing, circular questioning, and neutrality into the design and practice of research, they will avoid seeking out differences that merely confirm their preconceptions and they will be constantly reminded that they are not exempt from intervening in the research process. The systemic model offers an alternative to traditional, postivistic research methods by rejecting the dichotomy between the observer and the observed, embracing subjectivity and plurality of perspective, and focusing on intervention instead of control. Research, practiced according to the systemic model, would facilitate as well as account for change.

075. Millman, Marcia and Rosabeth Moss Kanter. "Editorial Introduction." In Another Voice: Feminist Perspectives on Social Life and Social Science, edited by Marcia Millman and Rosabeth Moss Kanter, vii-xvii (New York: Anchor books, 1975).

In the introduction to their book, Millman and Moss Kanter delineate six types of critiques that emerge in the discussions of research which follow: 1) the use of certain, conventional models have created a blindness to aspects of social reality: many sociological models, for example, do not use the person and her/his subjective experiences as the unit of analysis; sociology has too often emphasized agentic research in which the scientist controls and manipulates reality rather than letting it reveal itself; 2) sociology has focused on public, official, visible, and dramatic role players and events and ignored unofficial, supportive, private, and invisible spheres: because of this focus on the public, women's activities have been distorted and underexamined and the interplay between the informal and interpersonal and the formal and official has not been adequately understood; the genius or exceptional person has been the focus rather than the social structure that allowed the exceptions to occur; 3) sociology has treated men and women as inhabitants of a single world whereas they may actually inhabit different social worlds; 4) sex is often not taken into account as a factor, even in cases where it may be the most important explanatory variable: the way in which the physician's sex affects doctor-patient relations, for example, or the impact of women in a dominant position in the classroom and nowhere else have not been adequately studied; men have suggested a sexless rather than a masculine world and women have been the bearers of sex; 5) sociology has concentrated on explaining the status quo rather than exploring needed transformations; and 6) certain methodologies (often quantitative) and research situations (male scientists studying women) have systematically left important, often the most important, information undiscovered.

076. Neitz, Mary Jo. "Introduction to the Special Issue: Sociology and Feminist Scholarship." American Sociologist 20(1): 3-13 (1989).

In her introduction to a special issue of American Sociologist devoted to feminist research in sociology, Neitz makes the point that "the critical questions for feminist scholarship came out of the women's movement and not out of the disciplines." Early feminist scholars focused on the origins of women's oppression, and offered three different explanations: 1) the economic system; 2) women's roles in reproduction and child care; and 3) a separate sex/gender system. Feminist analysis, which has involved "putting women at the center of empirical analysis and watching to see how that forces a reconceptualization of sociological understandings," has resulted in critiques of traditional research methodologies. Neitz suggests that the past as well as the future needs to be revisioned if sociological theory is to be transformed.

077. Oakley, Ann. "Interviewing Women: A Contradiction in Terms." In Doing Feminist Research, edited by Helen Roberts, pp. 30-61 (London: Routledge & Kegan Paul, 1981).

In the process of conducting the interviews for her research on transition into motherhood, Oakley came to several conclusions concerning feminist interviewing: 1) use of the prescribed, hierarchical interviewing method is morally indefensible; 2) the textbook paradigm for interviewing includes irreconcilable contradictions; and 3) the goal of interviewing is best achieved when the relationship between the interviewer and the interviewee is non-hierarchical and both participants in the relationship invest their personal identities. The textbook paradigm of interviewing stresses that the interviewer is an instrument for data collection but at the same time demands that interviewees be manipulated, usually by a certain degree of inhumane treatment, into providing the needed information. Oakley chose to invest herself personally into the interviews she conducted with pregnant women because she believed the women should not be exploited and that a rule of thumb — "no intimacy without reciprocity" — must be adopted. She also believed that documenting women's own accounts of their transitions to motherhood, rather than documenting only answers to questions she chose to ask, would make a more valuable contribution to sociology and to society. Feminist research requires, Oakley says, that personal involvement be recognized as "more than dangerous bias — it is the condition under which people come to know each other and to admit others into their lives."

078. Oakley, Ann, and Robin Oakley. "Sexism in Official Statistics." In Demystifying Social Statistics, edited by John Irvine, Ian Miles, and Jeff Evans, pp. 172-189 (London: Pluto Press, 1979).

> Oakley and Oakley focus on the sexism inherent in official statistics collected in the United Kingdom. Their perceptions and conclusions, however, apply to statistics in general and suggest that researchers use care in applying statistical analyses and drawing conclusions from statistical results. Oakley and Oakley suggest that sexism can enter into the production of statistics: 1) in the areas chosen for statistical analysis (for example, employment, fertility); 2) in the concepts employed to organize and present the statistics (for example, head of household, family); 3) in the collection of data (for example, the kind of interaction that occurs between the statistics taker and the informant); 4) in the processing of the statistics (for example, the tabulations and breakdowns chosen for analysis); and, 5) in the presentation of the statistics (for example, which sex category is presented first). Statistics, like the discipline of sociology, can be examined for the visibility of women in three different ways. The first way examines the extent to which women are actually represented by statistical analyses. The second way refers to the match between how women are represented and the actual part they play in social life. The third examines the extent to which subject classifications and conceptual systems make sense from the perspective of women's particular situation. Oakley and Oakley use three case studies of head of household statistics, work statistics, and crime statistics to demonstrate their points.

079. Osmond, Marie Withers. "Feminist Research and Scientific Criteria." Journal of Family Issues 5: 571-576 (1984).

> In a commentary on Walker and Thompson's article, "Feminism and Family Studies" (see annotation below), Osmond argues that feminism's most important contribution to research lies with the variety of new research questions it raises and the many methods of explanation it opens. She objects to the duality between feminism and scientific methods that Walker and Thompson emphasize, and claims that, "when traditional methods and concepts do not invoke sexist assumptions," feminist researchers can and do rely on them. Feminist approaches to science "attempt to bridge the two polarities...[of] subjective and objective ways of knowing the world." Feminists are above all not empiricists who treat the world of appearances as if it were the real world. Feminist researchers, rather, try to demonstrate that what appears as reality "really rests upon the existence of conditions that are socially produced." Osmond proposes two broad criteria by which a feminist perspective can be

identified: 1) a research methodology must not limit our understanding of women's experiences; and 2) a research methodology must change the awareness of as many of those concerned with it as possible (for example, researchers, respondents, readers, etc.). Underlying these assumptions, Osmond says, is the "basic assumption that good feminist methodology takes the question of gender seriously," that gender occupies a central place in the research design, analysis, and discussion.

080. Roberts, Helen. "Some of the Boys Won't Play Any More: The Impact of Feminism on Sociology." In Men's Studies Modified: The Impact of Feminism on the Academic Disciplines, edited by Dale Spender, pp. 73-82 (New York: Pergamon Press, 1981).

Roberts takes a broad look at sociology in terms of historical antecendents of the more recent impact of feminism on the discipline, changes within the subject matter of the discipline, and changes in social relations within the profession. She cautions that women can be put back into sociology and still have little impact on the theoretical and methodological core of the discipline. An important place where women have been and continue to be made invisible revolves around categories of analysis, for example, when women are subsumed under studies of the family. Women sociologists must beware of using a language, theories, and methods that exclude women and, therefore, alienate the researchers from their own experiences.

081. Smart, Carol. "Researching Prostitution: Some Problems for Feminist Research." Humanity and Society 8: 407-413 (1984).

Smart uses the example of research on prostitution to demonstrate that "there is no ideal-type of feminist research which will remain true to a unified feminist ethic." Unquestionably, prostitution is a feminist issue as it is the prostitutes themselves who, in addition to being exploited through low wages and physical and sexual violence, "carry the blame and the consequences of prostitution" according to criminal law. With the effects of research in mind, however, prostitution as a topic for study presents some problems for feminism. Research which concentrates on changing the discriminatory laws will not have benefited women if clients as well as prostitutes are criminalised or if criminal laws are lifted altogether. Making prostitution, which supports the oppressive division of women into respectable and unrespectable, a less punitive and, therefore, more attractive alternative, violates long term feminist goals. To avoid the problematic focus on the prostitutes themselves, Smart studied the law and the agents of the law who dispense punishment for soliciting. This upward (rather than sideways toward other women or downward toward the disadvantaged) focus allowed Smart to expose magistrates' moral contempt for prostitutes but only at great personal cost. Oakley's (see annotation above) advice for a more feminist approach to interviewing and Stanley and Wise's (see annotation below) argument that feminist researchers make themselves as vulnerable as those they are researching were of little use to Smart in her interactions with respondents more powerful than herself. She feared that " in giving magistrates the opportunity to vent their sexist views unchallenged, [she] was condoning and perhaps reinforcing the ideological oppression of women." Smart suggests that feminist research methodologies have so far been based on the assumption that feminists will study only women or, at least, the stigmatized and relatively powerless groups in society. Such methodologies, as Smart's research with magistrates demonstrates, may not "adequately address the mechanisms of power most frequently (although not exclusively) exercised by men."

082. Smart, Carol. Women, Crime, and Criminology: A Feminist Critique. London: Routledge & Kegan Paul, 1977.

Women do constitute a topic in the research on criminology, according to Smart, but the quality of the work "leaves much to be desired." Studies which make explicit reference to female criminality assume a "natural" distinction between men and women criminals or ascribe female criminal acts to physiological causes. Studies which make implicit reference to female criminality tend to cataegorize women criminals with children and lunatics. In the literature of criminology, women as mothers or wives are often believed to be the behind-the-scenes cause of crime but the feelings and actions of the children and husbands are the focus of research. Studies of men sent to prison have investigated the emotional cost to the men of being separated from their families but no studies have been done on the emotional costs to the wives and children the imprisonment left behind. Women are invisible as victims as well as actors in the criminological literature. Battered wives and women seeking abortions, just like prostitutes and rape victims, should be studied as victims of individuals, organizations, or the law. Policies and practices in penal or local authority institutions need to be studied as they tend to reinforce a connection between independence, feminism, and crime. A feminist perspective would produce a criminology free from the traditional emphasis on social policy and control.

083. Smith, Dorothy E. "Institutional Ethnography: A Feminist Method." Resources for Feminist Research 15(1): 6-12 (1986).

Institutional ethnography as defined by Smith involves the discovery of objectively existing social processes by starting with individual women's lived experiences. The goal is a sociology "which provides for subjects means of grasping the social relations organizing the worlds of their experience," a sociology which offers a way, through moving out from the personal toward the political, of understanding institutional forces that affect individual lives. Smith says that institutional ethnography resembles consciousness raising because both the researcher and "those who want to understand the social matrices of their experience" learn from the research, and "objective correlates" are developed of what previously appeared to be "private experience of oppression." To illustrate the way institutional ethnography might be applied, Smith uses the example of a single parent mother articulating with the educational system. Starting with the assumption that the work a mother does determines the character of a classroom and thus the nature of the teacher's work, produces a different understanding for the single mother than the assumption that the irregularity of single parent households creates problems for children at school. Inquiry like institutional ethnography is open-ended. Smith compares it to making a piece of a quilt "which remains to be attached to the other pieces in the creation of the whole pattern."

084. Smith, Dorothy E. "A Peculiar Eclipsing: Women's Exclusion from Man's Culture." Women's Studies International Quarterly 1: 281-295 (1978).

Culture does not arise spontaneously but rather is manufactured by those in positions of dominance. Since men have manufactured culture, the means which women have available to them "to think, image, and make actionable their experience have been made for [them] and not by [them]." One of the most significant forms in which women's silence and exclusion has been practiced is through ordinary social organizational processes like socialization, education, work, and communication. Women have learned to live "inside a discourse which is not [theirs] and which expresses and describes a landscape in which [they] are alienated and which preserves that alienation as integral to its practice." Women have learned to view and describe themselves as other. To create different sorts of landscape and discourse "involves taking up the standpoint of women as an experience of being...which must be given form and expression in the culture as...knowledge, art, literature, or politically."

085. Smith, Dorothy E. "A Sociology for Women." In The Prism of Sex: Essays in the Sociology of Knowledge, edited by Julia A. Sherman and Evelyn Torton Beck, pp. 135-188 (Madison, Wisconsin: University of Wisconsin Press, 1979).

Womens' experiences have been separated from the social forms of thought available in which to express experience and make it actionable. Women as sociologists have worked "inside a discourse they did not have a part in making." Women could only appear as objects in relation to a sociological frame that was defined around the experiences of men. Smith suggests that sociological method be turned on its head by taking the everyday world as problematic. Rather than explaining behavior in relation to a predetermined set of concepts, theories, and definitions, sociology must begin from where people are in the world. According to this model, a sociological subject could be anyone "who is always located just as she or he is actually located in a particular material setting."

086. Smith, Dorothy E. "Women's Perspective as a Radical Critique of Sociology." Sociological Inquiry 44 (1): 7-13 (1974).

In a world where men govern, in the broad sense of the term meaning manage, administer, and create reality, women are alienated from their experience. Work, including sociological work and research, is based on objectivity, the separation of the knower from the known. Objectivity is predicated on the ability of the knower to separate himself not only from the subjects of his study but also from his own subjectively lived experience. Such a separation requires that his concrete and particular needs from the world of experience be taken care of. Women have been expected to "mediate for men the relation between the conceptual mode of action and actual...material conditions upon which it depends." Women who work, who practice sociology, are aware of the "chasm" separating the theories, concepts, and methods of the discipline from their own daily experience of the world. Smith says that women are "native speakers of this situation...and have that relation to it of knowing it before it has been said." Sociology must begin from the world as we actually experience it and take into account how this world is related to worlds which others experience from very different perspectives. It should be a means to anyone of understanding "how the world comes about for her and how it is organized..." rather than a privileged science that "has already discredited and deprived of the authority to speak, the voices of those who know the society differently."

087. Snyder, Eloise C. "The Selective Eye of Sociology." In The Study of Women: Enlarging Perspectives of Social Reality, edited by Eloise C. Snyder, pp. 39-78 (New York: Harper & Row, 1979).

Snyder takes a global look at sociology, examining "how well women fare" in the discipline. She first describes sociology as a male science of a male society in which the content has been weighted toward male interests and values. Such sociology typifies society, she says, only if women and other social minorities are excluded. With regard to methodology, Snyder points out that male behaviors have served as the standard against which female behaviors have been measured and sex differences have been exaggerated and attributed to biology rather than socialization. She compares sociology to language in that both reflect the sexist society in which they exist and both reinforce and perpetuate sexism by the form they have taken. Sociology has too often confused the descriptive with the prescriptive by purporting to describe, for example, marriage, while actually defining how marriage ought to be to perpetuate the status quo. Snyder is not seeking to replace the biased male perspective with a female one; she is, rather, trying to remove distortions by seeing that all perspectives are included. Using theories of society, social institutions, the sociology of deviant behavior, the sociology of minority groups, and social stratification as examples, Snyder demonstrates how women and their points of view have been ignored or misinterpreted by the selective eye of sociology.

088. Sprague, Joey and Mary K. Zimmerman. "Quality and Quantity: Reconstructing Feminist Methodology." American Sociologist 20(1): 71-86 (1989).

"In an ironical adoption of the very dualism [they] seek to avoid," say Sprague and Zimmerman, feminists have opposed qualitative and quantitative methods to one another, and have set forth the former as the only appropriate and prototypical methods for feminist research in the social sciences. They argue convincingly that both qualitative (including the new, critical qualitative methods) and quantitative methods tend to isolate facts from their contexts, to result in biased and selective observations, and to depend on the researchers' dominance over the respondents (see also Stacey (1989) below). Feminists have associated the quantitative with abstraction, which they have rejected as the transformation and, therefore, the distortion of reality. Sprague and Zimmerman claim that abstraction is essential because it provides an understanding of the relationship between choices at the social level and those at the individual level, because it makes it possible to understand the dynamics of a process, and because it is integral to the consciousness raising tool whereby individuals comprehend politics at a personal level. Since no single method can provide the satisfactory answer to any research question, Sprague and Zimmerman advise feminists to engage in collaborative research. Discussions of real world implications and relevance are necessary during the generation of the problem, the development of measures, and the analysis of the findings. Research must be reported in language that can be understood by any concerned, thinking individual. By rejecting quantitative methods out of hand, rather than attempting to transform them, feminist sociologists have restricted themselves to the periphery of their discipline and failed to alter its core (see also Stacey and Thorne (1985) below).

089. Stacey, Judith. "Can there be a feminist ethnography?" Women's Studies International Forum 11(1): 21-27 (1988).

Stacey's paper answers the question its title asks: there cannot be a fully feminist ethnography, she says, but there can be "accounts of culture enhanced by the application of feminist perspectives." Stacey undertook ethnographic research — research involving intensive participant observation — with optimism. Ethnography as a method resembles feminist methodology: it rejects the separations between researcher and respondent and between thought and feeling, and emphasizes lived experience and interactivity. However, once involved in the research, Stacey found herself faced with uncomfortable contradictions. "Precisely because ethnographic research depends upon the human relationship, engagement, and attachment, it places research subjects at grave risk of manipulation and betrayal [and desertion]...the lives, loves, and tragedies that fieldwork informants share with a researcher are ultimately data..." Ironically, Stacey points out, the ethnographic method "exposes subjects to far greater danger and exploitation than do more positivist, abstract, and "masculinist" research methods. In spite of the contradictions between feminist principles and ethnographic research, Stacey recommends the method for use with "rigorous self-awareness of the pitfalls." Less dangerous but more remote research methods cannot achieve the same "contextuality, depth, and nuance" essential to cultural accounts.

090. Stacey, Judith and Barrie Thorne. "The Missing Feminist Revolution in Sociology." Social Problems 32(4): 301-316 (1985).

Stacey and Thorne believe that feminism has affected sociology less thoroughly than it has affected history, literature, and anthropology. While feminists in sociology have succeeded in identifying and filling many gaps in sociological research, feminist research methodologies have been co-opted and ghettoized, leaving the dominant sociological paradigms relatively unchanged. Traditional history and literature had been so completely male-defined that the act of starting with women's experiences in either field had a profound effect on core theoretical assumptions. In neither discipline, however, has feminism managed to influence mainstream work in significant ways. Feminism has transformed core theoretical assumptions in anthropology and these transformations have achieved acceptance by mainstream scholars. Stacey and Thorne attribute the transformation of anthropology to the fact that more women have always been prominent in anthropology than in most other disciplines and that gender has always been central to anthropological inquiry. Feminism has been contained within sociology partly because "the subject matter of traditional sociology was neither totally male-centered nor basically gender-sensitive...." In addition, sociology has been fragmented as a discipline since the 1960s when functionalism was undermined as the dominant paradigm. Feminist transformations will need, therefore, to be multiple and diverse. Functionalism, with its emphasis on sex roles, focuses on individuals rather than social structure and continues to influence sociological analysis. Disciplines with strong traditions of interpretive understanding, such as history, anthropology, and literature, seem to be more easily influenced by feminism while those anchored in positivist epistemology, such as sociology, psychology, political science, and economics, have offered more resistance.

091. Stanley, Liz, and Sue Wise. "Back into 'the Personal,' or Our Attempt to Construct 'Feminist Research.'" In Theories of Women's Studies II, edited by Gloria Bowles and Renate Duelli-Klein, pp. 98-118. (Berkeley, California: Women's Studies Program, 1981).

Stanley and Wise object, like many other feminist researchers, to the positivist belief in a "reality" that can be discovered and in the subject/object dichotomy which supports a power relationship between the researcher and the researched. To a greater extent than many feminist researchers, they believe that the personal — women's, including women as researchers, experiences of their everyday lives — is basic to understanding women's oppression. Any account of feminist research must include, as a central component, a description of the process of the research, an explication of how/why the researchers came to know what they know. Researchers must make themselves vulnerable by sharing the reasoning procedures which underlie the knowledge they produce. Stanley and Wise draw from symbolic interactionism and ethnomethodology to applaud knowledge grounded in lived experience and oppose "de-corticated theory," by which they mean theory based on general principles arrived at independently of any detailed examination of the facts to be explained.

092. Tiefer, Leonore. "A Feminist Perspective on Sexology and Sexuality." In Feminist Thought and the Structure of Knowledge, edited by Mary McCanney Gergen, pp. 16-26 (New York: New York University Press, 1988).

Sexology, the study of human sexualities, has been based on an essentialist model, which views sexuality as something humans and animals have and do in accordance with biology, hormones, and brain-behavior relationships. A feminist critique of sexology would be anti-essentialist, rejecting the notion of sexuality as instinct or biological imperative in favor of sexuality as a social construction. Feminist research, Tiefer says, needs to begin with sexuality in the domain of interpersonal relations rather than in the medical domain of individualized response. Participants' subjective perceptions need to enrich objective measurement and the contextual aspects — the social, demographic, and cultural features — of their lives need to be taken into account. Feminist sexology would study sexualities and "looking for ways that all women are alike would play no part."

093. Walker, Alexis J., and Linda Thompson. "Feminism and Family Studies." Journal of Family Issues 5(4): 545-570 (1984).

Walker and Thompson list the following as characteristics of feminist family studies: 1) researchers will be overt about their ideologies rather than act as if research is objective; 2) researchers will acknowledge the role of the larger society in marriage and family relationships; 3) researchers will take gender and position into account as categories of analysis, exhibiting sensitivity to the similarities as well as the differences between genders; 4) researchers will reflect the diversity of individuals rather than form conclusions based on the groups to which individuals belong; 5) researchers will acknowledge complexity (i.e., dualities and contradictions, meaning and context) rather than assume linear processes and internal validity; 6) research will be communal rather than agentic and aim to improve the lives of women; 7) research will attempt to avoid the white, middle class, male bias; 8) research will avoid exploitation and strive to empower all individuals involved; 9) researchers will include the personal experiences of the researcher and the respondents as data; and 10) research will focus on issues and problems of importance to women. To evaluate the progress of feminism in family studies, Walker and Thompson analyzed the content of a sample of articles from the Journal of Marriage and the Family over the last 20 years. They selected randomly eight articles from each of the five years, 1963, 1968, 1973, 1978, and 1983, and coded them according to six dimensions of feminist approach: 1) consideration of the sex/gender system; 2) gender and/or position as category of analysis; 3) attention to complexity and patterning; 3) reduced control of data gathering; 4) inclusion of individual experience; 5) close relationship between participant and investigator; and 6) gender of first author. The year 1978 was a peak year for feminist conceptualization and content in family studies. Across years, only about ten percent of the articles in the Journal of Marriage and the Family rated as feminist according to the coding scheme. The gender of the first author was not related to feminist ratings in substance or methodology.

094. Ward, Kathryn B. and Linda Grant. "The Feminist Critique and a Decade of Published Research in Sociology Journals." Sociological Quarterly 26(2): 139-157 (1985).

Ward and Grant examined all full-length articles published in all issues of ten major sociological journals for the years 1974-1983 to determine if the feminist critiques of sociological research written in the early to mid-1970s had had a fundamental or merely ephemeral effect on research topics and practices. The effects for which they searched were related to four major themes consistent throughout the feminist critiques: 1) omission and underrepresentation of women as subjects; 2) concentration on topics more central to men's than women's lives; 3) use of paradigms, concepts, models, and methods which distort women's experiences; and 4) use of male experiences as the norm. While Ward and Grant saw evidence that previously ignored areas of the female world have been studied and that non-sexist language, concepts, data collection and analysis techniques, and theories are more frequently being used, they conclude that "making inroads is not the same as establishing footholds." They found evidence that the most radical articles were being ghettoized, i.e., being ignored in future research. They also found a disturbingly high percentage of single-gender studies still being published. Their study suggested "an association between women's participation in the journals' publication processes and the quantity" and character of gender-related articles. Ward and Grant conclude that they "are not yet convinced that the mid-1970s critiques have had a forceful enough impact within mainstream sociology to ensure gender equity in published articles if women are not active in the publication process."

4

ANTHROPOLOGY

INTRODUCTION

Feminist anthropologists began their assault on traditional methodology with an advantage because anthropology has always concerned itself with "tackling hitherto unquestioned assumptions about sex and gender." (Atkinson, 1982) But the feminists attempting to change mainstream anthropology want to do more than simply tackle another set of assumptions. According to Shapiro (1981), they want to make it "as impossible for social scientists to avoid dealing with gender in their studies of social differentiation as it is for them to avoid dealing with...rank, class, and kinship." A feminist approach to anthropology means not the study of women but the study of gender.

Feminist anthropology approaches sex roles and gender as historical and societal creations rather than as reflections of biological or sexual natures (Atkinson, 1982). This hard won approach has required feminist scholars to do battle with two influential and tenacious myths: that woman is to man as nature is to culture, and that males are universally dominant.

Women, Culture and Society, edited by Michelle Rosaldo and Louise Lamphere (Stanford, California: Stanford University Press, 1974), inaugurated what Lamphere (1987) calls the first phase of feminist anthropology when it gatherered together several essays that examined "universal sexual asymmetry." In her contribution to the volume, Ortner (1974) argues that the "pan-cultural fact" of women's secondary status results from the association of women with nature. Women's involvement with procreation and species perpetuation ties them to the natural world, leaving men free to develop higher order culture. Rosaldo (1974) explains universal male dominance by what she calls a structural opposition between the domestic and public domains of activity. Women's preoccupation with giving birth and raising children confines them to the domestic sphere while men, lacking any such preoccupation, involve themselves in institutions, policy, and professions.

In its subsequent phases, the feminist critique of anthropology rejected not so much explanations like Ortner's and Rosaldo's but rather the whole idea of universal male dominance. MacCormack (1981) cautions Western anthropologists, feminist and non-feminist alike, to avoid imposing on non-Western societies their own associations of male with culture and female with nature. While the notion of a "universal sisterhood of womankind immediately recognizable across class, cultural, and ethnic boundaries" is politically appealing (Scheper-Hughes, 1983), it is biologically damaging in that it rests on the assumption that "woman's place in human social life is...in a direct sense a product of the things she does (or...what biologically, she is)." (Rosaldo, 1980) Carey (1987) advises that in each society in which women's and men's roles appear rigidly defined and divided, an anthropologist must try to understand the specific system of beliefs and attitudes that holds the roles in place.

Rogers (1978) believes that, cross-culturally, the most common pattern of sex differentiation involves both ideological and behavioral distinctions. When the two sexes differ in terms of ideology and behavior, they will be opposed but will be mutually dependent, creating a balance of power. Western colonization has tended to emphasize behavioral over ideological distinctions by giving males more access to resources and thus destroying the balance of power. Patterns of male dominance seen in aboriginal societies can often be attributed to Western practices and attitudes resulting from colonization and modernization (Quinn, 1977). Historical approaches, tracing how far back dichotomies like the domestic and the public extend and tying such separations to modernization where appropriate, can help distinguish universal from colonially imposed patterns (Nicholson, 1982).

It is not only the effects of colonization and modernization that anthropologists' cross-cultural comparisons have failed to take into account. Ardener (1975) first pointed out the bias that the overwhelming presence of male anthropologists, ethnographers, and informants has on the information recorded and conveyed about cultural dynamics. Golde (1970) and Reiter (1975) both produced collections of the writings of women ethnographers. Golde's collection reveals ways in which "the characteristics of the ethnographer may indirectly and inadvertently affect the process of research." Reiter's more explicitly feminist volume aims at correcting the "double male bias [male anthropologists interviewing only male informants] which has trivalized and misinterpreted female roles for so long."

Ethnographers, handicapped by male-defined frameworks, have gathered data in ways guaranteed to corroborate their own cultural distinctions between "insignificant" female domains, such as socialization and household economy, and "important" male domains, such as politics and law (Scheper-Hughes, 1983). But feminists move beyond explaining sexual asymmetry with seemingly universal dichotomies of behavior or ideology and focus instead on the limited anthropological vision.

Feminists have demonstrated the subjectivity of ethnographic observation and have called for increased ethical responsibility. Christman (1988) questions the ethics of using "a woman's [intimate] words about her life" to construct a research argument. Finch (1984) cautions researchers to anticipate whether information about respondents' lives could ultimately be used in ways counterproductive to women's best interests (see also Stacey, 1988, in the Sociology chapter).

In addition, Slocum's (1975) theory of Woman the Gatherer — an alternative to the traditional, aggression-dominated Man the Hunter view of evolution — calls anthropological ethics and objectivity into question. She interprets the female-infant bond as the source of organization and communication skills, and gathering as the source of tool development. Following Slocum's lead, feminist anthropologists have revised other male interpretations. For example, women's tasks in society have traditionally been viewed as secondary to the demands of child care. Feminists have shown quite the opposite: child-spacing and child-tending have been accomodated to other important tasks that women perform (Stack, et al., 1975).

Sexist errors in interpretation also have created what Conkey and Spector (1984) call a "presentist" approach to archeology. The linking, without sufficient supporting data, of certain activities and artifacts with males, and detailed descriptions of male activities compared to vague references to female ones have led archeologists to impose contemporary gender dynamics on past cultures. Fieldwork in general has been viewed as a masculine pursuit, a bias which Gero (1988) points out may now be to women's advantage. At a time when museum collections begin to outnumber remaining archeological sites, women already accustomed to analyzing, sorting, and preparing archeological materials, may be in the best position to move research forward.

Feminist scholars in other disciplines praise anthropology for the degree to which it has been open to and influenced by feminist theories and methods. Stacey and Thorne (1985, see annotation in Sociology chapter) claim that feminism has transformed the core theoretical assumptions in anthropology. Langland and Gove ("Editors' Notes," In A Feminist Perspective in the Academy: The Difference It Makes, Chicago: University of Chicago Press, 1981) laud anthropology for its responsiveness to the conceptual shifts demanded by feminism. Feminist anthropologists themselves, however, remain cautious and disagree about the extent of their discipline's openness and of their own influence.

MacCormack's (1981) descriptions of the contributions of several early women anthropologists illustrate the extent to which anthropology has been more welcoming to women researchers than many disciplines. Atkinson (1982) stresses the focus on gender that feminism and anthropology have in common. Moore (1988) considers the feminist critique central to anthropology's theoretical and methodological developments. Strathern (1987), on the other hand, views feminism as just one of many theoretical viewpoints. Because feminism is interdisciplinary, working across disciplines rather than parallel to them, it cannot, Strathern says, achieve paradigm shifts. Radicalisms, such as feminism, she claims, abound within social anthropology. Sanday (1988) warns feminist anthropologists engaged in the process of "myth making for change" to beware of burying the subjects of their study under their own political concerns.

Lamphere (1987) credits feminism with transforming the thinking of many (mostly female) anthropologists and of creating the subfield of gender studies. However, she says, feminism has had little effect on introductory textbooks or on how general anthropology is taught. She believes that feminism has as much to learn from anthropology as it has to teach. Through an awareness of anthropology, feminists can learn to avoid the dangers of universalizing and concentrate on the development of more complex theories that take into account differences as well as similarities.

ANNOTATIONS

095. Ardener, Edwin. "Belief and the Problem of Women" and "The Problem Revisited." In Perceiving Women, edited by Shirley Ardener, pp. 1-27 (London: Malaby Press, 1975).

> In the paper, "Belief and the Problem of Women," which he first wrote and presented in 1968, Ardener criticizes methods of social anthropology that have "purported to crack the code of a vast range of societies, without any reference to the female group." He compares the treatment of women in fieldnotes to Nuer's cows — they were observed but did not speak. Because of the greater degree to which men are involved in the political aspects of society and are more accustomed to dealing with strangers and foreigners, they are more likely to be the ones with whom ethnographers converse. Aside from, or in addition to this technical aspect of dealing with the two sexes, ethnography seems biased towards the kinds of models men are ready to provide. Ardener suggests this is because men "consistently tend...to give a bounded model of society" while women "do not so readily see society bounded from nature." Women are muted by male dominance which blocks their actualization. According to Ardener, women anthropologists, perhaps because they are limited "by the 'maleness' of their subject," and perhaps because they sense that its

consideration would "split apart the very framework in which they conduct their studies," appear to be reluctant to deal with the problem of women.

096. Atkinson, Jane Monnig. "Review Essay: Anthropology." Signs 8(2):236-258 (1982).

Atkinson's review identifies major feminist trends in social and anthropological work and evaluates the impact of feminist theory on the writing of ethnography. Outstanding trends Atkinson identifies include: 1) the assertion that sex roles and gender concepts are products of history and society not a reflection of inherent human sexual natures; 2) a strong commitment to historical analysis; 3) a strong commitment to comparative study; and 4) a concern with interplay among situation, context, and meaning that reveals "the complexities of cultural experience pertaining to gender." Atkinson says that, when feminist anthropology "begins to shape significantly the ethnographies we write," it will have reached maturity. Cultural ethnographies must avoid the tendency to force the anthropologist's cultural stereotypes of gender constructs (for example, passive, active, victim, agent) onto the culture being observed. Gender constructs must be understood in the context of the culture in which they occur. "Given criticisms of androcentric analyses," feminists must beware of failing to relate claims about women to the "wider context of female-male relations." Feminist anthropologists must establish gendered analysis as "not merely a supplement but a sine qua non of social inquiry." The split between "analyses of women's personal lives...and male dominated social structure and ideology" must be replaced by feminist ethnographic work. Atkinson believes that "feminism and anthropology have taken well to each other" because they both focus on "tackling hitherto unquestioned assumptions about sex and gender."

097. Carey, Colleen Ballerino. The Anthropology of Women: An Advocacy Position. ERIC Document #ED 156 543 (1987).

The central questions raised by an anthropology of women relate to male "anthropological bias and perpetuation of the ideology of social inequality." At its worst, androcentric anthropology results from a "male anthropologist looking at male-dominated institutions through the eyes of a male informant and assuming his results to be representative of the entire fabric of social reality." The discovery of cross-cultural sexual stratification must neither be universalized nor singularized. In the case of each society in which stratification seems to appear, an anthropologist must seek to understand "the specificity of the role of ideology in a social situation, thereby explicating not only its action upon and relation to women but also its profound and determined action in the broader context of [the] society in general."

098. Christman, Jolley Bruce. "Working in the Field as the Female Friend." Anthropology and Education Quarterly 19(2):70-85 (1988).

In writing her dissertation on returning women graduate students while a returning woman graduate student herself, Christman conducted interviews and observations with twelve other students. Her article, by describing how her personal reactions and experiences influenced and enriched the course of the research, argues for a feminist approach to ethnography in which the researcher claims no scientific detachment but rather accepts responsibility as an actor in the research process. She also raises the ethical concerns that become pronounced when respondents share the intimacies of their lives. Christman's "greatest source of conflict revolved around using a woman's words about her life to construct" a dissertation argument. The findings of her study of returning women graduate students, Christman said, represent what could be learned by a returning woman graduate student trained in ethnography about her own group.

099. Conkey, Margaret W. and Janet D. Spector. "Archaeology and the Study of Gender." Advances in Archaeological Method and Theory 7:1-38 (1984).

Conkey and Spector review archeological literature to demonstrate that archeology has imposed present-day, culture-specific beliefs about the meaning of masculine and feminine and the power and roles of men and women upon reconstructions of the past. This "presentist" approach to the past allows archeologists to emphasize continuities in evolution and behavior and to assume that contemporary gender dynamics are preordained through evolutionary processes. Interpretive biases commonly found in archaeological literature include: 1) persistent and consistent linkage of certain activities and artifacts (for example, projectile points with males and bowls with females) with each sex without any supporting data to justify the links; 2) detailed descriptions of male activities compared with vague, passive recountings of female tasks; and, 3) explanations that view males as the makers and females as the users of the same tools found in burial contexts. Ethnoarcheological approaches to gender are promising if they are based on "a theory of social life that explicitly acknowledges the parameters and variations in gender arrangements, the possible material manifestations of those arrangements, and above all the ways in which material culture...actively structures not only gender arrangements but many other sociocultural phenomena." Conkey and Spector propose a task-differentiation framework, which focuses on the social and spatial dimensions of male and female activity patterns, and they insist that archeologists must "understand gender dynamics...if we are to continue to pursue the research objectives we have set for ourselves...."

100. Finch, Janet. "'It's Great to Have Someone to Talk to': The Ethics and Politics of Interviewing Women." In Social Researching: Politics, Problems, and Practice, edited by Colin Bell and Helen Roberts, pp. 70-87 (London: Routledge & Kegan Paul, 1984).

Finch uses the example of two research projects she conducted with clergy wives and with working class women running and using preschool playgroups to demonstrate the moral problems that arise when women researchers interview women respondents. She found that using a non-hierarchical, relatively unstructured interviewing technique resulted in an amazing amount of comfort and disclosure from the women interviewees. The fact that Finch herself was a woman, and therefore, powerless in similar ways to the women she interviewed, combined with the facts that the interviews were conducted in the interviewees' homes and that housewives are relatively isolated and lonely contributed to the extent to which the women Finch interviewed were willing to make themselves vulnerable. Finch learned by experience that disclosures on her part that allowed the interviewees to "place" her resulted in more comfort and more disclosures. The ease with which Finch was able to obtain extremely confidential information from the women she interviewed made her apprehensive about the degree to which such information could end up being used in ways that were not in women's collective best interests. While a feminist researcher herself may not expose individuals to whom she has guaranteed confidence or misuse their information, it is difficult for any researcher to control or predict ways in which her research findings may be used. Finch warns that the researcer "who produces work about women...has a special responsbility to anticipate whether it could be interpreted and used in ways quite different from her own intentions." (See also Christman above and Stacey (1988) in the Sociology chapter).

101. Friedl, Ernestine. Women and Men: An Anthropologist's View. New York: Holt, Rinehart and Winston, 1975.

Friedl is "convinced that the best tactic for understanding what flexibility exists as well as what has been constant throughout our known history in the role of the sexes is to be found rather in an examination of diversity than in a concentration upon similarities." Just a listing of the variety of roles taken by men and women in different cultures will not be sufficient, however; it is necessary to know "under what social, cultural, and physical environmental conditions variations in sex roles exist and what limits there are on diversity." In her book, Friedl describes the variety of roles available to men and women in hunter and gatherer and in horticulturalist societies, suggests hypotheses for the causes of these roles, and examines the dominance of the sexes in a variety of contexts. Her descriptions and analyses revolve around "five basic propositions:" 1) the types of energy used to procure food have crucial consequences for the sexual division of labor, the allocation of power and recognition between men and women, and the quality of the relationship between the sexes; 2) the spacing of children and the patterns of child-rearing are adjusted to the kind of work women customarily do rather the other way around; 3) power and prestige are gained in all societies by those who have the right to distribute and exchange valued goods and services; 4) the roles men and women play in special events influences the overall relationships between the sexes and their respective power and prestige; and 5) attitudes toward sex and the actual social relations between men and women are expressed in symbol and ritual. Friedl draws parallels between hunter gatherer and horticulturalist societies and modern industrialized cultures with respect to these five propositions.

102. Gero, Joan M. "Gender Bias in Archeology: Here, Then and Now." In Feminism Within the Science & Health Care Professions: Overcoming Resistance, edited by Sue V. Rosser, pp. 33-43 (Oxford: Pergamon Press, 1988).

Gero relates the exclusion of women from "productive processes in the archeological enterprise" to the ways in which "unexamined assumptions about gender" have affected interpretations of the past. She points to the asymmetry in the amount of attention given to female and male activities and the different language in which male and female activities have been described (see Conkey and Spector above) to illustrate why the "very basis of human existence now rests on reconstructions of a strict sexual division of labor that is extended back to a proto-human era." Archeologists behave according to the "same ideology that is adopted to explain the past." Fieldwork has been defined as an inherently male undertaking while analyzing, sorting, and preparing archeological materials for museum presentation has been left to women. Gero examines publications, funding records, and professional affiliation records to document the disproportionate amount of support that males receive for pursuing fieldwork. She advises women archeologists not to strive for validation via fieldwork at a time when museum collections are coming to outnumber remaining archeological sites. Women, already accustomed to the "analytic ghetto," may well be in the best position to "spearhead" this "more insightful, less costly, and longer-sighted route to understanding the human past," providing the guidance and the opportunities for archeology to mature into the social science it claims to be.

103. Golde, Peggy. "Introduction." In Women in the Field: Anthropological Experiences, edited by Peggy Golde, pp. 1-18 (Chicago: Aldine Publishing Company, 1970).

Women in the Field is a precursor to feminist critiques of anthropological research and ethnographic methods. Golde's intent in collecting the field experiences of twelve female anthropologists was to "portray the subjective impact of moving into a new culture, presenting an individual sightline on a unique experience...[and to] illuminate the recurring problems, choices, and solutions that are common to the encounter between the woman as a stranger and a foreign culture." Not only does Golde suggest that the essays in her collection be used as an "ethnography of ethnographers," she also hopes they will reveal the ways in which "the characteristics of the ethnographer may indirectly and inadvertently affect the process of research." Her honest appraisal of the subjectivity of ethnography laid the foundation for the feminist critiques of male bias in what had previously been considered objective ethnographic classics.

104. Lamphere, Louise. "Feminism and Anthropology: The Stuggle to Reshape Our Thinking About Gender." In The Impact of Feminist Research in the Academy, edited by Christie Farnham, pp. 11-33 (Bloomington, Indiana: Indiana University Press, 1987).

Lamphere reviews more than a decade of feminist research and writing in anthropology to conclude that "feminism has certainly transformed the thinking of a number of anthropologists (largely women), and gender studies is a thriving subfield within the discipline." Feminism cannot claim, however, "to be solely responsible for the transformation of other subfields like kinship and politics..." and it has not substantially changed the information in introductory textbooks or the way general anthropology is taught. According to Lamphere, the feminist approach to anthropology occurred in three phases. The collection of essays in Women, Culture, and Society (see Rosaldo, 1974 and Ortner below) inaugurated the first phase by posing the issue of "universal sexual asymmetry" for and against which arguments were made. Other first phase themes included Sally Slocum's (see annotation below)

"Woman the Gatherer" challenge to the evolutionary thesis of "Man the Hunter" and a general critique of male bias in anthropology. The development of "frameworks for looking at diverse women's roles within a particular society and for comparing societies with one another in a more complex way" characterized the second phase. During the third phase, feminists have concentrated on critical self-evaluation in which "the conceptual tools used in early feminist analyses have come under attack." Lamphere believes that anthropology has much to teach feminism about the danger of universalizing and the necessity for developing complex theories that take differences and not just similarities into account. The anthropological project — and, by implication the feminist project — is "the 'tacking back and forth' between one culture or social structure and our own, attempting to make sense of another way of life using our own language and concepts — but stretching them to better make the translation."

105. Lamphere, Louise. "Review Essay: Anthropology." Signs 2(3):612-627 (1977).

In her review of the anthropological literature emphasizing women's roles, Lamphere focuses on four trends: 1) a clarification of positions related to a belief in women's universal subordination versus the existence of sexual equality in some societies; 2) the search for appropriate cross-cultural frameworks through which to analyze sex roles and women's status; 3) an interdisciplinary approach to regional studies of women's roles; and 4) an awareness of the need to understand, in the case of both historical and comtemporary women and families, the impact of changes such as modernization, development, migration, and colonialism. Lamphere uses most of her article to criticize the literature related to the subordination versus equality debate. She believes that "the possibility that inequality lies in the division of labor and the marital relationship created through exchange" needs to be tested.

106. MacCormack, Carol P. "Anthropology: A Discipline with a Legacy." In Men's Studies Modified: The Impact of Feminism on the Academic Disciplines, edited by Dale Spender, pp. 99-110 (Oxford, Pergamon Press, 1981).

MacCormack describes the contributions of several early women anthropologists (for example, Matilda Cox Stevenson, Elsie Clews Parsons, Ruth Benedict) to illustrate her statement that anthropology "has been relatively welcoming to women researchers from its beginning as a discipline." She attributes this welcoming atmosphere to anthropology's "focus on every-day life in integrated whole societies that unquestionably include women and children." In spite of the presence of women researchers, however, and of the presence of women and children in societies, many functionalist case studies have revolved around the "thoughts and acts of politically elite males only" and a male bias in general has characterized the anthropological literature. The women's movement has resulted in the collection of new field data on gender roles and a reassessment of "the models used to generate hypotheses and analyze data." The debate about universal male dominance continues to revolve around issues concerning how dominance is defined and how women's more covert influence should be taken into account. MacCormack cautions that the Western association of male with culture and female with nature should not be "imposed upon the whole world as a universal structuralist explanation of gender roles."

107. MacCormack, Carol P. and Marilyn Strathern, eds. Nature, Culture and Gender. Cambridge: Cambridge University Press, 1980.

MacCormack and Strathern invited contributors to Nature, Culture and Gender "to reflect upon the manner in which anthropologists especially have used the concepts of nature and culture in the exegesis of other people's gender symbolism." The need for the volume, which appears to "go over again ground long traversed by other disciplines and by anthropology itself in the old nature-nuture debate," grew out of new conceptualisations of gender resulting from the "discovery of 'women' as an analytical category." The essays make clear the degree to which Western culture is preoccupied with the idea of culture in antithesis to nature, "in the same way as many attempts at feminist analysis are predicated upon a self-consciousness about the category 'woman' in antithesis to man."

108. Milton, Kay. "Male Bias in Anthropology." Man 14:40-54 (1979).

Milton dismisses the feminist concept of male dominance as being "of little value in anthropological analysis, not only because it is ill-defined, but also because it is based on the assumption that differences between men and women indicate the superiority of the former and inferiority of the latter." She argues that the male bias that feminists (i.e., universal male dominance and cultural devaluation of women) and Edwin Ardener and his followers (i.e., overwhelming prevalence of male anthropologists, ethnographers and informants) claim to find in anthropological methods has been inadequately defined. This lack of clarity forces the proponents of male bias into the position of implying that "the theories of anthropology are biologically determined." According to Milton, "if we were to accept the proposition that anthropology, as it has been practised up to now, is 'male' in character, then it would be difficult to imagine how anything that supposedly eliminated that male bias could ever be recognized as anthropology."

109. Moore, Henrietta L. Feminism and Anthropology. Minneapolis, Minnesota: University of Minnesota Press, 1988.

Moore hopes her book will "demonstrate that the feminist critique in anthropology has been, and will continue to be, central to theoretical and methodological developments within the discipline as a whole." The book is structured according to what she calls "a certain narrative historical form:" it summarizes the history of the relationship between feminism and anthropology, discusses the debates around gender, sexual asymmetry, and male dominance, describes the relationship between Marxist and feminist anthropology, deals with debates concerning the rise of capitalism and its effects on the sexual division of labor, and presents material on women and the state, the area, Moore argues, that is the newest and most exciting in feminist anthropological scholarship. In its examination of the interrelations between kinship structures and state structures, feminist anthropology has found that women "are located on a boundary between kinship relations and state structures," that the emergence of the state transforms kinship relations so that women are increasingly under the control of men, and that "the modern state is predicated upon gender difference, and this difference is inscribed into the political process." Feminist anthropology deconstructs, or takes the meaning out of, universal generalizations like the "oppression of women" or "patriarchy," and demonstrates that the nature and consequences of oppression or patriarchy have to be specified in each instance. "The distinctive contribution of feminist anthropology is the way in which it demonstrates that gender relations are central to any sustained analysis of class and historical relations...[and the way in which it points to] the value of comparison and to the importance of acknowledging difference."

110. Nicholson, Linda J. "Comment on Rosaldo's 'The Use and Abuse of Anthropology.'" Signs 7:732-735 (1982).

Nicholson agrees with Rosaldo that the theoretical model which explains sexual inequalities by the opposition of the "domestic" and "public" spheres "hides the diverse causes and content of gender roles." Such a theory, she says, leads us much too easily to "deduce the political from the biological." Nicholson disagrees, however, with Rosaldo's objections to a search for origins, seeing in such objections a move toward a rejection of explanations in favor of a variety of descriptions. Since the opposition of the "domestic" and "public" spheres does help structure gender relations in contemporary society, "it seems worthwhile at least to explore how far back the separation extends, where and how its meanings change, and what the connections are, if any, with the politics of gender."

111. Ortner, Sherry B. "Is Female to Male as Nature Is to Culture?" In Woman, Culture, and Society, edited by Michelle Zimbalist Rosaldo and Louise Lamphere, pp. 67-88 (Stanford, California: Stanford University Press, 1974).

Ortner uses the nature versus culture argument to support her belief that "the secondary status of woman in society is one of the true universals, a pan-cultural fact." In every society, culture, the "process of generating and sustaining systems of meaningful forms" is viewed as a way of transcending nature and asserting control over natural existence. Culture, therefore, is perceived to be superior to nature. Women are seen as being closer to nature than men because woman's body and functions are more involved with procreation and with perpetuation of the species, woman's social roles are seen as being of a lower order than men's, and woman's psychic roles (i.e., concreteness, personalism, particularism, subjectivity), a product of her social roles and physiology, are seen as being more worldly and less transcendent than men's. The cultural construct that associates women with nature and men with culture creates a hierarchical social reality. Social institutions and cultural views must both be changed, and "both men and women...must be equally involved in projects of creativity and transcendence" before women will be seen as aligned with culture.

112. Quinn, Naomi. "Anthropological Studies On Women's Status." Annual Review of Anthropology 6:181-225 (1977).

Quinn reviews and evaluates the logic of "the various explanations which have been proposed to account for observed similarities and differences in women's status from society to society." A political issue — feminists' desire to improve women's low status — influences many of the anthropological explanations to focus on what Quinn calls a "key" to lower status across societies. If women's oppression is universal and a cross-cultural explanation for that oppression can be found, then a solution and ultimate equality seem possible. Quinn believes that, in this case, politics has led explanation in the wrong direction. She suggests that it is "more accurate, and more helpful to future research to treat women's status as a composite of many different variables, often causally independent one from another." In any given culture, women's status may be lower than men's in some domains, equal to men's in others, and higher than men's in yet others. Research should concentrate on single aspects of women's position in society, for example, political participation, control over economic matters, or personal autonomy, rather than "conditions purported to influence women's status overall." By failing to include women as informants and by judging the status of women only from accounts of men, ethnographers have often introduced male bias into research and provided an inaccurate picture of women's importance and social standing. Colonialism and modernization have introduced Western practices and attitudes regarding women that may not have been characteristic of the aboriginal societies themselves. Quinn concludes that "what is clearest in the literature reviewed is the need for further investigation into each of the separate claims which has been made about women's status, and the conditions under which each claim holds true."

113. Reiter, Rayna R. "Introduction." In Toward an Anthropology of Women, edited by Rayna R. Reiter, pp. 11-19 (New York: Monthly Review Press, 1975).

The collection edited by Reiter begins to correct what she describes as "the double [male] bias which has trivalized and misinterpreted female roles for so long." The essays it includes focus on women in order to "redefine the important questions, reexamine...previous theories, and be critical in...the acceptance of what constitutes factual material." Focusing on women is essential to reorient anthropology to a study of humankind rather than mankind. The double male bias includes the bias researchers bring into their ethnographic studies and the bias researchers receive if the societies they are studying express male dominance. Much of the information that previously existed about women came from questions asked of men; many of the conclusions drawn about a group's reality were based only on male information. Reiter suggests that, in ways similar to the "theoretical perspective that separates biology from culture in the investigation of race," anthropology can develop "discrimination with regard to gender" that will overcome male bias.

114. Rogers, Susan Carol. "Woman's Place: A Critical Review of Anthropological Theory." Comparative Studies in Society and History 20(1):123-162 (1978).

Rogers reviews the anthropological literature related to "sexual differentiation and the relative status of men and women..." and formulates an analytic framework to help deal with the problems the literature poses. She asserts that the status and power of women can only be understood in terms of the relationship between women and men. Sex differentiation may be behavioral, in that each sex acts out different roles and participates in different activities, or it may be ideological, in that females and males view themselves as different entities or species. In any society, these two kinds of sex differentiation can occur together, just one type can occur, or there can be no sex differentiation, resulting in four possible varities. Each varation produces a different kind of "power relationship between the sexes," power being measured by control over significant resources, where resources is interpreted broadly to include ritual knowledge, specialist skills, information, etc. Rogers suggests that when both ideological and behavioral differentiation exist, a balance of power is most likely between the two sexes as they will be opposed to but dependent on one another. When behaviorial differentiation exists without ideological differentiation, "a clear imbalance of power becomes more probable." Cross-culturally, Rogers believes, the existence of both behavioral and ideological differentiation occurs most commonly. The power balance related to this variation of differentiation is often destroyed by colonization, when males are given more access to resources by the colonizing (Western) society. Rogers believes that sex differences based only on ideology or the lack of sex differences altogether are virtually non-existence.

115. Rosaldo, Michelle Z. "Moral/Analytic Dilemmas Posed by the Intersection of Feminism and Social Science." In Social Science as Moral Inquiry, edited by Robert Bellah, et al., pp. 76-95 (New York: Columbia University Press, 1983).

One of the contributions feminists have made to social science research has been to question the argument that nature provides the basis for the separation of male and female worlds and to support, instead, explanations based on social forces. Feminists have done a better job, however, at revealing the limitations of categories based on nature than of radically revising or replacing these categories. Because no such revision or replacement has occurred, Rosaldo believes that feminists themselves end up being heirs to the traditional arguments. Feminists have tended, just like their enemies, to turn to anthropology "to answer troubling ideologies or to give voice to universal human truths," and have thus fallen prey to the social scientific biases of individualism (in which individuals' social forms are givens of their reproductive physiology) and dualism (in which categories like domestic/political, biology/culture, individual/social, or woman/man are seen in opposition). In their search for universal "sisterhood, feminist researchers must avoid the tendency to stress 'deep,' essential commonalities in women's styles, relationships, and strengths. Feminists can best help their fellow social scientists to learn: the very real cross-cultural variety in views of gender and, more broadly, in conceptions of the self; their roots in different forms of social life; and their implications for human action and relationship in diverse societies."

116. Rosaldo, Michelle Z. "The Use and Abuse of Anthropology: Reflections on Feminism and Cross-cultural Understanding." Signs 5(3):389-417 (1980).

Rosaldo's reflections take the form of criticisms of a theoretical model she herself had helped create. The model she criticizes explains differences in status between men and women by the opposition between the "domestic" and "public" spheres. While there is much that is compelling about a model that suggests how "'brute' biological facts have everywhere been shaped by social logics," its weaknesses lie with the assumptions it makes that "woman's place in human social life is...in a direct sense a product of the things she does (or...what, biologically, she is)." Biological sex, Rosaldo says, like biological race, is an excuse for, not the cause of, existing sexist behavior. Counteracting the unbalanced account of Man the Hunter with an account of Woman the Gatherer broadens our understanding of the contributions women have made but does little to provide us with an "understanding of how these women organized their lives and claims in any actual society." Women and men function as partners and competitors in on-going social processes which must be analyzed to reveal why, "in a world where people of both sexes make choices that count, that men come to be seen as the creators of collective good and the preeminent force in local politics." Feminist anthropologists must avoid casting questions in "universalizing terms" that lead to a search for "universal truths and origins."

117. Rosaldo, Michelle Zimbalist. "Woman, Culture, and Society: A Theoretical Overview." In Woman, Culture, and Society, edited by Michelle Zimbalist Rosaldo and Louise Lamphere, pp. 17-42 (Stanford, California: Stanford University Press, 1974).

In this early paper, Rosaldo proposes a theory of universal sexual asymmetry which she later refutes (see Rosaldo, 1980 and 1983 above). While women are often important and sometimes powerful, she writes here, in every human culture they are subordinate to men in that they lack "generally recognized and culturally valued authority." Rosaldo attributes the asymmetry between women and men to the fact that "a good part of a woman's adult life is spent giving birth to and raising children," thus confining her to the domestic sphere. Men, who lack any "single commitment as enduring, time-consuming, and emotionally compelling — as close to seeming necessary and natural — as the relation of a woman to her infant child," are free to involve themselves in the institutions, activites, and forms of association that make up the public sphere. The structural opposition between the domestic and public domains of activity produces the characteristic aspects of male and female roles in social, cultural, and economic systems. The most egalitarian societies are ones in which "men value and participate in the domestic life of the home." Women will be recognized as men's equal not when the latter can participate in public life but rather when the former "help to raise new generations by taking on the responsibilities of the home."

118. Sanday, Peggy Reeves. "The Reproduction of Patriarchy in Feminist Anthropology." In Feminist Thought and the Structure of Knowledge, edited by Mary McCanney Gergen, pp. 49-68 (New York: New York University Press, 1988).

Sanday describes the two sides in what she calls a debate between feminist anthropologists who "evoke ethnographic examples of sexual symmetry, sexual equality, or matrifocality" and those who "claim the universality of 'male dominance' or 'gender hierarchy'." In spite of their differences, Sanday says, the two sides are united by a common goal: to change Western patriarchy. Since it appears that "all anthropology is a form of comprehending self and society through a detour of the comprehension of other selves in other societies," feminist anthropologists, engaged in the process of "myth making for change," must be careful not to bury the subjects of their study by their own political concerns.

119. Scheper-Hughes, Nancy. "The Problem of Bias in Androcentric and Feminist Anthropology." Women's Studies 10:109-116 (1983).

The brief history of feminist anthropology has, according to Scheper-Hughes, several phases. The first phase occurred when feminist anthropologists recognized the universality of male dominance and the consequent subordination and devaluation of women. In the second phase, which actually occurred simultaneously with the first, feminist anthropologists pointed out the gender bias in anthropology. This bias has produced "inaccuracies, omissions, and distortions in ethnographic descriptions," and has lead to the tendency to view female domains (for example, socialization, healing, household economy) as less important than male domains (for example, politics, warfare, law). Women have often been ignored as potential informants resulting in an underrepresentation of the female point of view. The third phase resulted when the second phase (i.e., that classical ethnographies have been subject to gender bias) made the assumptions of the first phase (i.e., the universality of male dominance) suspect. Rejecting the assumption of universal male dominance forced feminist anthropologists to also reject the "existence of a universal sisterhood of womankind immediately recognizable across class, cultural, and ethnic boundaries." There is no "shared experience of womanhood" which is likely to result in a worldwide feminist revolution. The fourth phase, which begins with the assumption of an androcentric anthropology based upon male theoretical frameworks, struggles with the ability of feminist anthropologists to ask questions that are not structured and determined by these very frameworks they are trying to avoid. Feminist anthropologists are struggling, in other words, not to lose hold of their subjectivity. Scheper-Hughes suggests, however, that "traditional male socialization for dominance and achievement might present itself as more of a barrier to the practice of fieldwork than female socialization." The qualities that allow ethnographers to succeed — empathy, intuition, intimacy, patience, self-effacing humor, an ability to listen not to talk, to follow not to lead, and to respect tradition rather than innovate — are by Western standards stereotypically feminine traits. Feminist ethnographers have exposed the myth of the invisible self which allowed traditional ethnographers to avoid examining the "subjective bases of the questions they asked and the kind of data they collected."

120. Shapiro, Judith. "Anthropology and the Study of Gender." Soundings 64:446-465 (1981).

Shapiro sees the task before feminist scholars as "one of making it as impossible for social scientists to avoid dealing with gender in their studies of social differentiation as it is for them to avoid dealing with such things as rank, class, and kinship." In the form of a literature review, she examines how the study of gender fits within symbolic anthropology, the theoretical problems that gender studies raise for understanding social hierarchy or inequality, and "how the study of gender brings to the fore issues concerning the sociology of knowledge." Shapiro stresses the importance of defining a feminist approach to anthropology as the study of gender rather than the study of women. She borrows the term "markedness" from linguists and semioticians to make her point, explaining that a "marked" term is the more restricted of two terms that constitute complementary opposites within a larger class. Man as a term is unmarked since, in relation to its complementary term, woman, it can be used to refer to a wider class — people — as a whole. Woman, on the other hand, is marked because it is more restricted in meaning. To insist that women be studied, then, marks the enterprise as a separate and restricted one outside of the the traditional fields of study. To study gender, however, implies that both men and women will be examined in an unmarked fashion.

121. Slocum, Sally. "Woman the Gatherer: Male Bias in Anthropology." In Toward an Anthropology of Women, edited by Rayna R. Reiter, pp. 36-50. (New York: Monthly Review press, 1975).

Slocum believes that the "basis of any discipline is not the answers it gets, but the questions it asks." Asking, "What were the women doing while the males were out hunting?" reveals basic male bias in the theory of Man the Hunter and suggests a more compelling theory of Woman the Gatherer in its place. Slocum rejects the Man the Hunter theory, which links aggression and killing with culture and which insists that hunting formed the basis for "the psychology, biology, and customs of our species." She suggests that the female-infant bond resulted in the sharing of food within families, which consisted of females and their children. Organization and communication skills evolved from the necessity to raise young. Tools and other cultural inventions evolved from the gathering of food and from the need for mothers to carry their young while gathering. Big game hunting grew out of "a complex of changes which included sharing the products of gathering among mothers and children, deepening social bonds over time, increase in brain size, and the beginnings of cultural invention for purposes such as baby carrying, food carrying, and food preparation."

122. Stack, Carol B., Mina Davis Caulfield, Valerie Ester, Susan Landes, Karen Larson, Pamela Johnson, Juliet Rake, and Judith Shirek. "Review Essay: Anthropology." Signs 1(1):147-159 (1975).

Stack et al.'s review of anthropological research on women concentrates on the four major areas of human evolution, symbolism, linguistics, and social organization. In the area of human evolution, feminists brought forward evidence that women's role as gatherer and sharer of food was the "critical hominid innovation" and that hunting and the sexual division of labor emerged relatively late in the evolutionary process (see also Slocum above). With regard to symbolism, feminists have concentrated on describing and analyzing the significance of female initiation rites in various cultures. The separation of menstruating women may not be an isolation inflicted on women by men but rather a desirable and exclusive withdrawal. Feminist anthropologists have questioned the traditional association of women with nature and men with culture. Feminist linguists have investigated "both the sexual categories inherent in a language and the significance of language as an agent for conveying information about role relationships in interaction." Research on language has emphasized the semantics of words referring to people, the sex-typed characteristics of speech, and different speech behaviors of males and females. Feminist approaches to social organization and the status of women have raised questions concerning some fundamental assumptions. Power relationships can no longer be assumed to represent the "primary organizing principle of human society." Rather than seeing women's tasks as those adjusted to the demands of child care, researchers are examining "how child-spacing and child-tending are accommodated to the requirements of the woman's tasks." The attempt to understand women's status has lead to a search both for cross-cultural universals and for historical explanations for women's position, racism, and sexism. The anthropological study of women has arisen out of the realization that "the importance of roles assumed by women in many cultures could not be accurately accounted for by traditional models emphasizing formal structures in societies...."

123. Strathern, Marilyn. "An Awkward Relationship: The Case of Feminism and Anthropology." Signs 12(2):276-291 (1987).

Strathern disputes the claims of Stacey and Thorne (1985, see annotation in Sociology chapter) and of Langland and Gove (Langland, Elizabeth and Walter Gove. "Editors' Notes," pp. 1-6. In A Feminist Perspective in the Academy: The Difference it Makes, edited by Elizabeth Langland and Walter Gove, Chicago: University of Chicago Press, 1981) that the discipline of anthropology has been more responsive than other disciplines to conceptual shifts as a result of feminism. According to Strathern, feminist scholarship works across disciplines rather than parallel to them and thus cannot in reality accomplish the "paradigm shifts" to which feminists working within traditional disciplines frequently allude. Especially within social anthropology, radicalisms abound; feminist anthropology, then, represents just one of several conflicting theoretical positions. Strathern describes the relationship between feminist scholarship and anthropology as "awkward" because "each, in a sense, mocks the other..." (see also Stacey, 1988, in the Sociology chapter). Feminism challenges "stereotypes that misrepresent women's experiences." It is based on the struggle to discover oneself, within the sociocultural constraints of one's own society, through destroying "the authority of other persons to determine feminine experiences." Anthropologists attempt to establish themselves as vehicles for interpreting the experiences of others through acknowledging their own personal experiences and through involving the others in the creation of their study reports. Feminists can claim — in a way that anthropologists can only envy — shared experiences with the women they study; anthropologists can achieve — with an ease that feminists can only envy — a distance from their own society. Feminist scholarship and anthropology are not substitutes for one another: they "offer [each other] not challenge but...mockery."

124. Tsing, Anna Lowenhaupt and Sylvia Junko Yanagisako. "Feminism and Kinship Theory." Current Anthropology 24(4):511-516 (1983).

Tsing and Yanagisako summarize the results of a conference held in August, 1982, which gathered together nineteen anthropologists from the United States, Europe, and Australia to "explore new perspectives on kinship arising from feminist investigations of gender." Three strategies were suggested at the conference for redirecting feminist analysis. The first strategy involves "detailed attention to the symbolic organization of gender." No assumptions can be made about what it is to be a man or a woman in any culture and conclusions regarding gender asymmetry must be based on an understanding of what constitutes power within that culture. The second strategy involves "the investigation of gender in the context of power and inequality." The third involves "the investigation of historical transformations in gender systems." The conference raised questions concerning "linkages between gender and kinship once thought to be universal," particularly the distinction between the domestic and the political-jural domains and cross-cultural comparisons of descent categories like patrilineality.

5
PSYCHOLOGY

INTRODUCTION

Objectivity

For its treatment of women, psychology has long been under attack. Leta Stetter Hollingworth's (1886-1939) research, published between 1913 and 1927, for example, demonstrated that sexual bias rather than scientific fact led to the assumption that women's performance deteriorated during menstruation. Hollingworth had faith that truly objective research was the key to eliminating social misconceptions (Shields, 1975).

More recent critiques of traditional psychology continue to bemoan the lack of true objectivity. Examinations of studies published between the late 1950s and the early 1970s (Carlson and Carlson, 1960; Harris, 1971; Dan and Beekman, 1972; Schwabacher, 1972; Greenglass and Stewart, 1973; Maccoby and Jacklin, 1974) reveal that traditional researchers used male subjects much more frequently than female ones, treated males as representative of all people, frequently failed to test for or report the presence or lack of sex differences, and frequently quoted one-sex studies to substantiate a claim of differences between the sexes.

Weisstein (1971) ties psychology's lack of objectivity to its focus on inner traits rather than social context. Social expectations for the two sexes must be equal, she claims, before researchers will be able to identify accurately their differences.

With its emphasis on experimental, laboratory research, psychology has sought partnership with the hard sciences. Ironically, as Sherif (1979) points out, the discipline has been shot through with unscientific sex bias, which runs contrary to the standards of scholarly inquiry. She encourages feminist psychologists to use a variety of research methods and techniques, take into account the influence of cultural institutions and social values on individuals, and draw on disciplines other than biology.

The Addition of Women

Parlee (1975, 1979) distinguishes the psychology of women, which applies special laws and theories to female behavior, and the psychology against women, which distorts facts and perpetuates pseudoscientific data, from psychology for women. She urges feminist psychologists to avoid adhering strictly to the context-stripping methods of traditional psychology and, instead, to seek the "best possible truth."

Vaughter (1976) sees placing research within its political and social context as one of the primary characteristics of the feminist perspective in psychology. Other characteristics include an interdisciplinary and collaborative approach, public involvement in decisions concerning research priorities, data collection, and data interpretation, and a cooperative instead of competitive model for expanding knowledge.

Weisstein is representative of feminist psychologists who believe that properly designed experiments will demonstrate to traditionalists the sexist error of their ways (Van Leeuwen, 1984). Wine (1982) calls such feminists imitators or protestors because they use traditional methods to correct women's under-representation or to attack misogynist bias. But simply adding women or identifying sexism will not change what Unger (1983) calls positivism's transformation of people into "object-like-subjects." According to Walker (1981), if feminists continue to work within the methodological and theoretical framework of psychology, they will never change the discipline. She advises them to abandon the scientific method in favor of a more flexible alternative.

Even armed with a flexible alternative, feminists will have difficulty transforming psychology unless their alternative is widely disseminated among mainstream practitioners. After analyzing ten issues of the Journal of Personality and Social Psychology, Lykes and Stewart (1986) found that feminist research published in feminist journals was cited far less frequently than feminist research published in mainstream journals. But if "methodological orthodoxy" is the price feminists pay for appearing in mainstream publications, then wider readership may not represent any gain (Squire, 1989).

Types of Feminist Approaches

Kahn and Jean (1983) divide feminist approaches to psychology into three types. "Integration and elimination" feminists explain all differences between men and women as socialization, use traditional methods, and advocate incorporating the psychology of women into traditional psychology as quickly as possible. "Integration follows equality" feminists believe that differences between women and men are differences in status and power. When women and men have equal status, a separate psychology of women will no longer be necessary. "Separation and self-definition" feminists see men and women as fundamentally different. The psychology of women must remain a separate discipline using different methods, theories, and ethics from traditional psychology.

These three approaches correspond to possible futures for feminist psychology: integration, an expansion of traditional psychology, or separation. Because of the experimental, predictive, and controlling approach of traditional psychology, Parlee (1985) rules out the first two alternatives. She encourages feminist psychologists to continue asking the questions they believe will "lead to psychological truth" even though "the methods and concepts by which psychology defines itself" will not be able to provide the answers.

ANNOTATIONS

125. Ballou, Mary B. "Approaching a Feminist-Principles Paradigm in the Construction of Personality Theory." Women & Therapy 9(1-2):23-40 (1990).

> Ballou outlines five methods of generating and validating knowledge used in the psychology of women literature: 1) the experimental method with its emphasis on objectivity, a single universal truth, public and repeatable measurement, and context-independent pheonmena; 2) experiential methodologies or phenomenology, which "holds that truth is in the experience or in the perception of the experience;" 3) reasoning, which uses consensual rules of logic and an adversarial method; 4) appeals to authority, which tries to make new ideas legitimate by associating them with old, accepted ideas; and 5) nonrational knowledge generation, associated with intuition, the mystical, or the spiritual. Instead of arguing for a single replacement method of knowing, she recommends the use of " a multiple method based on feminist principles." General systems theory, says Ballou, avoids shaping reality and distorting truth by proposing "a connective nexus among many methods of knowing and their shaping of reality." As an "organizing and normative base" for handling questions related to the generation and validation of knowledge, Ballou suggests the following principles: 1) valuing women's experience; 2) pluralism; 3) "equalitarian relationships;" and 4) external forces influencing causation.

126. Baumrind, Diana. "New Directions in Socialization Research." American Psychologist 35(7):639-652 (1980).

Positivist social psychology attempts to "infer unambiguously the existence and direction of causal relations." Traditional experimenters manipulate variables in artifical contexts and simplify them for measurement. Such behavior introduces deterministic bias into research. Baumrind suggests that it is not only impossible but also wrong for scientists to be objective. "Empirical work directed at describing and explaining what is should do so within a framework of clarifying and justifying what ought to be." Investigators must define the "Good" before they begin their research.

127. Boukydis, Kathleen McGuire. Existential/Phenomenology as a Philosophical Base for a Feminist Psychology. ERIC document #ED 206 966 (1981).

Meaningful variables, claims Boukydis, "must be developed out of and refer back to experiencing." Psychological exploration must begin with "somebody's felt sense of a phenomenon." Logical positivist psychology discriminates against women because it excludes inner experiences as subject matter for study. The principles underlying the phenomenological methodology state that: 1) feeling and intuition are basic existents; 2) the body is a source of knowledge about the world; and 3) the body is inherently relational.

128. Carlson, Earl R. and Rae Carlson. "Male and Female Subjects in Personality Research." Journal of Abnormal and Social Psychology 61(3):482-483 (1960).

Carlson and Carlson conducted their study in response to three problems: 1) imbalance in sampling research; 2) infrequency of tests for sex differences; and 3) failure to report sex composition of research samples. They examined 298 studies published in 14 issues of the Journal of Abnormal and Social Psychology from volume 56, number 1 (1958) through volume 60, number 2 (1960). 113 of the studies used male subjects exclusively, 15 used only female subjects, 108 used both, and 65 failed to specify the subjects' sex. Only 32 of the 108 studies using subjects of both sexes reported tests for sex differences. In 22 of the 32, sex differences were found at a level of statistical significance. Based on these results, Carlson and Carlson recommend that researchers test and report sex differences as a standard procedure. Failure to so has led to "implied generalizations as a function of consistent biases entering into the selection of the samples."

129. Carlson, Rae. "Understanding Women: Implications for Personality Theory and Research." Journal of Social Issues 28(2):17-32 (1972).

Carlson examines "ways in which studying femininity might contribute to enrichment of our presently impoverished approaches to the study of persons." She suggests that "current, preemptive, agentic" research paradigms, "incapable of meeting genuine scientific requirements for personological study," be integrated with communal types of research. As directions for future work, she lists: 1) duality in human nature; 2) typology and qualitative patterning; and 3) biological bases of personality.

130. Dan, Alice J. and Susan Beekman. "Male Versus Female Representation in Psychological Research." American Psychologist 27(11):1078 (1972).

Dan and Beekman draw on their own studies and studies of others to conclude that psychological researchers not only use male subjects much more frequently than female ones but are also more likely to overgeneralize conclusions drawn from male-based research. They caution that "the habit of mind which allows that males are more representative of the human race than females should be recognized as a potentially serious bias in our psychological research and theory." Most researchers who use both sexes in their studies fail to check for or to report on sex differences. Computerized information systems, which make abstracts rather than full articles widely available, may make it even less likely that information on sex differences will be widely disseminated. While both-sex studies which pay careful attention to sex differences are most likely to avoid research bias, carefully designed one-sex studies that fit conclusions to a specific population can also contribute to knowledge.

131. Denmark, Florence, Nancy Felipe Russo, Irene Hanson Frieze, and Jeri A. Sechzer. "Guidelines for Avoiding Sexism in Psychological Research." American Psychologist 43(7):582-585 (1988).

The Board of Social and Ethical Responsibility for Psychology formed an Ad Hoc Committee on Nonsexist Research. The Board charged the Committee to "develop materials to educate psychologists about ways to eliminate gender bias in research." This article provides examples of common avoidable problems and offers suggestions for eliminating gender bias. Denmark, Russo, Frieze, and Sechzer point out that values and assumptions related to race, ethnicity, disability, sexual orientation, or socioeconomic status, as well as to gender, can produce biases in research; their guidelines can help researchers avoid all forms of bias. Problems of bias related to question formulation include: 1) associating gender stereotypes with the topic being studied; 2) deriving questions from or constraining them by bias inherent in existing theory or research; 3) assuming that topics relevant to white males are basic while questions related to other groups are specialized or applied; and 4) conducting reviews of previous research without taking gender biases into account. Problems of bias related to research methods include: 1) selecting research participants based on stereotypic assumptions; 2) using convenience as the rationale for selecting only one sex for participation in research; 3) dropping female research participants from analysis when unanticipated gender differences emerge; 4) failure to specify the sex or race of participants, experimenters, and others in contact with research participants; 5) confounding gender with other participant variables such as job status, age, or race; 6) affecting performance by selecting gender-stereotyped measures; 7) labeling variable or response measures to suggest negative evaluations of women or nontraditional choices; and 8) allowing stereotypes to influence the development of operational definitions. Problems of bias related to data analysis and interpretation include: 1) failure to report a finding of no gender differences; 2) inaccurate magnification of gender differences; 3) asserting gender differences incorrectly; 4) formulating research conclusions in terms of innate biological differences; and 5) failure to address misleading implications of gender difference findings. Problems of bias related to conclusions include: 1) generalizing results based on one sex to both; 2) interpreting gender difference in performance on a specific task as an indication of global differences; 3) advocating different opportunities for males and females based on statistically significant sex difference findings; 4) using evaluative labels for results; and 5) using broad titles that obscure the limitations of study participants.

132. Favreau, Olga Eizner. "Sex Bias in Psychological Research." Canadian Psychological Review 18(1):56-65 (1977).

Using examples from the research literature, Favreau describes the occurrences of sex bias in psychological research on sex differences. Review articles frequently state that "what men are better at is better than what women are better at." Authors often make "large inferential leaps" that the data cannot justify: for example, by connecting interest in objects with coping and achievement motivation. Bias often occurs in the way previous studies are used: only studies supporting sex differences are cited; only studies citing the differences are credited as valid; and findings are reported erroneously. When no statistically significant sex differences are found, this fact frequently will not be reported. The language in which differences are reported — "females are better at Y than males" — is inappropriate. Reported sex differences should indicate the range of performance for both males and females and the degree of overlap. Favreau concludes that "biological sex alone is an inappropriate predictor of performance." The task should be to understand variables other than sex and to help change behavior, in either sex, if it is in any way undesirable.

133. Fine, Michelle. "Reflections on a Feminist Psychology: Paradoxes and Prospects." Psychology of Women Quarterly 9(2):167-183 (1985).

Fine analyzes the methods and conclusions of articles published in Psychology of Women Quarterly from 1978 to 1981. Feminists advocate research that is contextually valid. They point out that single sex designs, overreliance on laboratory research, and gender examined as an explanatory rather than a descriptive result distort the psychology of gender and justify gender inequities. In feminist research, gender and its social inequities frame theory, research, and analysis; conflicts and contradictions, rather than consistencies and harmonies, organize the inquiry; and findings are understood within the context of women's lives. Fine lists four criteria of feminist research: 1) samples must represent women of varying social and ethnic groups, sexual orientations, and lifestyles; 2) research must focus on topics meaningful to the respondents; 3) perspectives of numerous respondents from the same setting must be used and outcomes studied must involve units of analysis larger than the individual; and 4) research conclusions must "map psychological findings onto prevailing contexts." Fine cautions feminist researchers to avoid coming to "unduly optimistic conclusions," confusing social ideologies about women with their personal realities, or promoting "idiosyncratic or overdetermined models for social change." She concludes by listing strategies to enhance contextual validity.

134. Gergen, Mary M. "Building a Feminist Methodology." Contemporary Social Psychology 13(2):47-53 (1988).

In promoting feminist research, Gergen questions the "cardinal attributes associated with objectivity." She rejects the researcher's independence from the subject matter in favor of interdependence between the researcher and the subject. Gergen advocates taking social and cultural factors into account as opposed to isolating a subject and ignoring the life circumstances of the scientist. She believes that feminist research, which acknowledges its perspective, is better than androcentric research, which pretends the impossible: that no perspective is involved. Established facts, she argues, are a product not of reality but rather of an "a priori linguistic framework." All steps in research require interpretation. According to Gergen, feminist researchers differ from empirical researchers by considering themselves equal rather than superior to research subjects and readers.

135. Gilligan, Carol. "Introduction." In In a Different Voice: Psychological Theory and Women's Development, pp. 1-4 (Cambridge, Massachusetts: Harvard University Press, 1982).

Gilligan associates ways of thinking about relationships with male and female voices, as these voices appear in psychological and literary texts and in the interviews she uses to gather her data. According to Gilligan, "the way people talk about their lives is of significance [and]...the language they use and the connections they make reveal the world that they see and in which they act." To understand respondents, researchers must be sensitive to voice.

136. Gould, Ketayun H. "Old Wine in New Bottles: A Feminist Perspective on Gilligan's Theory." Social Work 33(5):411-415 (1988).

Gould suggests that Carol Gilligan's theories of gender and male and female ethics (see annotation above) "contribute inadvertently to the justification, rather than to the transformation, of professional and societal roles." She proposes a feminist perspective as an alternative. In her model, caring is associated with women, not because, as Gilligan implies, they are inherently caring, but rather because women are subordinate and because characteristics associated with caring are of secondary importance and, therefore, assigned to women. According to this model, resistance to women's devaluation becomes a political activity. Gould believes that "the incorporation of different voices is indeed the social work vision for the future." Her feminist perspective, instead of Gilligan's theory of moral development, has the potential to deconstruct "the core of individual and social reality."

137. Grady, Kathleen E. "Sex Bias in Research Design." Psychology of Women Quarterly 5(4):628-636 (1981).

The scientific method, with its "relentless" accumulation of facts designed to challenge ideas, should serve as an ally to revolutionaries of all sorts. The feminist critique of psychology has demonstrated, however, that science, practiced with a lack of awareness of the different social and economic conditions for men and women, can never realize its revolutionary potential. Sex bias has occurred in: 1) the kinds of topics researched and the kinds of research deemed worthy of publication; 2) subject selection, with a preponderance of males as research subjects; 3) operationalization of variables; 4) testing for sex differences; and 5) interpretation of research results. The central theme of the feminist criticism of methodology in psychology "involves the kinds of problems inherent in a research endeavor in a sexist society, one which has a pervasive romantic and anti-scientific ideology about men and women which is resistant to the 'objectivity' of science."

138. Greenglass, Esther and Mary Stewart. "The Under-representation of Women in Social Psychological Research." Ontario Psychologist 5(2):21-29 (1973).

Greenglass and Stewart examined randomly selected articles from the Journal of Social Psychology, the Journal of Personality, the Journal of Personality and Social Psychology, the Journal of Abnormal and Social Psychology, the Journal of Genetic Psychology, and Child Development for the years 1961-1970. Their examination revealed that "research in the social and personality areas is more likely to be based on the behaviour of male rather than female subjects." Twenty-two percent of the studies did not indicate the sex of the subjects. Only about half of the studies that included both sexes tested for sex differences. More than 60 percent of the studies using subjects of only one sex (either male or female) generalized the results to both sexes. While 30 percent of the American Psychological Association's members are female, under 20 percent of the articles' authors or co-authors were female. Greenglass and Stewart suggest that their study raises questions as to why psychologists study more males than females, why researchers don't test for sex differences even when they study both sexes, and how the findings based on one sex can be assumed to apply to the other.

139. Gutmann, Amy. "Freud Versus Feminism." Dissent 26(2):204-212 (1979).

Gutmann uses Juliet Mitchell's book, Psychoanalysis and Feminism (New York: Pantheon Books, 1974), as a springboard to discuss the relationship between Freudian and feminist ideas. Mitchell defends Freud's approach to women by claiming that his psychoanalytic theory explains rather than justifies women's situation in society. Freudian theory explains, claims Mitchell, why women who grow up in nuclear families accept their inferior status or rebel at the cost of "what is perceived to be their womanhood." Gutmann argues that Freudianism forces feminists to support the destruction of the nuclear family. She argues for a more existential view that gives women as victims of oppression an ability to change their situation.

Understanding the psychological dimensions of women's oppression within inegalitarian family structures is vital but so is understanding past and present economic and political barriers to women's equality. Mitchell's perspective, says Gutmann, "relieves women of responsibility for their situation but to be relieved of all responsibility may also entail being deprived of all dignity."

140. Harris, Sandra. "Influence of Subject and Experimenter Sex in Psychological Research." Journal of Consulting and Clinical Psychology 37(2):291-294 (1971).

Harris studied articles from the Journal of Abnormal Psychology and the Journal of Consulting and Clinical Psychology to demonstrate the extent to which experimenters fail to control for the influence of experimenter and subject sex and to show how this failure leads to unwarranted conclusions. Sex is not always a factor in psychological research. Because predicting when sexual differences will be important is difficult, however, sex should be considered in research design. Harris suggests one way to analyze experimenter and subject sex: use an adequate number of experimenters of both sexes and assign them equal numbers of male and female subjects.

141. Jacklin, Carol Nagy. "Feminist Research and Psychology." In The Impact of Feminist Research in the Academy, edited by Christie Farnham, pp. 95-107 (Bloomington, Indiana: Indiana University Press, 1987).

Jacklin discusses why feminists are interested in the research process and argues that women as researchers and as subjects have changed and will continue to change psychological research. Women, she believes, may be struggling to understand the research process because they have been excluded from it. Women as scientists and scholars will change the questions that are generated, and thus produce new research and new answers to old questions. Women's persistence and "threshold of convincibility" will differ from men's in terms of the time spent solving a problem and the effort invested in understanding or refuting previous research. Jacklin acknowledges feminists' preference for methods which bring researchers closer to their subject matter but asserts that the method chosen "should be the best possible for answering the particular questions chosen." She insists that the political consequences of science cannot be ignored through a pretence of research as value-free. The study of women and girls has brought sex differences to the fore and challenged the physiological/philosophical "representative individual" model of psychological research.

142. Johnson, Paula. "Doing Psychological Research." In Women and Sex Roles: A Social Psychological Perspective, edited by Irene H. Frieze, Jacquelynne E. Parsons, Paula B. Johnson, Diane N. Ruble, and Gail L. Zellman, pp. 11-27 (New York: W. W. Norton and Company, 1978).

Johnson suggests that exposing sex biases that influence the methods used in psychological research is important because psychology is a science and should move toward truth and because psychological findings affect people's lives. She lists eight common errors in methodology that result from biases in the study of women: 1) use of only male subjects in experiments; 2) the failure to test for sex differences; 3) building theories by eliminating data from women that do not correspond to data from men; 4) lack of knowledge of sex roles and their influence on behavior; 5) exclusive use of male experimenters and investigators; 6) ignoring experimental and situational influences and using male-biased tasks; 7) viewing behaviors as dichotomous rather than integrated (masculinity and femininity as mutually exclusive); and 8) incorporating the culturally-prevalent value system. These errors occur at all stages of the research process from formulation of the problem through operationalization and data collection to analysis and interpretation. According to Johnson, sexist methods in psychology stem from nonconscious assumptions about women and the belief that male behavior is normative.

143. Kahn, Arnold S. and Paula J. Jean. "Integration and Elimination or Separation and Redefinition: The Future of the Psychology of Women." Signs 8(4):659-671 (1983).

Kahn and Jean describe three different positions that feminists have taken toward the psychology of women and traditional psychology. The "integration and elimination" position advocates incorporating the psychology of women as quickly as possible into traditional psychology. Supporters of this position believe that all differences between women and men can be explained by socialization and social expectations. They also promote the use of traditional methods and topics for research related to women. The "integration follows equality" position believes that until women and men have equal status a separate psychology of women is essential. Differences between women and men are actually differences in status and power. Advocates of this position pursue research aimed at improving the status of women and promote women for influential positions in academia, agencies, and professional organizations. Psychology after women have equal status will be both feminist and nonsexist. The "separation and self-definition" position asserts that traditional psychology and the psychology of women can never successfully merge. Separatists view the differences between women and men as real. They envision the psychology of women as an independent field "with an agenda of political and social change, unfettered by the incomplete and biased notions of traditional psychology." Separatist researchers advocate new methods, theories, and ethics. Kahn and Jean don't promote any one of the three perspectives but they claim that their existence poses crucial questions: "whether, when, and how feminist scholarship should be integrated into mainstream academia." These questions are relevant not just to psychology but to all disciplines.

144. Kaplan, Marcie. "A Woman's View of DSM-III." American Psychologist 38:786-792 (1983).

In psychology, diagnostic assumptions guide and influence research. Kaplan's article details the extent to which masculine bias concerning healthy and crazy behaviors has shaped the Diagnostic and Statistical Manual of Mental Disorders (commonly known as DSM-III, in its third edition). Women are caught in a no-win situation. The criteria for healthy adults match male behavior. If women act as women are supposed to act, therefore, they are unhealthy adults. If they act as men are supposed to act, however, they are unhealthy women. DSM-III's definitions of mental disorder and social deviance make it impossible to determine when society should be labeled unjust and when an individual should be labeled crazy. Using dependency as an example, Kaplan shows how DSM-III singles out the ways in which women are dependent and labels these as problematic. It fails to address the ways in which men are dependent (for example, on others to take care of their houses and their children). Researchers must beware of designing research or drawing conclusions based on male-biased diagnostic assumptions concerning women.

145. Lips, Hilary M. "Toward a New Science of Human Being and Behavior." In The Effects of Feminist Approaches on Research Methodologies, edited by Winnie Tomm, pp. 51-70 (Waterloo, Ontario: Wilfrid Laurier University Press, 1989).

Lips describes the "very first and perhaps still primary" impact of feminism on psychological research methodolgy as "an increased sensitivity to sexist bias in theory and research and attempts to minimize such bias by doing better, more careful research." Early feminist psychologists, such as Helen Thompson and Leta Hollingworth, attempted, through the careful collection of data, to offer scientific proof that would eliminate gender stereotypes. More recently, however, feminists have begun to attack the biases that determine the research questions asked as well as the way the data are collected and interpreted. In framing their attacks, feminists have drawn a distinction between bias, as a source of error or distortion, and values, as commitments to particular goals. Lips lists several ways in which the influence of feminism has "cleaned up" psychological research methods: 1) many psychologists now include sex-of-experimenter-effects as a research variable; 2) researchers attempt more often to pick subjects respresentative of those about whom they wish to draw conclusions; 3) researchers less often generalize conclusions based only on people having difficulties with a normal process (for example, menopause, menstrual cycle); 4) researchers have become more sensitive to social context; 5) researchers have begun to report differences between women and men as simply differences rather than as ways that women need to improve; 6) researchers have begun to treat subjects as contributors to the research process; and 7) researchers more often look for many factors, rather than a single cause, when describing behavior. She encourages feminist psychologists not to reject quantitative approaches as masculine. Statistics, used with sensitivity, can "allow for a holistic and deeply exploratory approach to research." To remain self-critical, feminist theory and research must avoid choosing between alternatives such as subjectivity and objectivity or scholarship and advocacy. The "very tension...inherent in refusing to choose one side or the other," says Lips, will allow feminist researchers to remain critical of their own work as well as the work of others.

146. Lott, Bernice. The Potential Enrichment of Social/Personality Psychology Through Feminist Research, and Vice Versa. ERIC document #ED 241 872 (1983).

Lott lists two ways in which feminism can enrich scholarship in any field: 1) through self-conscious and critical analyses to uncover androcentric bias in content and method; and 2) by asking new questions and presenting new theories and hypotheses as a result of focusing on women's experiences and lives. Feminism can enrich psychology specifically by: 1) treating gender as a significant variable; 2) using both men and women in samples and noting similarities and differences; 3) avoiding an association between good mental health and fulfilling the "dictates of the gender stereotype;" 4) exploring new fields of inquiry that result when women are of interest in themselves rather than in relation to men; 5) using control groups that reflect diversity rather than the investigator's assumptions; 6) making explicit the differences in power and status between the sexes; 7) using new sources of information to study women's lives; 8) recognizing that behavior is a function of both the person and context; 9) reporting the magnitude of the effect as well as the statistical significance when dealing with gender differences; and 10) challening objectivity. "To understand the learning or acquisition of behavior," says Lott, "is to understand how culture constructs gender."

147. Lott, Bernice. "Separate Spheres Revisited." Contemporary Social Psychology 13(2):55-62 (1985).

Lott acknowledges gender "as a central organizing principle" in society, a principle that determines prestige and power. She opposes, however, the "separate sheres" approach to gender adopted by feminists as well as by Freud and Erikson, Erik H. Arguing that women and men behave in certain ways because of gender limits the opportunities for all people and sets a dangerous precedent for legal decisions and social change. "No human behavior is exclusively the province of one group of persons rather than another...." Psychologists must study the cultural arrangements that associate gender with different expectations, opportunities, and consequences, rather than examine the gender differences themselves.

148. Lykes, M. Brinton and Abigail J. Stewart. "Evaluating the Feminist Challenge to Research in Personality and Social Psychology: 1963-1983." Psychology of Women Quarterly 10(4):393-411 (1986).

After examining 156 articles from ten issues of the Journal of Personality and Social Psychology, Lykes and Stewart identify methodology "as the gatekeeper of mainstream psychological research, the point of most resistance and least change." Feminists are developing alternative research methods but they are shared through explicitly feminist journals. Research published in these feminist journals is cited far less frequently than feminist research published in mainstream journals. Lykes and Stewart advise feminists to "nourish [their] roots in the larger community of women and men" if they hope to transform "a psychology rooted in men's questions into a feminist psychology rooted in the questions emerging from all people's experience...."

149. Maccoby, Eleanor Emmons and Carol Nagy Jacklin. The Psychology of Sex Differences. Stanford, California: Stanford University Press, 1974.

Maccoby and Jacklin undertook a comprehensive review of the literature of sex differences to determine what differences exist, how these differences came about, and whether or not these differences are inevitable or products of social stereotypes. Their review aimed at testing "the null hypothesis that...assigning cases to groups by sex is no more meaningful for purposes of understanding the behavior of the subjects than assigning them at random." The literature Maccoby and Jacklin reviewed exhibits several methodological problems: 1) the information is often incomplete; 2) findings of no sex differences, and less often, of sex differences, are not reported; 3) findings not in agreement with the accepted view are kept out of print; 4) differences are reported without an explanation of the conditions eliciting these differences; 5) positive findings are frequently cited while negative findings are ignored; 6) studies of only one sex report conclusions, which are later cited, of differences between the sexes; 7) differences in the correlations of the two sexes are reported as if there were a significant difference between the correlations themselves; and 8) different patterns within each sex are reported as differences between the sexes. Maccoby and Jacklin warn that "the basic problem with research on sex differences is that it is almost always impossible for observers to be blind to the sex of the subjects." Because objectivity is impossible, they acknowledge that their feminist perspective colored their approach to the "value-laden topics" discussed in their book.

150. McHugh, Maureen C., Randi Daimon Koeske, and Irene Hanson Frieze. "Issues to Consider in Conducting Nonsexist Psychological Research." American Psychologist 41(8):879-890 (1986).

McHugh, Koeske and Frieze distinguish between sex-fair research, which does not discriminate against women, and feminist research, which works actively for the advancement of women. They view sex-fair research as only one goal of feminist psychologists. Much of the bias that occurs routinely may not be intentional or conscious. It results, rather, from the "accumulated 'common experience' of being a member of a particular group." Psychological findings influence "societal solutions to problems of living." Psychologists, therefore, must conduct sex-fair research. The recommendations McHugh, Koeske and Frieze offer to help eliminate sexist bias in psychological research include: 1) the careful examination of underlying values and assumptions in all research; 2) the use of alternative and nonexperimental research methodologies; 3) care in the use of terminology to avoid confusing sex with gender or description with explanation; 4) a consideration of all possible explanations, including social-cultural, biological, and situational factors, for sex-related phenomena; 5) give equal emphasis in publication to findings of sex similarities and sex differences; 6) avoid language that implies biological or social causation not demonstrated by the research; 7) base conclusions about male and female behavior on research in multiple contexts; 8) consider the role of the researcher and others present on the behavior, response, and performance of the participants; 9) generalize to both sexes only when samples of both sexes have been used in research; and 10) ensure that topics of interest to women are supported and accorded equal status with topics of interest to men.

151. Mckenna, Wendy and Suzanne J. Kessler. “Experimental Design as a Source of Sex Bias in Social Psychology.” Sex Roles 3(2):117-128 (1977).

McKenna and Kessler discovered evidence of sex bias in experimental design from examining abstracts of 312 experiments on interpersonal attraction and 244 experiments on aggression. They found that the topic being studied influenced the proportion of male-only and female-only experiments. Aggression, as indicated by the overwhelming choice of males as respondents, is clearly a masculine area. Interpersonal attraction is less masculine than aggression but the respondents are still predominantly male. McKenna and Kessler also found that, with female respondents, the independent variables were less likely to involve active treatment and the dependent variables were less likely to involve active behavior on the respondents' parts. “The pattern of results,” they claim, “indicates that experimenter's choice of subjects, variables, and manipulations or measurements are interdependent [and]...reflect sex-role stereotyping.” The development of a psychology of women seems, to McKenna and Kessler, to offer a solution to the problems that result when conclusions about sex differences are based on “unexamined assumptions about the relationship between sex of subjects and experimental design.” New concepts and theories “specifically based on what is valuable and relevant to women” will expose the biases inherent in current psychological research.

152. Meyer, Joan. “Feminist Thought and Social Psychology.” In Feminist Thought and the Structure of Knowledge, edited by Mary McCanney Gergen, pp. 105-123 (New York: New York University Press, 1988).

Feminist scholarship is rooted in social developments and social psychology is the study of the influence of society on the individual and of the individual on society. It seems reasonable to expect social psychologists to be among the most advanced users of feminist insights. However, clinical, therapeutic, and developmental psychology have been influenced to a greater extent by feminist scholarship than social psychology. The reason for this, according to Meyer, is that social psychology lacks “a genuine 'reality testing point' and a legitimate place for the subjective experience.” Feminists have been particularly concerned with the “invisibility of women” or “pars pro toto” syndrome characteristic of social psychological research. Women have been omitted not only as subjects in research studies but also when areas are chosen for theorizing, research questions are formulated, and hypotheses are developed and operationalized. A methodology is needed that will "make explicit the limitations of any particular research question, area, group, and generalizability." Models of human relationships must allow for "ambivalence, ambiguity, and inconsistencies." Meyer lists four principles on which she believes feminists base their research practice: 1) a researcher must take the material context (i.e., the availability of resources) into account; 2) the researcher must take the cultural and social norms into account; 3) the researcher must give subjective experience, both her own and the subjects', a legitimate place; and 4) the researcher must be aware of the impact of the research on society.

153. Miller, Frederick D. and Baila Zeitz. "A Woman's Place Is in the Footnotes." Personality and Social Psychology Bulletin 4(4):511-514 (1978).

Miller and Zeitz examined all articles published in the 1976 and 1977 volumes of Journal of Personality and Social Psychology and Journal of Experimental Social Psychology (a total of 357) to determine if "sex is used as a basis for awarding authorships." They found the vast majority of sole authors, first authors, and second authors to be male. On the other hand, they found more female than male research assistants thanked in footnotes. Unequal representation of men in the profession may explain their dominance among sole and first authors. The large difference, however, between the proportion of female secondary authors (26.8 percent) and female research assistants (51.2 percent) suggests that: 1) the work of men is valued more highly than the work of women; 2) women are choosing and being directed toward less significant tasks; and 3) women mentioned in footnotes may often be undergraduates rather than graduate students. Miller and Zeitz conclude that "women seem to be disproportionately carrying on the day to day work of social psychology while men receive the bulk of the credit."

154. Parlee, Mary Brown. "Appropriate Control Groups in Feminist Research." Psychology of Women Quarterly 5(4):637-644 (1981).

Control groups are used in psychological research to demonstrate the causal relationship between a manipulated independent variable and the dependent variable under examination. Subjects in experimental and control groups must be similar in all important ways for a causal relationship to be demonstrated. Parlee suggests that the choice of a control group is not simply a methodological issue but can determine "to a greater or lesser extent the nature of the conclusions that will be reached." Control groups also "implicitly define the theoretical perspective underlying research on a particular topic." Parlee lists three ways in which feminist psychologists can use control groups or discussions about them to promote a feminist perspective throughout the discipline of psychology: 1) control groups can be used to propose alternative theoretical frameworks for coneptualizing particular subject areas; 2) the issue of controls, broadened to include all sexes, races, ages, or classes could serve as a vehicle for broadening the perspective of the field as a whole; and 3) issues raised by control groups "may prompt psychologists to think...of moving outside a conceptual framework where the notion of such groups has any relevance."

155. Parlee, Mary Brown. "Psychology and Women." Signs 5(1):121-133 (1979).

Parlee identifies four kinds of work in the psychology of women: 1) critiques of traditional research on women; 2) research producing data on topics raised because of a feminist perspective; 3) development of theoretical concepts arising from a feminist perspective; and 4) research on topics with a psychological component (for example, domestic violence, conversational interaction) "which do not begin to be completely comprehended by any of the conceptual or methodological paradigms of traditional psychology." Feminist psychologists challenge traditional psychology because they seek the "best possible truth" about a subject rather than adhere strictly to a method. Mainstream psychology's context-stripping approach obscures the connections between individual experience and social roles and institutions. "The last thing wanted by traditional psychologists," Parlee concludes, "is clear thinking — focusing on context — about problems of social significance." So that is what feminists should do.

156. Parlee, Mary Brown. "Psychology of Women in the 80s: Promising Problems." International Journal of Women's Studies 8(2):193-204 (1985).

Parlee asks, now that psychologists interested in research on women have their own journals, texts, groups, and networks, what it is they want to do. In contrast to most other areas of psychology, the reasons feminists do research on the psychology of women "are importantly related to the kinds of questions [they] ask." Subject matter and questions, Parlee insists, should determine the methods of knowing instead of the other way around. She describes four kinds of psychological research now being done about women: 1) critiques of traditional psychological research on women; 2) research that generates new data on topics of interest to feminists but not traditional psychologists; 3) research focused on the theoretical development of concepts; and 4) research on domestic violence, rape, housework, pregnancy and other topics important to women's lives that cannot be understood using the paradigms of traditional psychology. For the future of the psychology of women in relation to the rest of psychology, Parlee suggests three models: 1) a total integration model, and the dissolution of the psychology of women as a subfield; 2) teaching and research in the psychology of women as extensions of models and concepts basic to psychology as a whole; and 3) the existence of the psychology of women alongside traditional psychology, as a separate field. Given that traditional psychology has modeled itself after the experimental, prediction, and control approach of the physical sciences, Parlee doubts that the first and second models are possible. "If asking questions that we think will lead to psychological truth means we cannot use the methods and concepts by which psychology defines itself,...we should...continue to ask those questions and seek the answers by whatever scientific methods are appropriate."

157. Parlee, Mary Brown. "Review Essay: Psychology." Signs 1(1):119-138 (1975).

Parlee borrows from Nancy Henley ("Resources for the Study of Psychology and Women," RT: Journal of Radical Therapy 4:20-21 (1974)) to divide the literature she reviews into psychology of women, psychology against women, and psychology for women. Much of the psychology of women literature is "conceptually chaotic" and "methodologically unsound." In addition, the phrase "psychology of women" misleads by implying the need for "a special set of laws and theories to account for the behavior and experience of females." The psychology against women literature includes studies which indicate that some psychologists have "distorted facts, omitted problems, and perpetuated pseudoscientific data relevant to women." Feminist psychologists have conducted research classified as psychology for women. Parlee separates the feminist literature into three categories: 1) studies that demonstrate some aspect of women's experience and behavior that has gone unnoticed by traditional psychologists; 2) studies that force a reinterpretation of traditional theories or bodies of data; and 3) studies that "put some aspect of women's behavior and experience...in the context of a reasonably well-developed theory from an established area of psychology." The latter studies contain no traces of the antifeminism that pervade some of the psychology of women literature and they do not involve procedures or practices that ignore or distort women's experience.

158. Pyke, S. W. and C. Stark-Adamec. "Canadian Feminism and Psychology: The First Decade." Canadian Psychology 22(1):38-54 (1981).

Pyke and Stark-Adamec survey the state of women and psychology in Canada. They list a "plethora of methodological...forms of bias in academic psychology:" 1) androcentric bias characterizes the historical development of psychology; 2) textbooks and research studies demonstrate a bias toward subjects of interest to men; 3) researchers have generalized to women findings based on male samples; 4) evaluation and inference biases have led researchers to conclude that tasks at which women excel are simple and that women's abilities equip them for lesser tasks; 5) through selection and distortion of evidence, researchers have used findings to justify sex discrimination; and 6) journals have published only sex differences research involving statistically significant findings. A feminist approach to psychology has encouraged new research on sex-role socialization and stereotyping, achievement, sex differences, psychobiology, androgyny, and feminism itself. To the concern that feminist psychology will remain an esoteric speciality isolated from real psychology, Pyke and Stark-Adamec respond that "the psychology of women is an exemplar of integration since it encompasses almost the entire range of psychological content...[from] an interdisciplinary generalist orientation." They believe that a multidisciplinary approach is necessary if psychology generally is not to remain parochial.

159. Reinharz, Shulamit. The Future of Feminist Psychology. ERIC document #ED 227 399 (1982).

Reinharz distinguishes participation in the network of psychology of women scholars from participation in traditional scholarly networks. Participating in the psychology of women network requires a rethinking of socialization and training. The domain of inquiry for the psychology of women is "all phenomena relating to women and girls and a reevaluation of all other research in the framework of its relation to women and girls." Feminist scholars criticize traditional psychological research on the three grounds of bias, limitation, and oppression. On research previously identified as objective, misogynist bias has been demonstrated. Research has suffered limitation by insufficiently studying girls and women, by ignoring issues of concern to women, and by not explaining women's personal experiences. Research has oppressed women by evolving from and sustaining a sex-stratified society. Feminist psychology "treats a field of science as itself a dependent variable." Risk-taking and imagination will help feminist scholars examine and understand cognitive differences between men and women that could have methodological repercussions.

160. Schwabacher, Sara. "Male Versus Female Representation in Psychological Research: An Examination of the Journal of Personality and Social Psychology, 1970, 1971." Catalog of Selected Documents in Psychyology 2:20-21 (1972).

After examining articles in all 1970 issues and two 1971 issues of the Journal of Personality and Social Psychology, Schwabacher concludes that "the indicated lack of attention of psychologists to women should be a major concern and an area for further research." She found males overrepresented as authors and subjects. She also found that studies using only male subjects most often applied their results to women as well as to men. Only 42 percent of the studies using both sexes as subjects tested for sex differences.

161. Sherif, Carolyn Wood. "Bias in Psychology." In The Prism of Sex: Essays in the Sociology of Knowledge, edited by J. A. Sherman and Evelyn Torton Beck, pp. 93-133 (Madison, Wisconsin: University of Wisconsin Press, 1979).

The existence of sexist bias in psychology has been recognized for almost a century and yet theory and research practice continue to reflect such bias. Sherif attributes the lack of change to "highly restricted notions of what science is." In order to be called a science, psychology has modeled itself after hard rather than soft disciplines and has respected experimental, laboratory research above research conducted in natural settings aimed at changing social life and individual conditions. Psychologists have assumed that: 1) the causes of an event can be determined by breaking down the event into component parts; 2) the events to be studied could be completely removed from their context and placed in the here-and-now of the researcher's observation; 3) causes can be discovered by understanding the relationships between variables; 4) sex is an independent not a dependent variable; 5) the more a researcher has manipulated the circumstances of the experiment the more valid the research is; and 6) individuals and social differences should be treated as errors in the sense that experiments and laws would not try to explain them. Sherif advises psychological researchers to: 1) broaden the framework within which knowledge is sought; 2) use a variety of methods and research techniques to relate events; 3) focus on a cross-disciplinary study of the human self-system rather than continue to build on trait theory; 4) take into account the pervasive influence of cultural institutions and social values on individuals;

and 5) extend cross-disciplinary borrowing beyond the biological sciences.

162. Sherif, Carolyn Wood. "What Every Intelligent Person Should Know About Psychology and Women." In The Study of Women: Enlarging Perspectives of Social Reality, edited by E. C. Snyder, pp. 143-183 (New York: Harper & Row, 1979).

According to Sherif, "what every intelligent person should know is that the 'causes' of human experiences and actions are much more complex than any of the traditional schools of psychology" have allowed. Sherif's essay is a chapter in a textbook addressing the study of women, and the essay's broad scope reflects its textbook-like intent. It covers historical background, defines the psychology of women, and discusses the re-examinations of traditional areas that the inclusion of women has caused. Sherif advocates interactionism, which sees the human individual as "shaped by the social environment, but also contemplating it, actively dealing with it, and, at times, deliberately trying to change that environment." The psychology of women seeks to eliminate the sex bias that has characterized psychological research "because such bias is contrary to the standards of scholarly inquiry, not to mention science."

163. Shields, Stephanie. "Ms. Pilgrim's Progress: The Contributions of Leta Stetter Hollingworth to the Psychology of Women." American Psychologist 30:852-857 (1975).

Shields describes Leta Stetter Hollingworth's (1886-1939) contributions to the psychology of women. The latter's careful research provided empirical evidence for the inaccuracy of assumptions concerning variability and the performance of women during menstruation. She demonstrated that social beliefs, rather than scientific facts, lay behind the educational and job-related discriminations against women and their occupational segregation as wives and mothers. Hollingworth had faith that truly objective research, which demonstrated that women were as capable of achievement as men, would overcome social restrictions. Her observations and suggestions, however, remain timely and relevant over 50 years later.

164. Squire, Corinne. Significant Differences: Feminism in Psychology. London: Routledge, 1989.

"The combinatory, egalitarian approach which most feminists favor," says Squire, "often repeats traditional psychological methods' own procedural macho." Feminists maintain "methodological orthodoxy" to ensure that they will be taken seriously as psychologists. Because, in the same way as the conventional method, feminist method centers on the "concept of the subject as a purely psychological entity," it represents only a cosmetic change. Methods so centered cannot deal adequately with differences between same-sex subjects.

165. Stark-Adamec, Cannie and Meredith Kimball. "Science Free of Sexism: A Psychologist's Guide to the Conduct of Nonsexist Research." Canadian Psychology 25(1):23-34 (1984).

Stark-Adamec and Kimball claim that sexist research is usually unintentional. Nonetheless, it is unscientific and unethical because it affects women's opportunities, psychological health, and quality of life. Sexist research is research that misrepresents sex differences or that excludes women or issues relevant to their lives from the body of psychological knowledge. Sexist research assumes that men and male behavior patterns are "superior to and more representative of the human experience" than women and their behaviors. To help researchers, directors of research, funding agencies, editors, and reviewers avoid unintentional sexism, Stark-Adamec and Kimball provide guidelines and a checklist on reviewing background literature, formulating research questions, designing and conducting research, balancing alternative explanations, avoiding oversimplification, using responsible language, theorizing, and making public statements.

166. Unger, Rhoda K. "Advocacy Versus Scholarship Revisited: Issues in the Psychology of Women." Psychology of Women Quarterly 7(1):5-17 (1982).

Unger examines the conflict between research and social values that arises for feminist psychologists socialized according to the traditional approach to science. She lists four incorrect assumptions shared by most psychologists: 1) science involves the objective pursuit of truth; 2) disciplines develop or advance as researchers accrue data, which determines valid models and theories; 3) competent researchers are rewarded by advancement and collegial relationships center around competence in the pursuit of knowledge; and 4) researchers, formally and informally, judge each other's work rather than each other's personal characteristics. Feminist psychology threatens the relationship between the theory and practice of science by questioning psychological definitions and assumptions about women, questioning the methods that generated these definitions and assumptions, and redefining the "means by which data are examined and validated." Unger asks why work in the psychology of women is ignored and undercited: because it is done by women, because it is about women, or because it represents a new theoretical perspective? She concludes that the psychology of women "appears to possess power without authority." Those who define appropriate scholarship have conferred deviance upon feminist psychology. While the question remains concerning the desirability or possiblity of incorporating feminist research into traditional disciplines, the psychology of women will exist "on scholarly boundary lines" until feminist psychologists possess the legitimacy to define themselves.

167. Unger, Rhoda K. "Psychological, Feminist, and Personal Epistemology." In Feminist Thought and the Structure of Knowledge, edited by Mary McCanney Gergen, pp. 124-141 (New York: New York University Press, 1988).

Unger begins her essay by saying that "psychology, more than other social sciences, has been largely unaware of the way its definition of appropriate methods and content has created the phenomena with which it deals." The positivist-empiricist model that has guided behaviorism assumes general laws of behavior exist to be discovered and narrows the scope of appropriate questions that can be asked about males and females. Assuming current social reality as the norm, behavioral researchers seek psychological and behaviorial sex differences that naturally accompany biological differences. Feminists tend to look at sex as a cognitive rather than as a biological variable. Maleness and femaleness are social stimuli and behaviorial differences between men and women result from attempts to behave in a socially desirable manner. Questions concerning when specific social norms are activated and what social processes cause individuals to conform to social norms harmful to themselves "require an analysis that recognizes the existence of contradiction at all levels of human existence." An example of such an analysis involves the nature and function of the double-bind, a situation in which a woman incurs social penalty regardless of her behavior. The importance of the analysis is to demonstrate that double-binds are the result of situational constraints rather than personal flaws. Feminist psychologists themselves are caught in a double-bind. A unique contribution of psychology as a discipline is its attempt to "infer cause-and-effect relationships about human behavior using the tools of empiricism." In their move away from logical positivism and toward a more cognitive perspective, feminist psychologists have moved away from cause-and-effect like methods. Unless they use such methods, however, they are unlikely to be taken seriously by the rest of the discipline. Unger concludes by suggesting that empirical methods can be useful to feminists within the cognitive paradigm. "The tools of psychology are of less significance in themselves than by whom they are used."

168. Unger Rhoda K. "Through the Looking Glass: No Wonderland Yet! (The Reciprocal Relationship Between Methodology and Models of Reality)." Psychology of Women Quarterly 8(1):9-32 (1983).

Unger wonders whether methodological issues are not actually conceptual ones. Early feminist psychologists concentrated on exposing the omissions in the positivist empiricist approach. They pointed out, for example, the neglect of women as research subjects, the effect of the sex of the researcher on the subjects' performance, and the tendency to generalize to all people from male samples. But rectifying these omissions does nothing to change the transformation of people, by the positivist approach, into "object-like subjects." Techniques of quantification and experimentation are "devoid of much significance in themselves," but researchers much be aware that they make "epistemological commitments" when they use these tools unthinkingly. Unger outlines the characteristics of a moral or value-imbued social science: 1) researchers would claim no methodology as the sole source of the truth; 2) research would emphasize the reciprocal, interactive relationship between people and reality; 3) research would recognize experimenter and subject bias as inevitable accompaniments of research not as "transient procedural contaminants;" 4) research subjects would be involved in the analysis of the research results; 5) the researchers' as well as the subjects' behaviors would be examined; 6) research would be helpful to the target population; and 7) researchers would be wary of proof.

169. Van Leeuwen, Mary Stewart. "The Female Reconstructs Psychology." Journal of Psychology and Christianity 3(2):20-32 (1984).

Van Leeuwen compares the work of four feminist psychologists. She describes Naomi Weisstein's (see annotation below) approach as "behaviorist scientism." Weisstein proposes that the right kind of experiments can demonstrate and transcend ideological bias concerning sex differences, and that environmental factors can change human behaviors. Weisstein uses positivist research to illustrate to traditional positivist researchers the sexist error of their ways. Carol Tavris, like Weisstein, appeals to the "authority of experimental science as the final arbiter of truth." Carol Gilligan (see annotation above) ignores the origins of sex differences to ask what the advantages of women's experience might be. She focuses explicitly on the female subculture as one that traditional psychology has neglected. Nancy Chodorow departs most radically from mainstream psychology. She reanalyses and reinterprets some of the authoritative case studies to examine the repercussions of women's primary role in parenting. As a comparison of these four psychologists demonstrates, there is no single feminist psychology of women.

170. Vaughter, Reesa M. "Review Essay: Psychology." Signs 2(1):120-146 (1976).

Vaughter defines the psychology of women as a discipline that "employs methodology appropriate, meaningful, and congruent with the lives of women as well as men; that develops theories that predict female as well as male behavior; and that studies questions of interest to women as well as to men." Its goal is to develop "a nonsexist science, a psychology of human behavior." A feminist perspective in psychology involves: 1) placing research and theoretical models within political and social contexts; 2) engaging in interdisciplinary, collaborative research; 3) engaging the public in decisions concerning research priorities, data collection, and data interpretation; 4) integrating research training and practice with quality of life and self-growth; and 5) working cooperatively instead of competitively and valuing teaching as well as research.

171. Walker, Beverly M. "Psychology and Feminism - If You Can't Beat Them, Join Them." In Men's Studies Modified: The Impact of Feminism on the Academic Disciplines, edited by Dale Spender, pp. 111-124 (New York: Pergamon Press, 1981).

Walker takes a dim view of the effects of the feminist critique on psychology. "Feminists," she says, "have continued, in the main, to work within the inherently conservative framework of methodology and theory of their discipline without substantial revision of its structure." She lists as the main points of the feminist critique: 1) psychology is not objective but rather is a value-laden discipline; 2) the male is the standard in psychoanalytic theories, in generalizations made to everyone from all-male research samples, and in assumptions that equate maleness with normal; 3) sex differences have been magnified and similarities ignored; 4) measures, tests, and theories reflect ingrained sex-role stereotypes; and 5) a psychology of women is needed to balance the prevailing "psychology against women." To change psychology, feminists must attack "the nature of the scientific method as used by psychologists" and reject "psychological practice which preserves the status quo in favour of a more flexible alternative."

172. Wallston, Barbara Strudler and Kathleen E. Grady. "Integrating the Feminist Critique and the Crisis in Social Psychology: Another Look at Research Methods." In Women, Gender and Social Psychology, edited by Virginia E. O'Leary, Rhoda Kesler Unger, and Barbara Strudler Wallston, pp. 7-34 (Hillsdale, New Jersey: Lawrence Erlbaum Associates, 1985).

> Social psychology has been slow to adopt feminist methods because of its "continued emphasis on narrowly defined experimentalism..." claim Wallston and Grady. The study of women has improved social psychology in terms of question formulation, sample selection, design, operationalization, statistics, and interpretation. The experience of a researcher often determines the questions the researcher asks. As more women and minorities have become psychologists the nature of questions asked has begun to broaden. Correlational methods, qualitative approaches, and triangulation allow researchers to study more variables. Generalization on the basis of male subjects has characterized psychological research. The implications of selection by and controlling for sex need to be investigated further. The study of women has moved social psychology toward a relativist approach in which "the conditions under which people label are at least as interesting as the labels themselves." Research reports should include a section describing experimenters similar to the section describing subjects. Because statistics restrict the questions asked, alternative statistics may need to be found. The "adequacy of inference is a function of how the data are produced not how they are analyzed."

173. Weinreich, Helen. "What Future for the Female Subject? Some Implications of the Women's Movement for Psychological Research." Human Relations 30(6):535-543 (1977).

> Weinreich describes the women's movement as "a dangerous truth that cannot be ignored, not only because the issues it raises for psychology concern half the human race, but because so many aspects of it as a phenonmenon challenge the basic assumptions of positivistic psychology." The women's movement brings politics and science together and contributes to a reexamination of interpretation, methodology, and the nature of evidence. Questions have arisen concerning: 1) assumptions regarding sex role stereotypes and their biological origin; 2) the study of women as not-men rather than as themselves in their own right; 3) narrowness of sampling in psychological studies; and 4) the premises and assumptions concerning the nature of the female that inhibit analysis and interpretation in research studies.

174. Weisstein, Naomi. "Psychology Constructs the Female." In Women in Sexist Society: Studies in Power and Powerlessness, edited by Vivian Gornick and Barbara K. Moran, pp. 207-224. (New York: Basic Books, 1971.)

Weisstein shows how psychology has been strangled and deflected by its association of human potential with "accidents of individual development of genitalia...." Two failures have led psychology astray: 1) psychology has looked for inner traits rather than examined social contexts, and 2) psychologists have developed and applied theories without evidence. Weisstein cites studies which have demonstrated that researcher bias "creates a changed environment in which subjects actually act differently," and that people's behavior changes when the social context changes. She refutes biological arguments based on primate behavior by demonstrating that "there is no one biologically natural female or male behavior...." Psychologists must understand social expectations about women if they intend to understand or characterize women's behavior. For differences between women and men to be accurately identified, social expectations for the two sexes must be equal.

175. Wine, Jeri Dawn. "Gynocentric Values and Feminist Psychology." In Feminism in Canada: From Pressure to Politics, edited by Angela R. Miles and Geraldine Finn, pp. 67-87 (Montreal: Black Rose Books, 1982).

Wine claims that "male-stream" psychology's rigid adherance to "a naive brand of logical positivism" and its consistent documentation of the inferiority of women make it a particularly hostile discipline for the development of feminist work. Many feminist studies reflect the highly controlled experimental, objective, context-stripped, and detached values characteristic of traditional psychological methods. Wine argues for more flexible, contextual, and interdisciplinary research. Drawing on the work of Elain Showalter ("Is There a Female Aesthetic," in Women, Advocate and Scholar: Proceedings of the Conference at Montclair State College, 1974), she characterizes most of the feminist research that has occurred as imitative or protesting. By imitative, Wine means research which intends to rectify the under-representation of women as objects of research but does not question androcentric values. Protest research attacks the misogynous bias in the body of psychological knowledge but still does not actually question underlying values. According to Wine, feminist psychologists are just beginning to perform research that explores "female experience guided by androcentric concerns and values," and their findings focus on "relationality," or a sense of connectedness to responsibility for others. While she believes that research on rape, pornography, women-battering, etc. is useful to the feminist struggle, Wine considers it "problematic from a gynocentric perspective." Social power research reveals more about strategies males use to maintain power than it does about ways that women relate.

6
HISTORY

INTRODUCTION

Precursors and Women's History Defined

Contemporary feminist historians have precursors. Nineteenth century feminists turned to history for an explanation of their oppression. New Viewpoints in American History, a 1922 publication by Arthur Schlesinger, blamed women's failure to gain equal rights on historians' "pall of silence" about women's achievements. In 1929, Virginia Woolf called on female students to rewrite history. The "lop-sided" historical record needed correcting with a "mass of information" about women drawn from newly discovered sources. Women have been a "force" in history, argued Mary Beard in 1946, "indispensable to the maintenance and promotion of civilization in the present age."

Natalie Zemon Davis (1976) stretches back to Plutarch to demonstrate that "women's history is no newcomer on the scene." She applauds two early twentieth century studies, Alice Clark's Working Life of Women in the Seventeenth Century (1919) and Léon Abensour's La Femme et le Féminisme en France Avant la Révolution (1923), as models for good women's history. The two studies use primary materials, treat social groups of women separately rather than generalizing from one to another, distinguish between prescribed behavior and women's actions, use theory to relate women and power, work, and property, and respect their research subjects.

In contrast to Davis, who turns to precursors to understand how women's history ought to be done, Ann Gordon, Mari Jo Buhle, and Nancy Schrom (1971), Linda Gordon (1972), and Gerda Lerner (1969) build their definitions of women's history by pointing out where precursors went awry. Gordon, Buhle, and Schrom (1971) reject both nineteenth century feminist writers' "endless history of subjection," which treats women as objects of history, and Mary Beard's woman as "civilizing force." They argue for history as a record of women's movement toward a consciousness of self. Linda Gordon (1972) modifies the nineteenth century oppressed group approach. She defines radical feminist history as the attempt to understand any situation from the perspective of the most oppressed group. Our impressions of entire societies are warped when the historical record includes only the politics and war traditionally defined as power.

Nineteenth century feminist writers' biases — preoccupation with the middle class and with women's oppression — provoked Lerner's description of a feminist historical perspective. The power women have had, she argues, is more important to understand than their oppression. Economic, social, and political subcategories of women are meaningful; woman as a uniform category is not. How society told women to act is one thing; how they have acted is another.

Critique of Traditional History

By naming the "pall of silence" and the "lop-sided" historical record, Schlesinger and Woolf suggested that all was not well with conventional historical research. Contemporary feminists mine these suggestions to expose a tradition of bias and omission. Along with social historians, feminist historians object to the content of history. When historians focus on the intiative and mastery of public life (Gordon, Buhle, and Schrom, 1976), women are objectified and the record is left incomplete. History that includes what Smith-Rosenberg (1975) calls "private places" — the household, the family, the nursery, the bed — examines the relationships between individuals and social institutions, between personality development and social arrangements. To understand such relationships, historians must take an interdisciplinary approach, reinterpret traditional sources, and turn to new ones.

By asking "Did Women Have a Renaissance?" Joan Kelly-Gadol (1977) demonstrates that perspectives, rather than social, economic, or cultural realities, have defined historical periods. The assumption that the relationship between the sexes is a natural one permeates traditional categories of social analysis and theories of social change (Kelly-Gadol, 1976). Exposing male and female as social constructions upsets the traditional apple cart. Bridenthal and Koonz (1977) redefine politics as "a complex set of conflictual power relations between classes, regions, and religious systems struggling for control over scarce resources." Such a definition makes diaries as relevant as political agreements.

Seeing women as a distinct sociological group (Smith, 1976), provokes new questions. Historians have never asked, but now must, what men think of women and whether or not women are allowed to develop freely and hold positions of power and responsibility. Bridenthal (1976) suggests examining history in terms of women's participation in and control over production and reproduction. Women's progress toward freedom, according to Arthur (1976), is a "general evaluation of society."

Critical Self-Reflection

By the late seventies, feminist historians had produced a body of women's history large enough to encourage critical self-reflection. As they reviewed what they had produced, feminists identified four basic approaches (Diner, 1979; Lerner, "Placing Women in History," 1979; Evans, 1982). The contribution or great woman approach concentrates on women who have achieved in the areas (for example, politics or a profession) that men have defined as important. The victim approach, occupied with the origins of women's oppression, focuses on patriarchy and tends to see women as passive sufferers. The women's rights approach studies organized feminism and, in so doing, fails to describe the economic conditions of most women's lives. The preconceived pictures of the past with which all of these approaches begin prevent them from becoming universal and from addressing fundamental questions about social organization or cultural change.

Woman-centered history is the fourth approach, the only one, according to Lerner (Placing Women in History, 1979), which takes history, for women, beyond "prehistory." The woman-centered approach studies women as a separate culture, uses new categories, and explores women's achievements without ignoring their oppression. Kelly (1984) calls the woman-centered approach "doubled vision" because its practitioners treat work and sex as two interrelated spheres. Women no longer occupy a separate domain outside of the patriarchal order.

Feminist historians' self-reflection generated advice. Smith-Rosenberg (1986) cautions women's historians to beware of "historical nihilism." History, she claims, consists of more than subjectively chosen words and individually chosen meanings. Grosholz (1988) warns feminists not to escape into relativism, where history becomes an "emanation of [the historian's] subjectivity...one self-limiting, self-justifying story."

In 1979, Gerda Lerner, on a very hopeful note, summarized the challenges made by feminist history to traditional history. The challenges include exposing patriarchal values, overcoming androcentric bias, redefining categories and periodization, understanding women's devaluation and oppression, and encouraging a paradigm shift toward a new universal history. But more recent literature has been less optimistic. Based on a review of research, Smith (1985) concludes that feminist historians have not been successful at using what they know about women's lives to "re-evaluate historical writing generally." Linda Gordon (1986) limits the contributions of feminist history to one: expanding what counts as evidence. The "feminist reconstitution of knowledge" is a rearrangement of relationships within old stories not a radical break with existing scholarship. Dumont (1989) believes that women's history is still relegated to the periphery, ineffective in modifying "the lenses" historians use to look at the past.

Whatever the state of historical lenses, Virginia Woolf would be delighted with the information about women available today. Sixty years ago, in A Room of One's Own, she despaired of ever knowing the details of earlier women's lives: when they married, how many children they had, what their houses were like, whether or not they had servants. Contemporary feminist historians answered Woolf's call to rewrite history or, at least, to add a supplement.

ANNOTATIONS

176. Arthur, Marylin. "Women in the Ancient World." In Conceptual Frameworks for Studying Women's History, section, I, pp. 1-15 (Bronxville, New York: Sarah Lawrence Publications, 1976).

> Arthur proposes a model of historical change for women's history based on the categories of politics, economics, and social relationships between the sexes. She contrasts her model to the "patriarchalist view" of women's history, and suggests that the two models complement one another. Patriarchalist history assumes that civilization has been patriarchal. The study of women within this model is an "account of the ways and means whereby women have adjusted to, entered into complicity with, or resisted their own subjugation." Arthur's model defines progress as "simultaneous advance" politically, economically, and in terms of the social relations of the sexes. The progress of women toward freedom serves as a "general evaluation of society." Incorporating women into history does more than shine "the flashlight into dark corners...it completes history and makes it true."

177. Beard, Mary R. Women as Force in History: A Study in Traditions and Realities. New York: Octagon Books, 1981 (copyright 1946).

> A forerunner of current feminist history, Beard spoke for the importance of women to all historical human events. She suggests that they "have been a force in making all the history that has been made." Beard stresses — an emphasis for which current feminist historians often take her to task — women's contributions as a civilizing force. She writes that "an understanding of women's past

history...must be regarded as indispensable to the maintenance and promotion of civilization in the present age."

178. Bridenthal, Renate. "Towards a Feminist Marxism: The Dialectics of Production and Reproduction." In Conceptual Frameworks for Studying Women's History, section III. pp. 1-14 (Bronxville, New York: Sarah Lawrence Publications, 1976).

Bridenthal defines mode of reproduction as sexuality, reproduction, and socialization of children. The relationship between reproduction and production "is a dialectic within the larger historical dialectic." Historically, women have been pulled between the opposing forces of work and family. Synthesis will be achieved when both sexes control modes of production and reproduction equally. In women's history, describing "shifts" in women's participation in reproduction and production is more meaningful than describing "progress" or "regress." Feminist movements arise in response to shifts away from direct and toward mediated participation.

179. Bridenthal, Renate and Claudia Koonz. "Introduction." In Becoming Visible: Women in European History, edited by Renate Bridenthal and Claudia Koonz, pp. 1-10 (Boston: Houghton Mifflin, 1977).

Feminist history, say editors Bridenthal and Koonz in the introduction to this collection, must study women "within the complexity of their specific cultural contexts." Historians looking at women in context will need to discover new sources and reinterpret traditional ones. They will also need to redefine the categories used to analyze history. Redefining politics, for example, as "a complex set of conflictual power relations between classes, regions, and religious systems struggling for control over scarce resources" expands relevant sources beyond the traditional political agreements to include letters, diaries, and memoirs. Bridenthal and Koonz suggest that women's history focus on women's power in the family, women's control over property and over their own labor, and the effects on women of technological and social changes in nineteenth century Europe.

180. Bridenthal, Renate and Claudia Koonz. "Restoring Women to History." In Issues in Feminism: A First Course in Women's Studies, edited by Sheila Ruth, pp. 404-411 (Boston: Houghton-Mifflin, 1980).

While acknowledging Simone de Beauvoir's and Mary Beard's contributions, Bridenthal and Koonz describe these writers' categories as "too crude to aid us in interpreting the complexity of women's history." Primary and secondary sources written by men place women either on a pedestal or at a stake, reflecting male attitudes more than women's realities. Feminist historians must reinterpret traditional sources by "placing them in their appropriate setting[s]" and redefine "the categories within which we analyze history." Economic and social institutions, such as the family, have affected women's lives more than political action. An expanded definition of politics — "a complex set of coflictual power relations between classes, regions, and religious systems struggling for control over scarce resources" — expands the nature of historical sources and the number of important participants.

181. Davis, Natalie Zemon. "'Women's History' in Transition: The European Case." Feminist Studies 3(3-4):83-103 (1976).

Davis begins by demonstrating that "the genre of women's history is no newcomer on the scene," and that current feminist history is not new but rather one of many historical transitions. Since Plutarch, historians have written memorials of "Women Worthies" and biographies of individual women. Neither of these approaches influenced the main body of history and both treated women in isolation from their historical contexts. Late eighteenth and early nineteenth century historians began to include subjects, such as the laboring poor or prostitution, which considered women's activities explicitly. In addition, they realized that the family and relations between the sexes varied over time. Davis examines in detail two earlier women's histories: Alice Clark's Working Life of Women in the Seventeenth Century (1919) and Léon Abensour's La Femme et le Féminisme en France avant la Révolution (1923). Clark and Abensour 1) used primary sources and archival materials; 2) did not generalize to all women from the experiences of one social group; 3) did not assume that prescriptions for behavior corresponded to how women actually behaved; 4) used a theory to account for the changing relations of women to power, work, and property; and 5) respected their subjects by "treating them neither as passive victims of historical injustice nor as constant heroines struggling to change society." Davis claims that these two works compare favorably to much of present-day women's history. She believes feminist historians can improve on the work of Clark and Abensour, however, by 1) expanding the study of demographics; 2) using statistical information related to migration, crime, literacy, etc.; 3) studying sexual or erotic activity to provide more information about intimacy between and within the sexes and about patterns of social organization; and 4) setting more general and sweeping goals. Historians of women must not work only on women any more than "historians of class can focus exclusively on peasants." Historians must focus on "understanding the significance of the sexes, of gender groups in the historical past." Studying the sexes will force historians to rethink power, social structure, property, symbols, and periodization. Davis cautions historians to distinguish speculation from generalization, to avoid assuming that existing historical divisions will always be significant, and to "realize how difficult it is to decide what constituted a favorable context in the past for the improvement of the relations between the sexes."

182. Diner, Hasia. "Women and History: Doing Good History." In The Study of Women: Enlarging Perspectives of Social Reality, edited by E. C. Snyder, pp. 296-317 (New York: Harper and Row, 1979).

Diner examines the historiography of women's history by asking what we ought to know about women's status and lives in the past and why we don't know more than we do. She criticizes compensatory history, which aims at compensating for past omissions. Its political purpose results in "assumptions and premises [that] distort and skew..." Diner identifies four approaches to women's history: 1) the great women approach, which uses the lives of extraordinary women to understand social trends; 2) the victimization or oppression approach, which views men as perpetrators of oppression, links women's oppression with the oppression of other minorities, and often fails to compare women's situations with men's; 3) the women's rights approach, which studies organized feminism, and, therefore, fails to describe the social and economic conditions of most women's lives; and 4) the "most significant approach, which begin[s] with a fundamental question about social organization or cultural changes and then proceed[s] to seek answers to that question, without any overriding ideology" or preconceived picture of the past. Gaps in "our understanding of women and change" include: 1) cross-cultural and multicultural concerns; 2) studies of all-female institutions (for example, settlement houses, convents); and 3) studies of the effects on women of technology.

183. Dumont, Micheline. "The Influence of Feminist Perspectives on Historical Research Methodology." In The Effects of Feminist Approaches on Research Methodologies, edited by Winnie Tomm, pp. 111-129 (Calgary, Alberta: Wilfrid Laurier University Press, 1989).

Dumont claims that feminist history "has not modified the lenses by which historians look at the past," and that "women's history is still relegated to the periphery of history." In answer to the question "on what basis do women share an historical existence?" she examines three concepts: equality, difference, and oppression. Theoretical frameworks based on equality assume that reforming democratic institutions will quarantee social progress for everyone; feminist historians dispute the validity of this framework. Using difference as a framework, historians tied women's oppression to their physical characteristics. Although researching it is difficult, the relationship between the sexes is a more productive approach than the differences between them. The oppression framework examines the "powers" in which women's subordinate status has resulted. Historians studying women as subjects of history have made a fundamental break with traditional historical approaches.

184. Dye, Nancy Schrom. "Clio's American Daughters: Male History, Female Reality." In The Prism of Sex: Essays in the Sociology of Knowledge, edited by Julia A. Sherman and Evelyn Torton Beck, pp. 9-31 (Madison, Wisconsin: University of Wisconsin Press, 1979).

Dye examines the history of American historical writing to understand why historians have focused on public life and why they they have ignored women's existence. She suggests that ignoring women resulted in the political and public orientation rather than the other way around. In an attempt to explain how historians could "possibly have been ignorant of the realities of women's lives," Dye claims: 1) that "women's work," the background of everyday life, is easily blocked out; and 2) that women and men experience different realities, life cycles, and even cultures. The first professional historians, who founded the American Historical Association in 1884, tended to be wealthy, intent on practicing history as a science, and products of "a culture that made rigid distinctions between public and private aspects of life and the proper roles for men and women." As members of the social mainstream, they were unlikely to question cultural assumptions. Historians' blindness to women has distorted the record in two ways: 1) by establishing historical periods and explaining social and economic developments inaccurately; and 2) by obscuring our understanding of American society as women have experienced it. To correct the record, historians must "develop the ability to see women as actors in the past" and rewrite American history from a female perspective.

185. Evans, Sara M. "Visions of Woman-Centered History." Social Policy 12(4)46-49 (1982).

Evans begins by stressing the importance of history: "movements require history because history provides an explanation for oppression." Because the "history one learns depends ultimately on the questions one asks," the diversity of questions posed by feminism as a social movement have produced a variety of approaches to feminist history. The contribution approach identifies women's contributions to the historical activities in which men have prevailed. This approach accepts the traditional definition of historical importance and "discovers" only women whose contributions fall within this definition. The victim approach concentrates on the origins of women's oppression and the nature of patriarchy. It focuses more on the actions of men toward women than on the actions of women themselves, and tends to view women as "passive victims." The woman-centered approach to history is, to Evans, the most satisfying approach "both in political and historical terms." This approach explores what women have done, without ignoring the historical reality of oppression.

186. Falk, Joyce Duncan. "The New Technology for Research in European Women's History: 'Online' Bibliographies." Signs 9(1):120-133. (1983).

Falk introduces computerized searching of bibliographical databases as a research tool for feminist historians. Of particular benefit to researchers seeking information on women is the computer's ability to search every word in titles, abstracts, and subject terms. Terms can be combined using "and," "or," or "not" to narrow or broaden retrieval or to exclude certain concepts. The computer provides feminist scholars with access unavailable in printed indexes and abstracts.

187. Fox-Genovese, Elizabeth. "Placing Women's History in History." New Left Review 133:5-29 (1982).

There is not women's history, says Fox-Genovese, without male and class dominance. "Adding women to history is not the same as adding women's history" to history. The implications of adding women's history include: 1) gender as a fundamental category of historical analysis; 2) the understanding that forms of male dominance vary historically; 3) the understanding that substituting women's history for mainstream history leaves women "prisoners of the pernicious status of 'other';" 4) the understanding that capitalism and modern representative government have promised men of all classes public individualism and private dominance; 5) the realization that social theories are based on a hierarchical gender system; 6) the understanding that modern institutions incorporate gender difference as part of the social order; 7) class-and-gender-struggle-based explanations for the family and the sexual division of labor; and 8) the understanding that dominant social theories provide "no adequate way to assess the indispensable contributions of women to collective life in society, including class and racial dominance on the one side and the resistance of the oppressed on the other." Fox-Genovese warns historians of women to avoid rejecting all of official history as irrelevant. Such rejection establishes women as other and "perpetuates many of the most pernicious myths of official history." The "woman-as-other" myth lumps women's varied experiences under the oppression of womanhood and prevents the uncovering of "the history of women in all its tragic complexity."

188. Geiger, Susan N. G. "Women's Life Histories: Method and Content." Signs 11(2):334-351 (1986).

Geiger defines feminist method as "the collective critical reconstitution of the meaning of women's social experience, as women live through it." Such a definition demands that users of the method account for womens' diversity. Geiger reminds feminists that women make up seventy percent of the total illiterate population. She asks how the experiences of the "silent" can be uncovered and understood by researchers dependent on the written word. The characteristics of life histories that traditional researchers view as weaknesses — the representativeness of an individual life and the subjectivity of the sources — appear to feminists as strengths. Through life histories, feminists seek the link between experience and consciousness. Consciousness not only interprets but also constructs the social world. A condition of familial embeddedness central to the way women experience and construct the world is consistent across cultural, racial, and class lines. "The critical feminist question regarding consciousness as an act of social construction is whether and under what conditions such embeddedness is either internalized and taken for granted, or seen as problematic and questionable."

189. Gordon, Ann D., Mari Jo Buhle, and Nancy Schrom Dye. "The Problem of Women's History." In Liberating Women's History, edited by Berenice A. Carroll, pp. 75-92 (Urbana, Illinois: University of Illinois Press, 1976).

Gordon, Buhle, and Dye discuss four historical methodologies used to approach women and "feminist theory about women's collectivity." History "equates initiative and mastery with life." Such an equation creates women as objects rather than subjects of history and determines the way historians write about them. The "history of women in organizations" approach studies women's association with movements, primarily women's rights. Historians using this approach assume that 1) women merit study only when they behave like men; 2) organizations initiate change on their own, independent of the socioeconomic changes occurring around them; and 3) the linear pursuit of liberty characterizes American history. Availability of sources limits the "biographies of women" approach. While biography can be useful for understanding exceptional women, it fails to reconstruct a "history of the inarticulate." Historians too often apply psychological theories simplistically to explain the unique factors that encouraged outstanding women to reject their "natural roles." The "history of social ideas" approach studies the relationship between ideas and social practice by examining prescriptive literature such as etiquette books, sermons, or child-rearing manuals. By focusing on suggestions about how women ought to behave rather than how they actually did behave, this approach often fails to distinguish between women of different classes. The "social history" approach "holds the greatest possibility for future work." Historians using this approach ask how women's roles have changed over time and attempt to integrate women into the mainstream of American historical development. Gordon, Buhle, and Dye warn feminist historians that analyses of women based on their oppressed status "render history an external process, a force which presses against women's lives without a reciprocal interaction." While remaining conscious of experiences all women share, feminist historians must develop categories to fit women, who have changed over time and who differ by class, race, and sexuality, into history. The new history will encompass personal and subjective experience as well as public and political activities.

190. Gordon, Ann D., Mari Jo Buhle, and Nancy E. Schrom. "Women in American Society: An Historical Contribution." Radical America 5(4): 3-66 (1971).

Nineteenth century feminist writers tried explain their current situation by describing "an endless history of subjection." Mary Beard limited women's role to one of "civilizing force." Gordon, Buhle, and Schrom, wanting to avoid either of these approaches, say women's history "must transcend the imposition of contemporary institutions and values" by documenting the "underlying historical conditions of the subjection of all women." They object to the "caste" view of women as static and argue for history as a record of the movement of women toward a consciousness of self. A caste/oppression framework fails to explain the dynamic of women's lives or the historical conditions underlying them and ignores racial and social differences, making women "objects of history, bound by their peculiar situation as victims of oppression." Most women's history is either institutional, biographical or prescriptive. Institutional history examines feminist organizations; biographical history tends to focus on the elite and literate, and prescriptive history examines social institutions, such as marriage and the family. A woman today who turns to history will find "precious little" to help her get a sense of continuity or development outside of the feminist movement. History must describe the "totality of the female experience [to provide] the essential identification for women to recognize their collective fate and to build a force that can move forward."

191. Gordon, Linda. "Towards a Feminist History." Female Studies 5(2):49-52 (1972).

Gordon decribes radical feminist history as the attempt to understand any situation from the perspective of the most oppressed group concerned. By definition, things associated with power are historically noteworthy; history, therefore, excludes women. Without an analytical history of women, historians' understanding of "entire societies is warped." According to Gordon, the current university system, which excludes the oppressed or "trains them in the ideology of the dominant groups," will not support radical feminist history. Feminists must form a community of scholars independent of the financial, political, and intellectual support of established universities.

192. Gordon, Linda. "What's New in Women's History." In Feminist Studies Critical Studies, edited by Teresa de Lauretis, pp. 20-30 (Bloomington, Indiana: Indiana University Press, 1986).

Gordon has decided that the "feminist reconstitution of knowledge" is not a radical break with existing historical scholarship but rather a rearrangement of relationships within the old stories. She identifies two approaches taken by feminist historians. One approach focuses on rectifying past errors by discovering a more accurate historical truth. The other approach rejects objectivity and the possibility of truth and concentrates on history as humanistic and narrative, as a stimulus for the creation of "new myths to serve our aspirations." Gordon recommends a historical method that mediates between these two approaches, a method that will maintain a tension between "accuracy and mythic power." Such a method will enable feminist historians to move beyond the polarization between social and political history, to transcend the division between the theoretical categories of victim and heroine, domination and resistance, and to actually challenge traditional historical interpretations through new evidence. Gordon claims that feminist history has made only one significant contribution: redefining and expanding what counts as evidence.

193. Gordon, Linda, Persis Hunt, Elizabeth Peck, Rochelle Goldberg Ruthchild, and Marcia Scott. "Historical Phallacies: Sexism in American Historical Writing." In Liberating Women's History: Theoretical and Critical Essays, edited by Berenice A. Carroll, pp. 55-73 (Urbana, Illinois: University of Illinois Press, 1976).

The feminist movement of the late 1960s stimulated research and publication on the feminist movement of the late nineteenth century. Gordon, Hunt, Peck, Ruthchild, and Scott criticize the sexism characteristic of most of this research and publication. Historians too often write as if "the genital difference between men and women...explain[s] entire sets of social and cultural phenomena as emanating not from external forces...but from the nature of women themselves." Attitudes expressed by sexist historians include: 1) the belief that women cause their own oppression; 2) the belief that women's emotionalism misleads them; 3) the belief that women should be satisfied with the emancipation they have; and 4) the belief that class is always more significant than sex. Male historians write as if they were a "third sex, uninvolved in the struggle against male dominance and unaffected by the demands of the feminists that men give up their privileges."

194. Grosholz, Emily. "Women, History, and Practical Deliberation." In Feminist Thought and the Structure of Knowledge, edited by Mary McCanney Gergen, pp. 173-181 (New York: New York University Press, 1988).

Grosholz argues that "practical deliberation, not scientific theory, is the right model for understanding what we are about when we engage in feminist historiography." Instead of being a correct theory or a truth, feminism is an on-going assessment of the moral significance of actions, a method of social change. Grosholz borrows from Simone de Beauvoir to sketch a taxonomy of feminist history gone astray. The childish historian accepts traditional historical scholarship as fact; the serious historian seeks for what she assumes is the fixed meaning of history; the nihilist historian rejects history because all views are arbitrary; and the passionate historian makes history the "emanation of her subjectivity," enclosing herself in "one self-limiting, self-justifying story." This taxonomy warns feminist historians not to ignore history or let others write it for them. Feminist historiography must take what has come before into account, and must avoid escaping into relativism. Approached with forgiveness, the past, claims Grosholz, can become a resource for the future rather than "a prison and ensnarement."

195. Johansson, Sheila Ryan. "'Herstory' As History: A New Field or Another Fad?" In Liberating Women's History: Theoretical and Critical Essays, edited by Berenice A. Carroll, pp. 400-430 (Urbana, Illinois: University of Illinois Press, 1976).

Johansson bemoans feminist historians' choice of Simone de Beauvoir's ideas over Mary Beard's. She holds de Beauvoir responsible for the "Woman-the-Passive-Victim" approach, which dominates contemporary women's history. Beard's woman-as-agent approach, while just as one-sided as de Beauvoir's, deserves equal attention. To establish itself as "a legitimate and useful perspective on the past," the study of women must deal, not with "Woman," but with well-defined and differentiated groups of women. Johansson proposes the use of status patterns or "complex guides to assembling and organizing material pertinent to understanding the phrase 'status of women' in a comprehensive sense." She applies to women's history "an interpretive perspective which declares that decentralized, collective forms of decision-making and behavior are ultimately the main source of fundamental forms of social change."

196. Kelly, Joan. "The Doubled Vision of Feminist Theory: A Postscript to the 'Women and Power' Conference." In Women, History & Theory: The Essays of Joan Kelly, by Joan Kelly, pp. 51-64 (Chicago: University of Chicago Press, 1984).

In this essay, which originally appeared in Feminist Studies, volume 5, 1979, Kelly claims that feminist theory is transforming social vision by its "'doubled' view of the social order." Feminist scholarship has shown that "woman's place is not a separate sphere or domain of existence but a position within social existence generally." The two social spheres of work and sex do not operate, as has been assumed, side by side but instead are systemically bound to one another and operate simultaneously. Three consequences flow from such a "doubled" view of history: 1) it should resolve conflicts in feminist theory and practice over the place of sex oppression relative to race or class oppression; 2) it should help us understand better the persistence of patriarchy; and 3) it indicates that feminists are entering a new social and political position with respect to patriarchal order, a position from which they can end it.

197. Kelly-Gadol, Joan. "Did Women Have a Renaissance?" In Becoming Visible: Women in European History, edited by Renate Bridenthal and Claudia Koonz, pp. 137-164 (Boston: Houghton Mifflin, 1977).

Based on her study of women in the Italian Renaissance, Kelly-Gadol concludes that women did not experience a Renaissance. She bases her conclusion on: 1) a comparison between the regulation of male and female sexuality; 2) a comparison between the economic and political roles of men and women; 3) an examination of women's access to education and to other institutions that define cultural roles; and 4) the sex-role ideology expressed in the "symbolic products of the society," such as art, literature, and philosophy. Kelly-Gadol's conclusion suggests that historians' perspectives, rather than social, economic, or cultural realities, create historical periods.

198. Kelly-Gadol, Joan. "Notes on Women in the Renaissance and Renaissance Historiography." In Conceptual Frameworks for Understanding Women's History, section II, pp. 1-11 (Bronxville, New York: Sarah Lawrence Publications, 1976).

Histories of Renaissance women have sought out women who achieved in the way men achieved. Since exceptional women of that time do not represent what the Renaissance meant for the history of women, such histories are distortions. The traditional sense of historical periods and periodization must be reexamined. Kelly-Gadol calls the social relation of the sexes a "fundamental category of historical thought." Changes in the respective roles of women and men have always been consequences "direct or remote, of fundamental changes taking place in the mode of production." Like the relationship between progress and decline, the relationship between women and men is a dialectical one. To understand the free self in a society devoid of domination, historians must study the oppressed not the oppressor.

199. Kelly-Gadol, Joan. "The Social Relations of the Sexes: Methodological Implications of Women's History." Signs 1:809-824 (1976).

Women's history, according to Kelly-Gadol, must "restore women to history and...restore our history to women." The idea that the relation between the sexes is a social and not a natural one has upset traditional notions of periodization, categories of social analysis, and theories of social change. Historians now examine social periods in terms of the liberation or repression of women. Periodization has become relational as historians seek institutional reasons for the advance of one sex and oppression of the other. The assumptions that women do form a distinct social group and that their invisibility cannot be blamed on women's nature introduce sex as a category of social thought. Women's history raises questions about the connections between changes in class and sex relations. "A theory of social change that incorporates the relation of the sexes has to consider how general changes in production affect and shape production in the family...and the impact of family life and the relation of the sexes upon psychic and social formations."

200. Lerner, Gerda. "The Challenge of Women's History." In The Majority Finds Its Past: Placing Women in History, by Gerda Lerner, pp.168-181 (New York: Oxford University Press, 1979).

According to Lerner, materials and sources about women are readily available; methodology rather than availability creates the problems related to women and history. She lists seven challenges made by women's history to traditional history: 1) exposing the patriarchal values (for example, the natural, biological separation of human activities) that pervade culture and ideas and moving beyond them; 2) understanding women's oppression as the consistent devaluing of women's activities (for example, childbearing and rearing), a subordination in which women themselves have often collaborated; 3) adding gender as an analytical category to other historical categories such as race, class, ethnicity, and religious affiliation; 4) overcoming the androcentric bias that characterizes historical sources and the structure of information; 5) challenging the traditional periodization of history according to wars, conquests, revolutions, and cultural/religious shifts, and demonstrating that periods of advancement for men have often been periods of disadvantage for women; 6) redefining categories and values by asking what history would be like if seen through women's eyes; and 7) encouraging a paradigm shift that will "lead to a new universal history which will synthesize traditional history with women's history such that the historical interactions of men and women will be as much the subject of study as their historical differences." Women's history, Lerner claims, is not history about a past reality but rather a method by which to illuminate things traditional history has obscured.

201. Lerner, Gerda. "The Majority Finds Its Past." In The Majority Finds Its Past: Placing Women in History, by Gerda Lerner, pp. 160-167 (New York: Oxford University Press, 1979).

Women's history must include an account of women's struggle for autonomy. By autonomy, Lerner means "women defining themselves and the values by which they will live, and beginning to think of institutional arrangements that will order their environment in line with their needs." What would a history ordered by values women define be like? According to Lerner, female historical experience differs from male historical experience. Urgently needed are historical interpretations of experiences unique to women, such as women's community-building work. "What needs to be explained," claims Lerner, "is not why women were so little evident in American history as currently recorded, but why and how patriarchal values affected that history."

202. Lerner, Gerda. "New Approaches to the Study of Women in American History." Journal of Social History 4:333-356 (1969).

Lerner begins this early article by announcing that "the striking fact about the historiography of women is the general neglect of the subject by historians." A historical focus on the transmission and exercise of power, by definition, omitted women. Feminist writers, the first to systemically examine women in American history, "were hampered by a two-fold bias:" 1) they ignored anyone who didn't fit into "the middle-class, nativist, moralist approach of the Progressives;" and 2) they limited the importance of the history of women to the history of an oppressed group struggling against an oppressor. Economic historians, historians of reform movements, and historians of the family have studied women. Women, however, are spread throughout the population. To understand them as a group requires a new conceptual framework. The primary sources exist, Lerner claims; historians must develop a fresh approach by: 1) breaking women as a subject into subcategories by economic status, family status, and political-legal status; 2) exploring the various roles women have played in American history; 3) discarding the oppressed group model for a model based upon understanding the power that women have wielded, in spite of their exclusion from politics and economics; 4) examining the impact of depriving women of equal access to education; 5) comparing and contrasting women's actual status with society's notion of women's proper place; and 6) developing a scale, different from that used for men, by which to evaluate the contributions of women.

203. Lerner, Gerda. "Placing Women in History: Definitions and Challenges." In The Majority Finds Its Past: Placing Women in History, by Gerda Lerner, pp. 145-159 (New York: Oxford University Press, 1979).

Lerner describes two levels at which historians, trained in traditional history, approach women's history: 1) the compensatory level, which examines famous or deviant women and fails to account for the variety of women's experiences; and 2) the contribution level, which describes women's contribution to, status in, and oppression by male-defined society. Lerner sees these levels as an inevitable but transitional stage where women are still being forced into "categories and value systems which consider man the measure of significance. In order to move the history of women in the direction of examining the actual experience of women in the past, historians will need to add new categories (for example, sexuality, reproduction, the link between child-bearing and rearing) to those by which they organize their material, study women as a separate culture, and develop a "new universal history" based on the tensions between male and female cultures. Lerner concludes by stating that "all history as we now know it, is, for women, merely prehistory."

204. Lewis, Jane. "Women, Lost and Found: The Impact of Feminism on History." In Men's Studies Modified: The Impact of Feminism on the Academic Disciplines, edited by Dale Spender, pp. 55-73 (New York: Pergamon Press, 1981).

Lewis examines two approaches to women's history: one uses established methodologies to add information about women's behavior in the past, and the other "attempts to re-examine history from a 'woman-centered' point of view." The former approach includes studies of famous or exceptional women and studies of women's roles in historically established movements and events. "Woman-centered" history clarifies and reinterprets women's positions in the past but methodological problems have complicated its practice. Lewis recommends that historians using the "woman-centered" approach "combine an understanding of theoretical concepts (often drawn from other disciplines) with careful research." Theoretical concepts include a woman-centered perspective on social change and a consideration of gender in social history.

205. Nicholson, Linda J. Gender and History: The Limits of Social Theory in the Age of the Family. New York: Columbia University Press, 1986.

Feminism is one of several contemporary resources that can help historians understand that the idea of the family as the sphere of the "private" is a modern development. Nicholson encourages feminist scholars to use an "antipositivistic" methodology. Such an approach acknowledges the pervasiveness of women's oppression and acknowledges that that oppression has no singular cause. Nicholson argues that "it is only through adopting an explicitly historical methodology that contemporary feminism can resolve many of the theoretical dilemmas generated within it." An historical approach "gives coherence" to the feminist mistrust of the "distinctiveness of family, state, and economy."

206. Pierson, Ruth and Alison Prentice. "Feminism and the Writing and Teaching of History." In Feminism in Canada: From Pressure to Politics, edited by Angela R. Miles and Geraldine Finn, pp. 103-118 (Montreal: Black Rose Books, 1982).

Pierson and Prentice see examining the structures of women's oppression as the critical task of feminism. Feminists want to redress the inequality of visibility by analyzing, rediscovering, and revaluing the experiences of women. Feminist researchers must examine the "origins and perpetuation of patriarchy." Problems associated with feminist goals include the fear that autonomy for women will create "a further atomizing of society," and the suggested dichotomy between women's equality with and difference from men. Pierson and Prentice argue that women can be both different and equal and insist on "the full complexity of human lives and possibilities." They eschew a separation of scholarly research from personal and social reality. Feminist historians must retrieve women from obscurity, avoid plugging women into existing historical chronologies and outlines, establish new periodization, look beyond pronouncements of women's behavior to the way women actually behaved, approach old sources in new ways and seek new sources, and investigate the functional relationship between private and public worlds. In spite of the structure of the historical profession, which mitigates against the success of feminist history, feminist publications exist and archivists and funding agencies are becoming interested in women's history.

207. Purvis, June. "Reflections Upon Doing Historical Documentary Research From a Feminist Perspective." In Strategies of Educational Research: Qualitative Methods, edited by Robert G. Burgess, pp. 179-205 (Philadelphia, Pennsylvania: Falmer Press, 1985).

Purvis says that feminist research differs from "malestream" research according to the following premises: 1) women must not only be made visible but also heard; 2) the primary audience is women; 3) "malestream" assumptions must be questioned — for example, the distinction between objective and subjective knowledge, the hierarchies and classifications of knowledge, the language of academic research; and 4) research should be written up in an accessible style.

208. Rowbotham, Sheila. Hidden from History: Rediscovering Women in History from the 17th Century to the Present New York: Pantheon Books, 1974.

Rowbotham's ideas aim to help anyone interested in developing a Marxist feminist view of history. Researchers need to begin with the material circumstances of women's lives, keeping race, class, and the differences and similarities between men and women in mind. Because women's consciousness has "dwelt hidden in a twilight world," resarchers must borrow from anthropologists, who have devised ways of understanding philosophies which are not explicitly stated. Oral history can capture experiences, thoughts, and feelings from the immediate past. Historians studying women need new standards about what is important. For example, menstruation, pregnancy, menopause, reproduction, and housework have rarely been subjects of academic study but have been central to women's lives. A history including women means examining the role of women in movements usually described from the male point of view, understanding how periods of change and upheaval have affected women, and going beyond the scope of what history usually is.

209. Schlesinger, Arthur Meier. New Viewpoints in American History. New York: Macmillan, 1922.

Schlesinger blames historians for the "pall of silence" they "allowed to rest" over women's achievements and services and for the slow pace with which women have gained "equal rights with the men in this the greatest democracy in the world." In a chapter called "The Role of Women in American History," he recounts the many areas of women's contributions and describes their battle for suffrage. Schlesinger uses his catalog of women's achievements to assure readers that women "will use their new power [the vote] for the good of the nation and of humanity."

210. Schulenburg, Jane Tibbetts. "Clio's European Daughters: Myopic Modes of Perception." In The Prism of Sex: Essays in the Sociology of Knowledge, edited by Julia A. Sherman and Evelyn Torton Beck, pp. 33-53 (Madison, Wisconsin: University of Wisconsin Press, 1979).

Schulenburg warns historians of women to avoid, as they attempt to "right the scales," the myopic perception characteristic of traditional history. She cautions that knowing when something is "uniquely female" rather than simply human is not an easy task. Traditional approaches have been guilty of compartmentalizing history by focusing on politics, or the rise of people to universal power. Even the new social history, with its focus on the family, omits women from consideration. Conventional periodization obscures actual historical experiences. Schulenburg encourages feminist historians to bring new questions and methods to analyzing existing intentional and unintentional (censuses, wills, parish records, and more) data on women.

211. Scott, Joan W. "Gender: A Useful Category of Historical Analysis." American Historical Review 91:1053-1073 (1986).

Scott describes three theoretical positions feminist historians have taken to gender analysis: 1) an attempt to explain the origins of patriarchy; 2) a "material" explanation based on a Marxist interpretation of history; and 3) a psychoanalytic explanation of the "production and reproduction of the subject's gendered identity." She finds problems with each position. The first reduces historical scholarship to variations on a single theme, that is, history becomes "epiphenomenal." The second relegates gender to only "a by-product of changing economic structures," giving it no "independent analytic status of its own." The third limits the concept of gender to family and the household and fails to address the issue of inequality. Scott advises feminist historians to articulate gender as an analytic category. Her definition of gender includes two propositions: 1) gender is a constitutive element of social relationships based on perceived differences between the sexes; and 2) gender signifies relationships of power. She concludes that gender "provides a way to decode meaning and to understand the complex connections among various forms of human interaction."

212. Scott, Joan Wallach. "Women's History and the Rewriting of History." In The Impact of Feminist Research in the Academy, edited by Christie Farnham, pp. 34-50 (Bloomington, Indiana: Indiana University Press, 1987).

Scott discusses the assumptions and methods characteristic of three approaches to writing the history of women. Only one approach, the third, actually "rewrites history." "Her-story" narration assumes women have had different experiences from men and attempts to establish women's agency in the making of history. This approach substitutes women for men in the conventional historical framework. The social history approach focuses on economic variables by quantifying the details of everyday life, borrowing from other disciplines such as sociology and anthropology, defining family relationships, fertility, and sexuality as historical phenomena, and focusing on large scale social processes rather than on male leaders, as history-makers. The third approach, difficult to put into practice but most effective in raising critical questions about traditional historical methods, examines social definitions of gender and asks how the meanings of sexual difference are constructed and affected by economic and political institutions. Feminist historians must expose and explore the political structures and ideas that create and enforce power relationships, "the often silent and hidden operations of gender, which are nonetheless present and defining forces of politics and political life."

213. Scott, Joan Wallach. "Women's History: The Modern Period." Past and Present 101:141-157 (1983).

Scott outlines different approaches to the feminist rewriting of history. One approach, women's history as "her-story," narrates women's experiences separate from traditional historical frameworks and periodization. This approach does not challenge conventional history directly. The second approach borrows from social history in concentrating on women, who have customarily been ignored. Large-scale social processes, rather than male leaders, constitute the historical focus. Since women are just one of many groups affected by social processes, they have remained a department of social history, becoming subsumed "within received categories of analysis." The approach that can actually lead to the rewriting of history is one which examines social definitions of gender "as they are developed by men and women, constructed in and affected by economic and political institutions, expressive of a range of relationships," including class and power as well as sex. Studying gender is less a theory and more of a method or procedure for investigation. To make women the subject of history is not sufficient; historians must examine "what gender and sexual difference have had to do with the workings of power" in order to "find women and transform political history."

214. Sklar, Kathryn K. "Four Levels of Women's History." In New Research on Women at the University of Michigan, pp. 7-10 (Ann Arbor, Michigan: University of Michigan Center for the Continuing Education of Women, 1973).

Sklar says that "history is important because it seizes the power of definition over what has been done, and this very deeply affects our sense of what can be done." She lists four types of women's history that feminists should be writing: 1) histories of women who have achieved in categories usually attributed to men; 2) histories describing women's contributions to the "large scale forces of historical change;" 3) history that reconstructs the female perspective on experience; and 4) history, which sees in fresh ways, the structures governing both men's and women's lives. Sklar believes that good women's history can tell the "full truth about the past."

215. Smith, Hilda. "Female Bonds and the Family: Recent Directions in Women's History." In For Alma Mater: Theory and Practice in Feminist Scholarship, edited by Paula A. Treichler, Cheris Kramarae, and Beth Stafford, pp. 272-291 (Urbana, Illinois: University of Illinois Press, 1985).

Smith reviewed the articles appearing in ten major journals and the dissertations produced from 1975-1980, and she examined the recent monographic literature on women's history. Based on her reviews and examinations, she concludes that "women's history has evolved along lines both fruitful and treacherous." Feminist historians have concentrated on facts about women's traditional roles. They have not been successful at using what they know about women's lives to "re-evaluate historical writing generally." Smith says that two criteria distinquish women's history from works which merely include women: 1) while not insisting that all women have lived similar lives, women's historians must consider women as a group with a unique status; and 2) women's historians must ask questions relevant to women's group experience. She advises women's historians to avoid thinking of women only in relational and feminine terms, "secondary to the central action of the past," and to avoid fitting women into traditional historical categories. The emphasis on women's private lives developed in reaction to "compensatory" or "women worthies" history, which focused only on great women. It also developed, says Smith, because historians of women have been attracted to "the notion of women's autonomy over their own lives." Women's lives, however, must not be studied in a vacuum without regard for "the forces which have circumscribed and confined [their] autonomy to a single realm."

216. Smith, Hilda. "Feminism and the Methodology of Women's History." In Liberating Women's History: Theoretical and Critical Essays, edited by Berenice A. Carroll, pp. 368-384 (Urbana, Illinois: University of Illinois Press, 1976).

Smith defines feminism as "a view of women as a distinct sociological group for which there are established patterns of behavior, special legal and legislative restrictions, and customarily defined roles." When so defined and applied to history, feminism generates two questions: 1) what did men think of women at a particular period? and 2) were women allowed to develop freely and hold positions of power and responsibility? Women's historians must try to understand when pressure to conform to feminine ideals has forced women to work against their own best interests. Instead of simply designating important people, women's history recounts how the members of a particular society lived. Because women lived different lives from men, historians searching for material on women the same way they search for material on men are likely to come up empty handed.

217. Smith-Rosenberg, Carroll. "The New Woman and the New History." Feminist Studies 3:185-198 (1975).

Women's historians and new social historians have "redefined what is significant about our past." Their focus on private places, such as the household, the family, the nursery, the bed, and on the internal dynamics of nonpolitcal institutions, such as schools, churches, and factories, has "altered our methodology and our hierarchy of historical significance." Women's history goes beyond social history by emphasizing the male-female interaction, role discontent, and the relationship between role conflict and social change. "To explore the emotional quality of women's lives and at the same time make possible the formulation of...analytic models," Smith-Rosenberg proposes a combination of the ethno-historical and the psychological approaches. Ethno-history borrows from anthropology and sociology to examine the relationship between the individual and social institutions. Psychological history uses psychoanalytic theory, ego theory, group dynamics theories, and object relations to ask how social arrangements and belief systems affect personality development.

218. Smith-Rosenberg, Carroll. "Writing History: Language, Class, and Gender." In Feminist Studies Critical Studies, edited by Teresa de Lauretis, pp. 31-54 (Bloomington, Indiana: Indiana University Press, 1986).

Feminist historians must avoid "historical nihilism," which claims that historical evidence consists entirely of subjectively chosen words and individually imposed meanings. They must accept the challenge posed by feminist literary critics who believe that texts "can be understood only in terms of the world in which [they were] written." Smith-Rosenberg advocates "close reading" that traces the "process by which words are formed out of experiences and experiences are shaped by words." Words, even more than clothes, reflect the social locations and relative power of speakers. Historians who trace women's contributions to discourse and language will better understand "the role gender plays in class identity formation."

219. Woolf, Virgina. A Room of One's Own. New York: Harcourt Brace Jovanovich, 1957 (copyright 1929).

> Describing history as "unreal" and "lop-sided," Woolf calls for "a mass of information" about Elizabethan women: when she married, how many children she had, what her house was like, whether or not she had a room of her own, whether or not she had servants. She points out the lack of sources ("Aubrey hardly mentions her. She never writes her own life and scarcely keeps a diary; there are only a handful of her letters in existence. She left no plays or poems by which we can judge her."), and wonders why a student couldn't rewrite history or at least add a supplement.

7

POLITICAL SCIENCE

INTRODUCTION

Feminists have critiqued and proposed alternatives to traditional political science research methods for the last fifteen years. Increasingly sophisticated ideas and approaches demonstrate progress. But feminists appear to have influenced few political scientists other than themselves.

Four feminist scholars who wrote in the early 1980s complain about feminism's failure to influence the discipline. Carroll (1980) distinguishes academic from radical critiques but finds neither effective: traditional concepts influence the academic critiques more than the other way around, and the radical critiques, by socialist, anarchist, and lesbian feminists, remain isolated outside of the mainstream. Lovenduski (1981) claims that poor timing explains why "feminist initiative in the study of politics has been a cautious and not entirely successful one...." Writing a decade after feminists began critiquing political science, Keohane (1983) says that women finally were "being added, and the field ha[d] hardly begun to stir." Sapiro (1987) compares progress in political science unfavorably with progress in anthropology and psychology: feminist work, she laments, has accomplished little transformation.

And yet, the body of feminist literature dealing with political science research methods and epistemologies is an impressive one. Two ideas have shaped its development: first, that political behavior has been defined as male behavior, and second, that to accomodate women, the entire political science enterprise will need to be redefined. Both ideas can be traced back to the earliest feminist critiques.

Shanley and Schuck (1974) criticize the circular, self-serving nature of political science. Male behavior determines the standard for political behavior just as institutions already designated as political determine the proper object of political science inquiry. Political science defines women as deviant because they're not men and blames them for their inadequate political socialization. In reality, women are denied access to positions of political influence (Jaquette, 1974). Socialization questionnaires use blatantly sexist language and subject matter (Iglitzin, 1974) that give women respondents no real range of answers. Conclusions about all people are based only on male responses (Goot and Reid 1975). Biased instruments, says Boals (1975), not only produce untrustworthy results; questionnaires also create the political attitudes they purport to study. Political socialization and voting and elite studies examined by Bourque and Grossholtz (1974) take for granted rather than question the vast majority of male incumbents in public offices and tie feminine political behavior to women's social roles as wives and mothers.

Linking sex roles with political behavior, a logical consequence of defining politics as a masculine pursuit, creates destructive dichotomies. The public world of politics stands in opposition to the private world of family and home; the practical domain of political decision-making exists apart from the abstract realm of ethics and morality (Jaquette, 1974; Bourque and Grossholtz, 1974; Boals, 1975). These dichotomies will break down, claim some of the early feminist critics, as women move into politics in significant numbers. Iglitzin (1974) points to birth control abortion, and childrearing as examples of private issues that, since women have entered politics, have become public and political. Shanley and Schuck (1974) believe that with more women will come expanded political parameters and new data to be analyzed. But other early critics are less optimistic. Bourque and Grossholtz (1974) mourn the tragic similarities between male and female politicians: women who enter public life accept, rather than change, the norms and ideals already in place.

However tragic such similarities may be, they do disprove any link between sex roles and political behavior. Socialization has not kept women out of the polity; male control of the political sphere has. Politics must be conceived differently from the ground up to include concerns previously defined as private and apolitical. Competition and power must be replaced by values and interpersonal relationships. Politicizing must become synonymous with consciousness raising (Boals, 1975). A politics based on heterosexual domination, which defines women as the property of men, offers women only heterosexual privilege and, consequently, a stake in male supremacy and their own oppression (Bunch, 1975).

Keohane (1983) believes that sheer numbers of women politicians will force the political science discipline out of its silence on women. Because they are a social group different from men, Sapiro (1981) encourages women to develop a sense of their own interests and turn this sense into practical demands. Diamond and Hartsock (1981) protest that working within the conventional categories of political analysis — categories such as interests, rights, and individualism — women will never gain meaningful inclusion. If women are to become part of the political process, reproductive activity can no longer determine social divisions.

Feminist critiques written in the late 1970s and early 1980s focus on reproductive activities to redefine and reinvent the political. Elshtain (1981) promotes motherhood, "a rich, ambivalent, vexing, joyous activity," as a moral imperative for curing the ills of political life. For Sapiro (1981), women's responsibilities for reproduction and child care distinguish them as a social group from men. From her examination of the writings of Plato, Aristotle, Rousseau, and Mill, Okin (1979) traces women's economic, social, and political inequality to a functionalist association between women and the bearing and raising of children. Roberts (1984) links human connectedness with mothering. The separation of public, political life from private, reproductive life encourages "power over," leading to war and violence against women.

But some feminist political scientists view as dangerous an association between the mother-child relationship and women's political participation. Dietz (1985) warns that emphasizing the private realm as superior in every way to the public realm maintains the public-private dichotomy and fails to tranform a "politics in conflict with maternal values." Feminism must stress women's unique organizational styles and their distinctive modes of political discourse, with the goal of politicizing not maternalizing consciousness.

McKinnon (1982) draws on the ideas of Boals (1975) and Bunch (1975) when she advocates consciousness raising to expose sexuality as the "primary social sphere of male power." She ties objectification as a social process to objectivity as a methodological stance. Stiehm (1983) attributes another methodological stance to a "collective Aristotelian hangover." She demonstrates that treating women as a separate category rather than lumping them, as researchers have done since Aristotle, into the household category, produces different political participation results. Lovenduski (1981) encourages research that will challenge the positivist foundations of political science and introduce a "tradition of searching self-criticism...."

The most recent feminist critiques of political science sketch the outlines of a politics incorporating women. Jones (1988) states that "neither the blind demand for [women's] access, nor the uncritical embrace of 'maternal thinking' will be enough to transform the political process." The development of political theory that can grant the "individual personhood of women" requires a new vocabulary and new categories of analysis. Feminist research must explain, according to Sapiro (1987), how people come to accept — and even to perpetuate — a sex-gender system in which they have subordinate status.

Acklesberg and Diamond (1987) conclude that practicing the "personal is the political" would transform cultural and political institutions. Equating the personal and the political elevates the body from an encumbrance to "the locus, vehicle, and origin" of freedom (Brown, 1988). When the personal becomes the political, sex can no longer be displaced onto women, and women move from the margins of the political world to its center (Brown, 1987). Based on her examination of the political canon, Coole (1988) recommends aesthetic, erotic, and imaginative approaches to the demystification of political theory.

Hartsock (1987) believes in a feminist standpoint. The sexual division of labor has epistemological and ontological consequences. Theories and research "grounded in women's material activity" would produce a restructured and redefined society. The problem with the liberal epistemological tradition, say Kelly, Ronan and Cawley (1987), is the gap between disciplinary concepts and women's daily experiences.

Tronto (1987) observes that feminists have often been careless of applying theories, such as Carol Gilligan's "ethic of care," from other disciplines. She argues that putting the care ethic in proper historical context destroys any notion of caring as biologically female and asks what social conditions are necessary to foster a more caring polity. Grant(1987) argues against a feminist epistemology based on experience on the grounds that no category of "woman" exists except the stereotypical one defined by patriarchy. A rejection of reason leads to "authoritarian non-theories...akin to religions."

During almost two decades of critiquing and proposing alternatives to existing political science research methods, feminists have questioned norms, gathered new data, broadened the definition of the political, and narrowed the split between the public and the private. They have not, however, transformed the political science discipline.

ANNOTATIONS

220. Ackelsberg, Martha and Irene Diamond. "Gender and Political Life: New Directions in Political Science." In Analyzing Gender: A Handbook of Social Science Research, edited by Beth B. Hess and Mary Marx Ferree, pp. 504-525 (Newbury, California: Sage Publications, 1987).

> Ackelsberg and Diamond review the feminist literature that has stimulated rethinking in political science in three major ways: 1) by critiquing conventional views of women as reflected in the canon and in empirical studies of political participation and citizenship; 2) by attempting to fill in gaps and correct misconceptions by including women in existing bodies of literature; and 3) by exploring how a focus on women and their experiences transforms political theories, paradigms, and understandings. Feminists have pointed out that the definitions of masculinity and political were the same and they

have taken issue with the public/private split, exposing the political nature of making the split at all. They have objected to the extent to which political scientists "naturalized" differences between men and women, explaining their political participation on the basis of biology rather than sociology. Feminists have begun to examine women as political actors, women as objects of policy, and women's relationship to the welfare state. Feminists have criticized pluralist paradigms that fail to take the relationships of domination and subordination into account, and have suggested that politics may involve studying people in the communal context of their lives rather than treating them as "isolated individuals who come to 'political' life with no prior ties." Feminist criticisms demand the "creation of cultural and political institutions that live with, rather than flee from, the contingencies of the body." Reason and knowledge must be transformed to include emotion and experience and to take into account the extent to which the personal is the political.

221. Bartlett, Katharine T. "Feminist Legal Methods." Harvard Law Review 103(4):829-888 (1990).

Bartlett says feminists must be concerned with the "doing" of law because "methods shape one's view of the possibilities for legal practice and reform." Even though "feminist" is a difficult label to use, it is a necessary one. She analyzes three feminist legal methods: 1) asking the woman question; 2) feminist practical reasoning; and 3) consciousness-raising. Bartlett rejects the sharp dichotomy between abstract, deductive, male reasoning and concrete, contextualized, female reasoning. The differences are not ones of logic but rather of emphasis and underlying ideas about rules. After reviewing four theories of knowledge used by feminists (rational empiricism, standpoint epistemology, postmodernist knowledge, and positionality), she claims that "positionality offers the best explanatory grounding for feminist knowledge." Positionality suggests that "being 'correct' in law is a function of being situated in particular, partial perspectives upon which the individual is obligated to attempt to improve."

222. Black, Naomi. "'The Child Is Father to the Man': The Impact of Feminism on Canadian Political Science." In The Effects of Feminist Approaches on Research Methodologies, edited by Winnie Tomm, pp. 225-244, (Waterloo, Ontario: Wilfrid Laurier University Press, 1989).

Because political science focuses on power, it has been one of the disciplines most resistant to feminism. Black says that "power is the prerequisite for audibility," and, historically, women have not had a voice in politics. Among the very small group of women questioning political science, a feminist perspective can be identified but not a feminist methodology. In a field "which disregards the whole of private life — almost everything people do," a feminist perspective represents a radical change.

223. Boals, Kay. "Review Essay: Political Science." Signs 1(1):161-174 (1975).

Boals reviews literature in political science that illustrates the three functions which she believes feminist scholarship performs: 1) to expand empirical knowledge; 2) to critique existing theory; and 3) to reconceptualize core concepts. In addition to these scholarly functions, feminist research and theory must "help us engage in creative societal transformation." Her review of the feminist literature that is expanding empirical knowledge on women political elites shows that "the prevailing sex-role system affects not only how many women will enter politics, but also what kind of women will do so." She cautions that research aimed at expanding empirical knowledge must "be carried out within the context of a theoretical framework oriented to our long-range concern with full political equality." Boals also looks at feminist reexaminations of the literature on political socialization and political participation. Feminists have pointed out that questionnaires traditionally used to gather data are forumulated in ways that reflect conventional stereotypes and tend to elicit answers in line with the stereotypes and the status quo. In addition, the thinking of respondents to the questionnaires is affected so that the instruments tend to create the political attitudes they purport to study. Sex roles have been used to explain sex differences in political attitudes but no effort has been made to understand the derivation and implications of the sex roles themselves. Feminist scholars have also pointed out the extent to which research findings take the male as the norm and treat the female as deviant. Labelling women's activities as private and, therefore, non-political, has narrowed the definition of political to include only those activities in which men traditionally participate. Feminists must reconceptualize the nature and scope of politics rather than simply address the means by which more women may be assimilated into politics as it is currently defined. Boals identifies two themes that have appeared in feminist political writings: 1) the "need to see as political substantive concerns that have conventionally been thought of as private and apolitical;" and 2) the need to move away from a politics defined by competition for power and toward a politics based on shared values and interpersonal relationships. Boals suggests that "any human relationship, at any level from the intrapsychic to the international, provided it can be shaped and altered by human decision and action" should be defined as political. Such a definition would avoid the common tendency to identify "what exists at any given moment with the way things necessarily are" and would equate the meaning of politicize with consciousness raising.

224. Bourque, Susan and Jean Grossholtz. "Politics an Unnatural Practice: Political Science Looks at Female Participation." Politics and Society (Winter):225-266 (1974).

Bourque and Grossholtz address "the sexual definition accorded to politics and the manner in which the discipline of political science perpetuates this definition." The behavior of those who exercise power is accepted as the standard definition for political behavior, thus those who fail to participate are blamed for their own failure because they cannot approximate the behavior of those in power. To demonstrate the pervasiveness of political sexism, Bourque and Grossholtz examined the literature on socialization, voting studies, and elite studies. They found four categories of distortions that appeared consistently throughout the literature: 1) fudging the footnotes — misuse of data of earlier studies by removing qualifications; 2) assumption of male dominance — the failure to question the fact that males hold the vast majority of public offices and to worry about the implications; 3) masculinity as ideal political behavior — the unexamined assumption that male characteristics (for example, aggressiveness, competitiveness) are the norms of political behavior; and 4) commitment to the eternal feminine — feminine political behavior is a direct result of woman's social role as wife and mother and purity personified. There are very few differences between men and women in politics. Bourque and Grossholtz view this as a "tragedy," since it means that women who enter the polity accept the norms and ideals of the men who created it. But the fact that men and women are so similar means that the male dominance of the political sphere cannot be explained by conditioning or socialization. An alternative explanation, say Bourque and Grossholtz, is that "control is exercised over access to important roles in the political system so that women are excluded." The very definitions of political life and politics change if we assume that women are as interested in and capable of exercising political power as men. Political scientists need to try to define a "politics of real people" by looking at data without the blinders derived from preconceived notions of sex differences.

225. Brown, Wendy. Manhood and Politics: A Feminist Reading in Political Theory. Totowa, New Jersey: Rowman & Littlefield, 1988.

In the "Preface," Brown stresses that her book is "a feminist book about political theory...not a book about women." The distinction is important: confining feminist research to women's issues ghettoizes the research and keeps it at the margins rather than in the center. While the first emphasis of feminist scholarship had to focus on "documenting the omissions or outrageous depictions of women...and redressing these...," the second emphasis can build on the first to develop "critiques of the gendered quality of our inherited discourses, disciplines, institutions and practices." Brown examines the writings of Aristotle, Machiavelli, and Weber to demonstrate the relationship between politics and manhood. She sees her study as interrogating the hitherto "uninterrogated terrain" of the nature and quality of political life itself. In her conclusion, Brown explores freedom, desire, and power, and proposes ways in which these concepts could be applied in a "post-masculinist politics." She suggests that a feminist politics would involve "recognizing that the body is the locus, vehicle, and origin of our freedom rather than the encumbrance to it Western political theory has always claimed the body to be."

226. Brown, Wendy. "Where Is the Sex in Political Theory?" Women & Politics 7(1):3-23 (1987).

Brown says that a feminist critique of traditional political theory will "tell us a great deal about men and a socially male construction of politics and thinking, manhood and womanhood, values and desires." Feminist theory will also deliver "understandings of what has been excluded, degraded, or violated in the human endeavor of collective life...[and will] develop new parameters for thinking about human collective life and its possibilities...." But, in order to deliver these understandings and develop the new parameters, feminism must move toward the center of political theory without losing its perspective on the margins, where women have traditionally been placed in the political world. Brown explores the history of political theory to show what it has meant for political thinking and practice to displace sex unto women and what this displacement has meant for women. The gendered sexuality of politics must be recast as must gender and sexuality at the individual and social level.

227. Bunch, Charlotte. "Not for Lesbians Only." Quest 2(2):50-56 (1975).

Lesbianism, according to Bunch, is not simply a personal decision or a question of civil rights; lesbianism is political. "Lesbian-feminist politics is a political critique of the institution and ideology of heterosexuality as a cornerstone of male supremacy...an extension of the analysis of sexual politics to an analysis of sexuality itself as an institution...[and] a commitment to women as a political group which is the basis of a political/economic strategy leading to power for women...." Heterosexuality is based on the premise of men first.

Women are defined by and as the property of men. Heterosexual privilege gives women attached to men a stake in male supremacy and, therefore, a stake in their own oppression. Lesbianism and class are connected since lesbianism "means discovering that we have to support ourselves for the rest of our lives, something that lower and working class women have always known." The goal of lesbian feminist politics is not and should never be to make being lesbian acceptable within capitalist patriarchy. Lesbian strength lies in being outside of patriarchy; lesbian existence challenges patriarchy's life. Essential to the change which must occur in the entire system of capitalism and patriarchy is an end to heterosexual domination.

228. Carroll, Berenice A. "Political Science, Part I: American Politics and Political Behavior." Signs 5(2):289-306 (1979); "Political Science, Part II: International Politics, Comparative Politics, and Feminist Radicals." Signs 5(3):449-458 (1980).

From her review in two parts of the feminist literature in political science, Carroll concludes that feminist scholarship has not yet had a major impact on the discipline and that mainstream, academic feminist critiques and radical critiques have followed separate paths and had little effect on one another. The academic research conducted by feminists on women and politics continues to be influenced more by the traditional concepts of the discipline than by the challenges posed by the women's movement. Traditional authorities and stereotypes of women's political behavior have not been directly challenged, and sex role socialization, "with its implicit tendency...to place on women the burden of changing sex roles without changing the system which requires the existing sex-role patterns, rewards those who conform to it, and punishes those who defy it," remains the focus. Almost no attention has been given to unconventional forms of political action, which women often initiate. Marxist feminists have focused on reproduction and the sexual division of labor, housework, and the family but are restricted by the boundaries defined by the "sacred texts." The most comprehensive analyses of patriarchy as a political system are written by radical, socialist, anarchist, and lesbian feminists and appear "outside the ordinary channels of the discipline."

229. Coole, Diana H. Women in Political Theory. Boulder, Colorado: Lynne Rienner Publishers, 1988.

Coole's intention was to "integrate and make available in one text the sort of arguments and interpretations" feminist readings of the classic texts of political theory have offered. A thematic thread unraveled as her chapters unfolded: Western thought is fundamentally dualistic. Mind-body, subject-object, reason-passion, form-content, culture-nature, order-chaos, public-private are all dualities centered around the fundamental male/female dichotomy. The terms are not reciprocal; the second term is always associated with bad or inferior as opposed to the good, superior first term. In addition, the first term functions as a standard or norm and the second term is distinguished primarily by not being the same as the first. Depending on their approaches to these binary oppositions, all the thinkers analyzed in Coole's book could be divided into two categories. First category thinkers (for example, Aristotle, Aquinas, Hegel) argued for a "natural and unassailable difference between the sexes, which must be reflected in social place and function." Second category thinkers (for example, Plato, Augustine, Wollstonecraft, Mill, de Beauvoir, Firestone) spoke for sexual equality but only insofar as women could overcome their flawed natures and adopt the characteristics defined as male. The answer for feminist political theory is not to expel the characteristics associated with the male principle as unfeminine but rather to demystify and deconstruct traditional theory and research to include more aesthetic, erotic, and imaginative approaches.

230. Diamond, Irene and Nancy Hartsock. "Beyond Interests in Politics: A Comment on Virginia Sapiro's 'When Are Interests Interesting? The Problem of Political Representation of Women.'" American Political Science Review 75:717-723 (1981).

Diamond and Hartsock criticize Sapiro (see annotation below) for inconsistency relating to women's representation. Her inconsistency results, they claim, from her attempt to work within the conventional categories of political analysis (i.e., interests, rights, and individualism) and from her "hidden and untested assumption that women's demands can be integrated into political systems." Diamond and Hartsock question the appropriateness of the language of interests for understanding political life. "Close attention to women's activity rather than men's and the consequent thoroughgoing focus on whole human beings necessitates the development of more encompassing categories of analysis for political life." Female activities, such as motherwork, housework, and subsistence and survival work, have been defined as private and "unworthy of those who are fully human," while male activities associated with public life have been deemed important. Western cultural preoccupation with violence and death is a consequence of this "reversal" of the proper order of things. State policy must recognize the "profound implications of the social divisions deriving from reproductive activity." Inclusion of questions regarding reproduction and sexuality "might well lead to a profound redefinition of the nature of public life itself."

231. Dietz, Mary G. "Citizenship With a Feminist Face: The Problem With Maternal Thinking." Political Theory 13(1):19-37 (1985).

By critiquing the social feminism of Jean Bethke Elshtain (see annotations below), Dietz begins to articulate a feminist theory of political thought centered around women as citizens. Elshtain's social feminism "seeks to foster the identity of 'women-as-mothers' and to establish the moral primacy of the family, and so the private realm of human life." Social feminists see the family as, in every way, superior to the public realm of politics. The public-private dichotomy is maintained, therefore, with the private realm on top. Maternal thinking keeps "the reality of a single child before the mind's eye" and thus provides "the 'moral imperative' for countering the prevailing liberal-individualist world view." Dietz believes that Elshtain fails to show that maternal virtues are connected to or causal in bringing about the democratic values of active citizenship, self-government, egalitarianism, and the exercise of freedom. The mother-child relationship, in which the child is subordinate to the mother, is a particularly inappropriate model for citizenship, which depends upon equality among citizens. The bond between citizens is political not intimate. According to Dietz, "women who do not venture beyond the family or participate in practices beyond mothering cannot attain an adequate understanding of the way politics determines their own lives. Nor can they...help transform a politics that stands in conflict with maternal values." The goal of feminism must be to politicize consciousness, not to maternalize it. It is women's unique organizational styles and their distinctive modes of political discourse, not their role as (potential) mothers, that will transform political practice.

232. Elshtain, Jean Bethke. "Methodological Sophistication and Conceptual Confusion: A Critique of Mainstream Political Science. In The Prism of Sex: Essays in the Sociology of Knowledge, edited by Julia A. Sherman and Evelyn Torton Beck, pp. 229-252 (Madison, Wisconsin: University of Wisconsin Press, 1979).

Elshtain's essay "bring[s] the predominant presumptions of the discipline [of political science] to the surface...and subject[s] them to rigorous and unflinching scrutiny." She analyses the implicit but unspoken assumptions underlying the behavioralist approach that result in a separation of politics and morals and in the exclusion, by definition, of people of certain sexes, classes, races, and ages from political participation. The women's and other liberation movements have redefined political power to "include dimensions of unintentional power, and power as productive of unintended consequences." Unintentional power is power possessed by a group, for example, men, which derives benefits and privileges it did not intentionally seek to create. To "articulate serious moral claims which would serve to describe and to evaluate society and [the political science] discipline..., feminist research cannot take place within the presumptions of the dominant mode of political inquiry...."(see also Elshtain in the Communication chapter).

233. Elshtain, Jean Bethke. Public Man, Private Woman: Women in Social and Political Thought. Princeton, New Jersey: Princeton University Press, 1981.

Elshtain examines the concepts of public and private in the political thought of Plato, Aristotle, Machiavelli, Rousseau, Hegel, Marx, and contemporary feminists, and offers a reconstructed, critical theory of women and politics. Her theory centers around the primacy of the family and the private realm of human life. She puts motherhood forward as the "moral imperative" for countering the current ills of public and political life. Mothering is "a complicated, rich, ambivalent, vexing, joyous activity" that "carries profoundly resonant emotional and sexual imperatives." Elshtain extends and develops her argument for maternal thinking in other articles including, "Feminism, Family, and Community," Dissent 29(4):442-449 (1982); "Feminist discourse and Its Discontents: Language, Power, and Meaning," Signs 7(3):603-621 (1982); and "On Beautiful Souls, Just Warriors, and Feminist Consciousness" Women's Studies International Forum 5(3/4):341-348 (1982).(see also Elshtain in the Communication chapter).

234. Goot, Murray and Elizabeth Reid. Women and Voting Studies: Mindless Matrons or Sexist Scientism? Sage Professional Papers in Contemporary Political Sociology, no. 8. London: Sage Publications, 1975.

Goot and Reid examine the literature on the relationship between sex and voting behavior since World War II to demonstrate that several conclusions concerning women and politics — that children adopt the party preference of the father, that wives follow their husbands, that women are more conservative than men, and that women personalize politics — are based on sex role stereotyping rather than valid research data. Socialization, they argue, does not account for the political consciousness of women. They point out that much of the empirical work in political science has been designed around the assumption that "politics [should] at least primarily be left to men" and this assumption's corollaries, that only men are involved in politics and only the male electorate matters. Questionnaires have been structured to allow women respondents, when there have been any, no real range of responses. Studies intending to generalize about political behavior have been based on the responses of only men. A less biased interpretation of the data shows that the woman voter is not "an apolitical being...concerned with morality and insulated from work and politics...."

235. Grant, Judith. "I Feel Therefore I Am: A Critique of Female Experience as the Basis for a Feminist Epistemology." Women & Politics 7(3):99-114 (1987).

Grant says that many feminists have answered no when confronted with the question, "if reality and objectivity have heretofore been defined by men, do any existing theories, including epistemologies, have meaning for women?" In reaction to male-dominated reason and objectivity, feminists have formulated theories "based around the idea that women know from their 'experiences'." Grant describes three refutations of reason which "rest upon a leap of faith" that associates reason irrevocably with the male: 1) the fact that matriarchal religions and societies fell just as thinkers like Plato and Aristotle associated with the cult of reason rose in power; 2) metaphorical similarities between reason and the male body; and 3) the tendency of male thinkers to ignore the female body or associate it with irrationality. Even without the necessity for leaps of faith, the feminist epistemology of experience falters due to internal logic: how is it possible to theorize a female experience at once diverse and similar? The belief in an experiential epistemology "rests upon a category - Woman," whose characteristics are those assigned according to the patriarchal stereotype. It also ceases to stress the sex/gender difference so crucial to early radical feminism. The critical step missing from feminist theory is "an evaluation of the interpretation of experience." Theories which reject reason risk "devolving into authoritarian non-theories more akin to religions."

236. Hartsock, Nancy C. M. "The Feminist Standpoint: Developing the Ground for a Specifically Feminist Historical Materialism." In Feminism and Methodology: Social Science Issues, edited by Sandra Harding, pp. 157-180 (Bloomington, Indiana: Indiana University Press, 1987).

Hartsock argues that the fact that women's lives differ structurally from men's has epistemological and ontological consequences that result in a feminist standpoint. Like the Marxist argument that the correct vision of society is available only from the proletarian perspective, Hartsock's argument suggests that women's life activity in a society structured according to a sexual division of labor results in "the experience of continuity and relation — with others, with the natural world, of mind with body — [that] provides an ontological base for developing a nonproblematic social synthesis...which need not operate through the denial of the body, the attack on nature, or the death struggle between self and other...[characteristic] of abstract masculinity." Male and female experiences of self differ dramatically due to the sexual division of childrearing. The male experience of differentiation from the other produces a "hostile and combative dualism at the heart of both the community men construct and the masculinist world view by means of which they understand their lives." Women's oppression provides them with a standpoint based on "a duality of levels of reality, of which the deeper level or essence both includes and explains the 'surface' or appearance, and indicates the logic by means of which the appearance inverts and distorts the deeper reality." The existence of such a standpoint suggests the need for feminist theories and research to be "grounded in women's material activity." The outcome could be a society restructured and redefined on the basis of women's experience.

237. Hawkesworth, Mary E. "Feminist Epistemology: A Survey of the Field." Women & Politics 7(3):115-127 (1987).

Hawkesworth says that the concerns which have led feminist scholars to propose feminist epistemologies over the last few years include: 1) the tendencies to marginalize feminist scholarship within the dominant disciplines; 2) the quest for an "epistemological foundation which can rescue feminist claims from trivialization by demonstrating their truth and importance;" 3) the recognition that epistemological assumptions have "profound social, political, and methodological implications;" 4) continuing dissatisfaction with paternalistic politics; and 5) objections by third world women and women of color to the political priorities of white, Western feminists. Her bibliographic essay surveys the literature which expresses these concerns.

238. Hekman, Susan. "The Feminization of Epistemology: Gender and the Social Sciences." Women & Politics 7(3):65-83 (1987).

Hekman compares the feminist critique of Enlightment epistemology with the anti-foundational critique. Both argue against one, rationalist mode of knowledge and for a plurality of ways of knowing; both reject dichotomies like subject/object, subjectivity/objectivity; and both believe that all knowledge is engaged, involved, and tied to a certain perspective, and that no categories can be defined as universal. Feminism goes beyond anti-foundationalism by identifying the Enlightment epistemology as a male epistemology and by showing that dichotomies are all rooted in the male/female dichotomy. However, feminists who insist on replacing the male-centered epistemology with a female-centered one fall into the very dogmatism they criticize. Hekman draws on the concept of "supplementary logic" proposed by Jacques Derrida to "break the binary opposition of male/female that structures not only our epistemology but our social and political life as well." Feminist epistemologists are calling for the reinstitution of a truly human viewpoint "in which both ways of knowing...and moral qualities would be associated with persons, not sexes."

239. Iglitzin, Lynne B. "The Making of the Apolitical Woman: Femininity and Sex-Stereotyping in Girls." In Women In Politics, edited by Jane S. Jaquette, pp. 25-36 (New York, John Wiley & Sons, 1974).

While accepting the proposition that women are socialized to be less political than men, Iglitzin criticizes the existing tools and techniques of political socialization research for being biased and sexist, and thereby contributing to the creation of the apolitical female. Her examination of questionnaires revealed that both the language and the subject matter were blatantly sexist. The feminist movement has politicized many issues, such as birth control, abortion, and childrearing, that were previously considered private, individual, and psychological but traditional political science remains limited by its narrow view of politics as the exercise of power by government officials. To help children understand the "very real ways in which politics touch their lives at all times," socialization questionnaires they receive should include questions dealing with political aspects of their own lives in home and school.

240. Jaquette, Jane S. "Introduction." In Women In Politics, edited by Jane S. Jaquette, pp. xiii-xxvii (New York, John Wiley & Sons, 1974).

As a conclusion to her review of the studies of women and politics, Jaquette comments on the prevalence of male bias in political science. What start out as "objective stud[ies] of male/female differences all too often end up as diatribe[s] against female weaknesses and paean[s] to male virtues." Women are criticized for not being like men and no acknowledgement is given to the fact that they may be prevented from assuming male roles. The necessity or legitimacy of doing things the way male politicians have always done them is never questioned. Women's concern with ethics and morals in politics is rejected as unsophisticated and inappropriate. Political socialization research has methodological weaknesses that result from sexist biases. "As the definition of politics expands to include issues which were formerly relegated to the private sphere..., the examination of the role of women in politics and a conscious awareness of male bias may revitalize our thinking...."

241. Jones, Kathleen B. "Towards a Revision of Politics." In The Political Interests of Gender: Developing Theory and Research With a Feminist Face, edited by Kathleen B. Jones and Anna G. Jónasdóttir, pp. 11-32 (London: Sage Publishers, 1988).

Classical political theorists took questions of gender into account. Even though these theorists concluded that women were biologically and culturally unfit to participate in political authority structures, they realized that "understanding the world of women was critical to understanding the nature and aims of the political." Contemporary theorists, influenced by liberal theory, act as if women are "conceptually irrelevant to political discourse." The rationality essential to political involvement is a genderless capacity of all human beings; women, therefore, can strive to be as rational as men. Classical and comtemporary political theory has been predicated on a fundamental dichotomy between the public and the private or personal. The challenge facing feminist theory in political science is "how to construct a theory of political equality and citizenship that grant[s] the individual personhood of women without denying [that they have] differing needs and interests from men." The concept of a universal citizenship that includes everyone without prejudice "ignores the way in which gender, as a socially constructed, historical reality, reflects different ways of being and knowing that fundamentally affect the practice and meaning of civic duties and responsibilities...." Feminist political science research has tended to concentrate on exposing the sexist exclusion of women. While valuable, such research has used the epistemological and methodological frameworks established by traditional political scientists and has left the traditional categories of analysis unchallenged. Feminist political science must follow Gerda Lerner's advice and abandon the "oppressed group model" for women's roles and develop, instead, "a new vocabulary of politics so that it can express the specific and different ways in which women have wielded power, been in authority, practised citizenship, and understood freedom." The feminist future depends upon the development of categories of analysis that can describe adequately the diversity of women's political experiences. "Neither the blind demand for access, nor the uncritical embrace of 'maternal thinking'" will be enough.

242. Kelly, Rita Mae, Bernard Ronan, and Margaret E. Cawley. "Liberal Positivistic Epistemology and Research on Women and Politics." Women & Politics 7(3):11-27 (1987).

Kelly, Ronan, and Cawley identify two basic problems with how the liberal epistemological tradition has influenced research on women and politics. The first problem is the "incompatibility of many of our disciplinary concepts and action meanings with the reality of meaning lived by subjects we study and manifested in the 'real world.'" The second problem is the "inadequacy of relying heavily on a quantitative paradigm so dependent upon survey research methodology, public opinion and preference analysis to address the range and scope of human existence and social reality." These problems point to the need for "a broader epistemological and methodological base...and for an openness to new approaches to bridge the gap between qualitative and quantitative research."

243. Keohane, Nannerl O. "Speaking from Silence: Women and the Science of Politics." In A Feminist Perspective in the Academy: The Difference It Makes," edited by Elizabeth Langland and Walter Gove, pp. 86-100 (Chicago: University of Chicago Press, 1983).

Keohane writes that "in political science, women are just now being added, and the field has hardly begun to stir." The extent to which the public realm of politics has been male-dominated raises some questions: 1) why has the dominance of political life by men been taken for granted rather than studied as a research problem? 2) why haven't female exceptions to the rule been closely studied to determine if there are differences in the ways men and women exercise power, and, if so, what those differences are? and 3) why has power been studied only in the context of the state or the city and not in the context of institutions or associations like convents, harems, nursery schools, or prisons that would have revealed more about women in roles of authority? Since these questions have neither been asked or answered, women have been invisible in the study of politics, striking for their non-participation. This invisibility is beginning to change because of the unprecedented numbers of women now moving into positions of political authority and because of changes in "the way the discipline of political science understands its subject matter." Whether one subscribes to the theory that women in office will behave just like men or to the theory that women bring "a distinctive set of traits and concerns that will begin to alter the character of public life," sheer numbers dictate that political science can no longer remain silent on women. In terms of teaching and research, four different factors can make women visible: 1) the inclusion of articles and books by women; 2) the inclusion of articles and books about women; 3) attention to passages in political science classics and contemporary writings that treat women superficially or prejudicially; and 4) attention to and questioning of the occasions on which women are missing. Feminist research in political science is stimulating a re-examination of dichotomies like the public sphere/private sphere, of the association of authority with the father, and of language that perpetuates male dominance.

244. Lovenduski, Joni. "Toward the Emasculation of Political Science: The Impact of Feminism." In Men's Studies Modified: The Impact of Feminism on the Academic Disciplines, edited by Dale Spender, pp. 83-98 (Oxford: Pergamon Press, 1981).

In spite of political science's thoroughly honorable, multi-disciplinary, and wide-ranging history, which should have led to a "relatively untroubled union between a developed and confident [discipline]...and a radical, innovative Feminist Scholarship..., the feminist initiative in the study of politics has been a cautious and not entirely successful one...." Lovenduski explains, in part by timing, feminism's difficulties in political science. By the time that the second wave of American feminism was calling traditional scholarship into question, political science was dominated by a positivist, objective, self-satisfied model (as opposed to the "eccentric, self-consciously constructed" model that had been popular in the past.) Political science has been sexist both because it has excluded women from its concerns and from membership in the profession. Since politics has focused on public power, political elites, and the institutions of government, women were bound to be excluded, and "in an increasingly positivistic discipline, no-one thought to question this." Studies, like political participation studies, which did include women, were riddled with sexist bias. Masculinity, for example, was defined as ideal political behavior, and "feminine political behavior [was seen] as a direct product of women's domestic role." Most of the early feminist research in political science was "limited to the areas of reinforcement of existing method and the exposure of sexist...bias in the standard literature on political participation, political socialisation, and voting behaviour." Some new research may be moving in the direction of challenging the positivist foundations of polticial science but such a challenge will not be easy in a discipline that lacks "a tradition of searching self-criticism...."

245. MacKinnon, Catharine A. "Feminism, Marxism, Method, and the State: An Agenda for Theory." Signs 7(3):515-544 (1982).

MacKinnon begins part one of a two part article (see annotation below for second part) with the statement, "Sexuality is to feminism what work is to marxism: that which is most one's own, yet most taken away." She "explores the conflicts and connections between the methods" of feminism and Marxism as "theories of power and its distribution: inequality." Once sexuality has been identified as the "primary social sphere of male power," the question for feminism becomes is there a female sexuality, which "is the same as asking whether women exist." The feminist concept of the personal is the political — "that women's distinctive experience as women occurs within that sphere that has been socially lived as the personal...so that what it is to *know* the *politics* of woman's situation is to know women's personal lives" — is an attempt to answer this question, and "consciousness raising is its quintessential expression." Objectivity corresponds to the "power to create the world from one's point of view. "What is objectively known corresponds to the world and can be verified by pointing to it (as science does) because the world itself is controlled from the same point of view....Objectivity is the methodological stance of which objectification is the social process." Feminism, which encourages women to use consciousness raising to "grasp the collective reality of women's condition from within the perspective of that experience, not from outside it," challenges both masculine partiality and the universal imperative itself. Since "male power is the myth that makes itself true," women's oppression can neither be demonstrated nor refuted empirically. Consciousness raising confronts the fact that male power is real but that it is not the only reality. As "the collective critical reconstitution of the meaning of women's social experience, as women live through it," consciousness raising "has revealed gender relations to be a collective fact, no more simply personal than class relations."

246. MacKinnon, Catharine A. "Feminism, Marxism, Method, and the State: Toward Feminist Jurisprudence." Signs 8(4):635-658 (1983).

MacKinnon carries the theme of "objectivity as the epistemological stance of which objectification is the social process" into second part of her two part article (see annotation above). She uses the example of rape to demonstrate that liberal jurisprudence will be "most relentless in imposing the male point of view when it comes closest to achieving its highest formal criterion of distanced aperspectivity." Justice will be achievable only when "masculinity appears as specific position, not just the way things are." Feminist jurisprudence requires a new relation between life and law.

247. Okin, Susan Moller. Women in Western Political Thought. Princeton, New Jersey: Princeton University Press, 1979.

Okin asks two questions: 1) can the existing tradition of political philosophy sustain the inclusion of women in its subject matter; and 2) what can an analysis of the treatment of women in traditional political philosophy reveal about the fact that the enfranchisement of women has not led to substantive economic, social, or political equality between the sexes. To answer these questions, she examines the political writings of Plato, Aristotle, Rousseau, and Mill. She concludes that arguments developed long ago concerning women's role in the family continue to exert an oppressive, functionalist influence, tying women to child bearing and child raising. Men are viewed as complete persons with potentials and rights but women continue to be defined in terms of the functions they serve in relation to men.

248. Roberts, Barbara. "The Death of Machothink: Feminist Research and the Transformation of Peace Studies." Women's Studies International Forum 7(4):195-200 (1984).

Roberts connects sexism and war and claims that the root cause of both is the social and individual pathology of a masculinity based on competitive, hierarchical, context-stripping, and authoritarian principles. Most mens' "lived experience of exercising power is power over women," and most women's daily experience is associated with violence against themselves. Violence against women must become a peace research issue. Dominance, which "seems inextricably linked to violence," has been accepted by mainstream peace research as the definition of power. Roberts suggests a link between the human connectedness forstered by mothering and peacefulness. Since social pathology seems to result directly from inbalances of power, "any reduction of inequality between women and men should decrease the level of violence in society." Peace research must be recontextualised into human caring and connectedness...[and] regrounded in human experience."

249. Sapiro, Virginia. "What Research on the Political Socialization of Women Can Tell Us About the Political Socialization of People." In The Impact of Feminist Research in the Academy, edited by Christie Farnham, pp. 148-173 (Bloomington, Indiana: Indiana University Press, 1987).

Feminist work on political socialization has been critical of existing studies, and has supplied some corrections in terms of alternative viewpoints and additional data; it has not accomplished much actual transformation, however, especially when compared with other disciplines such as psychology and anthropology. Feminist criticism of political socialization research has indicated that there has simply not been enough research on women, and that what there has been has exhibited male bias and androcentric problems in method and interpretation of results. Gender differences research tended to view women as "relatively underdeveloped...political animals," but did not associate this with "any important structural problem in society or in the political system." Feminist research examines system persistence and maintenance in terms of power and authority patterns, and asks how people "can come to accept a sex-gender system that grants them subordinate and limited status" and even participate in supporting and perpetuating that system. Whereas sex-differences investigations have tended to concentrate simply on male and female behavior, feminist research puts theoretical emphasis on gender, using the contributions of research from other disciplines. Feminists have also broadened the definition of political, breaking down the sharply defined public/private dichotomy. They have questioned the norms established on the basis of male behavior for career patterns, political activism, and success, rejecting the evaluation of women according to a male standard. A feminist perspective "focuses attention on some problems and issues of personal and political life and learning that have been ignored by others...[and gives] rise to concentration on different kinds of research methods."

250. Sapiro, Virginia. "When Are Interests Interesting? The Problem of Political Representation of Women." American Political Science Review 75(3):701-716 (1981).

Sapiro explores what it means for women to ask for political representation on the basis of being members of the group, women. She attempts to answer the questions, "What is political representation of women?" and "To what degree and under what circumstances are political institutions and decision makers responsive to female citizens?" Without ignoring the diversity among women of different classes, races, ages, etc., Sapiro suggests that women as a group are in a different social position from men because they have different responsibilities for reproduction, child care, and other areas often defined as private. In this sense, they represent an interest group whose members must "develop a sense of their own interests and place demands upon the [existing political] system." According to Sapiro, political economy, ideology, feminist movements and interest organizations, and the effects of women as members of political elites can all result in change in public policies on women. Asking questions about the representation of women requires "renewed attention to the thorny problem of the limits of politics and government, the boundaries of and relationship between the private and public domains,...uncovers critical problems in democratic theory and research,...and criticizes and refines the basic tool of any type of research." (see Diamond and Hartsock, above, for a reaction to Sapiro).

251. Shanley, Mary L. and Victoria Schuck. "In Search of Political Woman." Social Science Quarterly 55(3):632-644 (1974).

In one of the earliest articles to address the issue of women and politics, Shanley and Schuck examine the political science profession before and after the advent of behavioralism to show "how the questions asked, the phenomena considered deserving of political analysis, and the tools of the trade led to...[the] ignoring of women as political beings." The focus on "the evolution of political institutions as the proper object of study for political science" seems to explain why political scientists virtually ignored women, even women's suffrage, which was finally granted in 1920. Behavioral political scientists strove to make the study of politics a science, emphasizing prediction and explanation rather than just description. In a very empiricist manner, the behavioralist seeks to discover rules and regularities of political behavior. While the study of behavior increased the likelihood that women would be studied, the concentration on regularities and the emphasis on a "value-free depiction of the facts of political life" led scientists to focus almost solely on "the behavior of those people within or aspiring to posts in those very same public institutions" which had fascinated behavioralists' predecessors. Political scientists have tended to define male behavior as the standard for political behavior and to dismiss female activities as non-political. The contemporary women's movement has affected political science because more women have entered the discipline resulting in more attention to issues concerning women. New data are being analyzed and the "parameters of what political scientists are willing to call 'political activity'" are being expanded. The suffrage movement "largely accepted the terms of American political life, and simply asked entry into one small part of that life..." but contemporary feminism has "called into question some of the basic assumptions about what, or who, is political...."

252. Stiehm, Judith Hicks. "The Unit of Political Analysis: Our Aristotelian Hangover." In Discovering Reality: Feminist Perspectives on Epistemology, Metaphysics, Methodology and Philosophy of Science, edited by Sandra Harding and Merrill B. Hintikka, pp. 31-43 (Boston: D. Reidel Publishing Company, 1983).

Stiehm argues that explanations for the differences between men's and women's political participation have been inadequate because of what she calls the "collective Aristotelian hangover." According to Aristotle's theory of the household, adult males can represent the interests of and act appropriately in the public arena for the slaves, children, and women over whom they rule. In the assignment of class or socio-economic standing, women are often unconsciously treated as members of a household (i.e., assigned their father's or husband's characteristics) rather than as individuals, indicating that "Aristotle lives [even though] he is not necessarily acknowledged." To demonstrate her arguments, Stiehm uses the data collected by Sidney Verba and Norman Nie for their award-winning book, Participation in America. Using three different methods to produce and compare male-female socio-economic standing, she demonstrates that substantial differences occur when women are assigned their own occupational status and when the category "housewife" is assigned occupational prestige. Since socio-economic status is the crucial variable determining political participation, handling data on men and women differently obscures the significant differences in behavior.

253. Tenenbaum, Susan. "Woman Through the Prism of Political Thought." Polity 15(1):90-102 (1982).

Tenenbaum criticizes the "negative and accusatory tone" that pervades the feminist attempts to "unmask patterns of sexual bias in the writings of 'great' political philosophers." She argues that the household/polity or private/public dichotomies that form the central constructs of feminist criticism "derive not from a thoughtful appreciation of the complex traditions of political theory, but from a highly selective reading that is often insensitive to context." She examines, as examples of political thought that offer alternative conceptions of women's role, Montesquieu's discovery of a highly pluralistic social universe, Mme. de Stael's celebration of the household as a moral agency, and the suffragists' belief that norms of domesticity should guide standards for political action. Tenenbaum believes that "an appreciation of the patterns of sexual bias in Western political thought represents only a necessary first step for feminist scholars...[and that] our philosophical heritage is both intricate and subtle, holding out to women visions of liberation as well as yokes of oppression."

254. Tronto, Joan C. "Political Science and Caring: Or, the Perils of Balkanized Social Science." Women & Politics 7(3):85-97 (1987).

Feminist political scientists, like all political scientists, frequently borrow theories from other disciplines. Using the example of the "ethic of care," borrowed from moral psychology, Tronto suggests that feminists must be careful to situate theories into a broad historical context before applying them to women and politics. She traces the predecessors of Carol Gilligan's "ethic of care" back to the Scottish moralists, Francis Hutcheson, David Hume, and Adam Smith, over whose theories Kant's criticisms triumphed. Putting Gilligan's ethic in a historical context "brushes away any biological claims about caring as innately female," and raises the more interesting question of "why a morality that grows out of context came to be associated with women." Instead of just attempting to plug current psychological research on caring into political analyses, researchers "probing accounts of the place of women in politics" can ask: what is the place of caring in a just society...[and] what social conditions are necessary to foster caring...."

8

ECONOMICS

INTRODUCTION

Early Optimism

When Esther Boserup's classic study, Woman's Role in Economic Development (1970), actually affected policies and practices in developing countries, feminism's influence on economics seemed assured. Miller (1972) believed that institutionalism, founded by Thorstein Veblen, pointed the way for economics to take women seriously

A decade later, a note of caution had crept in, but feminists remained optimistic. The title of Ferber and Teiman's (1981) article describes economics as the most established, most quantitative, and most male-dominated social science but the article itself focuses on past and predicted improvements. Eight percent of the Ph.D's in economics in 1979 were women compared with five percent in 1970. Before 1970, no woman had edited any of 375 economic publications; by 1979, 33 women occupied editorial positions. New editions of a standard textbook demonstrated that economists' consciousness had been raised.

Disillusionment

But during the 1980s, optimism sputtered and died. Calling economics the "dismal science," MacDonald (1984) saw only its shortcomings "on all levels relevant to feminism." Not even a fringe field focused on women could be found within the discipline. Driscoll and

McFarland (1989) answered the question, "what impact has feminism had on economics?" with none. Women fall completely outside of economic research and analysis. Mathematical models and econometrics shroud researchers in a protective coat of secondary data, immune from the actual conditions and experiences of women's lives. Greenwood (1984, 1988) lamented that, in spite of the progressive ideas of its founder, the "heterodox brand of economics" called institutionalism had ignored women as completely as the neoclassical approach.

Resistance to Feminist Influence

What makes the "dismal science" so resistant to feminist influence? Cohen (1982) argues that neoclassical economics, still the dominant paradigm, omitted women in its original conception. Alternative paradigms, not revisions, are needed to fit them in. The neoclassical model assumes perfect competition and studies only market behavior. It ignores housework, the largest single industry in number of workers and value, and can only explain wage differences between women and men as a product of women's lower worth or the improper behavior of economic man. Eyes wearing neoclassical lenses cannot "see" that women lack access to jobs and the freedom to move in search of wages.

In the 1960s, "the new home economics" (NHE) began addressing economic issues of interest to women by analyzing unpaid services in support of family life. Bergmann (1987) believes that NHE, with its seemingly relevant subject matter and sophisticated methods, "retarded the development of feminist economics." NHE uses the theory of comparative advantage to argue that women prefer to specialize in housework, that biological motherhood carries with it child rearing responsibility, and that authority rests with the "head of household."

Economics resists change, according to Bell (1974), by concentrating on roles instead of on human beings. Women, and the households they run, have been classified as consumers in contrast to male producers who earn wages in the marketplace. The work versus leisure approach to decisions about scarce resources fails to describe women, who choose between paid work outside and unpaid work inside the home.

Waring (1988) claims that economists' "obsession with numbers and the institutionalization of concepts based on scientific method has been a colonizer." Economists measure world production and growth using the United Nations System of National Accounts (UNSNA). Through a review of the statistics and tools on which it is based, Waring demonstrates that the UNSNA ignores women, children, and the environment. Household, food-related, reproductive, and preservation activities, which cannot easily be expressed in numbers, have been colonized.

Feminist Criticisms and Alternatives

Markusen (1977) is confident that feminists will eventually develop a "cohesive theory of political economy," but for now, they need to concentrate on women's economic oppression and weaknesses in traditional economic theory. Feminists have demonstrated that the economy is not sex-neutral (MacDonald, 1984). The value of housework equals one-quarter to one-half of the Gross National Product (GNP), yet households are not considered productive (Cohen, 1982). What is needed is an accepted occupation called human maintenance, which involves providing food, shelter, clean surroundings, clothing, and personal care (Bell, 1974). Markusen (1977) cites empirical facts — the small number of men who remain unmarried and the frequency with which divorced men remarry — as proof that men are more economically dependent on women than women are on men.

Taking women's experiences into account exposes errors in the theory of demand, which says that each person is the best judge of her own preferences, and in marginal productivity theory, which claims that a worker's return relates directly to her contribution (Markusen, 1977). The notion that a competitive market results in fair wages falls apart when researchers connect, as feminists have, women's earnings with their relative social position (Barrett, 1983).

Bergmann (1984) believes that the reality of women's lives will force economists to change. Traditional economic sex roles cannot survive when so many women work and raise children alone. She outlines a twelve-point agenda — admittedly liberal rather than radical — for a more equitable future. Points include ending discrimination against part-time workers, establishing publicly-funded, high-quality child care, establishing special unemployment insurance for single parents, and lowering the hours of daily work.

Feminist economics, as Waring (1988) sees it, will realistically describe the well-being of communities and their environments and will reflect real wealth and a range of values. She promotes Hilkka Pietilä's model that expresses work by number of workers or number of hours instead of by money.

Even though institutionaland radical paradigms have more potential than the neoclassical one to reshape economic thinking, Barrett (1983) believes that economics alone will never be sufficient to explain "why a sex-based status differential has been so deeply engrained in all societies." Only an interdisciplinary approach can piece together "a sexual political economy of production." (MacDonald, 1984).

From a feminist perspective, Driscoll and McFarland (1989) feel that economic methods, theories, assumptions, and ideologies are hopeless but, still, they encourage feminists to persist. Methods must be found to direct a discipline with such enormous influence on policy toward the improvement of women's lives.

ANNOTATIONS

255. Barrett, Nancy S. "How the Study of Women Has Restructured the Discipline of Economics." In A Feminist Perspective in the Academy: The Difference It Makes, edited by Elizabeth Langland and Walter Gove, pp. 101-109 (Chicago: University of Chicago Press, 1983).

Barrett promotes the importance of women's studies as an interdisciplinary activity because "the study of women through the perspective of any one discipline is likely to lead squarely into another." Economics alone can offer little toward "explaining the fundamental reason why a sex-based status differential has been so deeply engrained in all societies," and full economic equality for women cannot be achieved until this question has been answered and resolved at a basic level. The study of women in the work force demonstrates that economic status does not determine social status but rather reflects societal worth and status judgments. The entire neoclassical "invisible hand" theory that puts faith in the "inherent justice of wage outcomes in a freely functioning competitive market" is threatened by the institutionalist view that insists that relative wages of men and women mirror the relative positions of men and women in society. A human capital approach claims that remedies for inequality lie through legislation. Institutionalists realize, however, that "providing better access to human capital for all" will not solve sex-based inequality and discrimination. "What is needed is a complete societal revolution in sex roles."

256. Bell, Carolyn Shaw. "Economics, Sex, and Gender." Social Science Quarterly 55(3):615-631 (1974).

Bell defines economics as the study of "decisions about how to use resources that are limited by the nature of things," that are scarce. Economists pose alternatives and outline the implications of choices. Instead of concentrating on human beings, economics has concentrated on people's roles in economic activity: the roles of producer and consumer. While neither of these roles is inherently masculine or feminine, women as producers and consumers have been differentiated from men. Most adults combine the producing and consuming roles in themselves but economics has set households apart from the world of production. Women as producers have different choices from men as producers. Because women have responsibility for household care and child raising, "posing a choice-decision between work and leisure simply does not describe the alternatives open to women." Women's actual choice is between paid work outside the home and unpaid work within the home. Economics suggests that the basic consumer decision is between spending and saving. A large proportion of women, however, lack the income to make this type of consumer decision. With regard to households, economics has never asked where the authority lies in terms of decisions to purchase. The word "consumer" is used in ways that suggest it means "woman" and, even more narrowly, "housewife." Bell suggests that a new occupation, human maintenance, be recognized "to identify the considerable chores of providing food, shelter, clean surroundings, clothing, personal care, and the like."

257. Bergmann, Barbara R. The Economic Emergence of Women. New York: Basic Books, 1986.

Bergmann's book explores the repercussions of the "breakup of the ancient system of sex roles under which men were assigned a monopoly of access to money-making and mature women were restricted to the home." She outlines a twelve-point policy agenda that she admits is not radical. While her policies would initially benefit primarily white, middle-class women in the United States, Bergmann believes they are more achievable than the overthrow of capitalism and that the benefits would eventually spread to others. Her twelve policies include: 1) improving enforcement of fairness in placement and promotion; 2) realigning wage rates based on comparable duties; 3) ending sex segregation in vocational and engineering education; 4) ending discrimination against part-time workers; 5) campaigning against sexual harassment; 6) adopting nationally a deduction-based uniform child support plan; 7) setting up special unemployment insurance for single parents; 8) establishing a publicly funded, high-quality child-care system; 9) lowering standard hours of daily work; 10) establishing subsidies for apartment complexes with resident child-care facilities; 11) establishing a new ethic of sharing family-care work between men and women; and 12) helping families with an impaired child by an insurance fund. Bergmann's approach is liberal feminist: she advocates changes that would allow women to compete with men according to the rules and customs men have already established. "It is hard to change the rules of a club from outside the clubhouse. For now, competitive behavior is necessary to get into the clubhouse."

258. Bergmann, Barbara R. "Feminism and Economics." Challenge 27(3):46-49 (1984).

Three developments, says Bergmann, have forced economists to confront the different economic roles women and men have played and the consequences of this difference: 1) the increase in women's participation in the work force; 2) the increase in the number of women raising children alone; and 3) the revival of feminism. Throughout her article, Bergmann compares feminist economists with traditional economists. Feminist economists (of both sexes) have documented the severity of women's economic problems, are developing the outlines of a more equitable future, and are beginning to formulate policy changes that would result in a workable but more equitable system. They emphasize how choice is constrained by institutions, social conventions, styles, and sanctions, and that one person's choices may be less constrained than another's. Feminist economists view discrimination as the product of a system in which women are defined as servants of men. They refuse to explain away systematic differences in hiring and promotion practices as evidence of women employees' inferiority. Feminist economists oppose the new home economics, which uses the theory of "comparative advantage" to explain why women specialize and should continue to specialize in housework. "The major preoccupation of feminist economists is precisely to try to sketch visions of a system of work and family relations which will be fair to men, women, and children, and to try to devise methods, short of mayhem, to get us from here to there."

259. Bergmann, Barbara R. "The Task of a Feminist Economics: A More Equitable Future." In The Impact of Feminist Research in the Academy, edited by Christie Farnham, pp. 131-147. (Bloomington, Indiana: Indiana University Press, 1987).

Feminist economists, says Bergmann, are distinguished by their conviction that "the present assignment to economic duties based on sex is unfair and should be eliminated." Their goal is to "sketch visions of a system of work and family relations which will be fair to men, women, and children, and to devise methods, short of mayhem, to get us from here to there." The new home economics (NEH) developed in the 1960s may have slowed the development of feminist economics by preempting the subject matter of unpaid production of services for the family by family members. Proponents of NEH, however, support the concept of head of household and equate biological motherhood with responsibility for child raising. Technological change has been the major factor in changing economic sex roles. Women in increasingly large numbers are entering the labor force and it is unlikely that the old-fashioned family structure with women as lifelong housewives could be revived as the dominant form. Bergmann reviews the feminist standpoint on a number of economic issues including causes and consequences of the decrease in birth rate, controversies over the labor market, the causes of occupational sex segregation, the causes for low wages for women, the controversy over pay equity adjustments, housewives place in the economy, economic issues in divorce, and the support of single mothers and their children.

260. Boserup, Ester. Woman's Role in Economic Development. Brookfield, Vermont: Gower Publishing, 1986 (first published by Allen & Unwin, 1970).

Boserup's work is a classic. Not only did it articulate, for the first time, the particular problems women experience during economic development but it also influenced policies and practices in some developing countries. Boserup points out that the modernization of agriculture and the migration to the towns that accompany economic and social development disintegrate the traditional division of labor between the two sexes. If the result of the disintegration is that women "are deprived of their productive functions,...the whole process of growth will thereby be retarded." Economic development increases specialization, increases the quantity and quality of equipment and infrastructure, and improves the education and training of the workforce. Production moves out of the household and into private enterprises and public institutions. Women, who tend to receive less training and education than men and who retain more family responsibilities, end up at the "bottom of the labor market hierarchy." In a preface to the 1986 Gower edition of her book, Boserup hails the improvements in women's education that have occurred since Woman's Role in Economic Development first appeared in 1970. She expresses dismay, however, that "the general picture of women's work conditions presented [in the original edition] continues to be valid."

261. Cohen, Marjorie. "The Problem of Studying 'Economic Man'." In Feminism in Canada: From Pressure to Politics, edited by Angela R. Miles and Geraldine Finn, pp. 89-102 (Montreal: Black Rose Books, 1982).

Cohen's essay explains that "women's economic activity was not a part of the original conception of [neoclassical economics], and fitting them in the existing analysis does not work." Neoclassical economic theory was developed to study market behavior and is "an exceedingly blunt instrument" for studying non-market behavior. While housework is the single largest industry in terms of numbers of workers and estimates of its value are from one-quarter to one-half of the gross national product, economists have not traditionally counted housework as productive. Cohen suggests that whole notion of optimum use of resources in an economy becomes meaningless when such a large portion of economic activity is not counted. The neoclassical assumption that household decisions, similarly to other decisions, are made on the basis of maximum gain has created a cultural climate of consumption. Because it assumes perfect competition, neoclassical economics can only explain wage differences between men and women as the result of women's lower worth or the result of improper behavior on the part of economic man. Women have neither had freedom of access to jobs nor been free to move from place to place in search of wages. The economic methodology cannot "'see' women's economic behavior."

262. Driscoll, Kathleen and Joan McFarland. "The Impact of a Feminist Perspective on Research Methodologies: Social Sciences." In The Effects of Feminist Approaches on Research Methodologies, edited by Winnie Tomm, pp. 185-203 (Calgary, Alberta: Wilfrid Laurier University Press, 1989).

In answer to the question, "what impact has feminism had on economics?" Driscoll and McFarland reply "in short, none." Women have fallen "outside of the purview of economic analysis." Economists have focused on economic man, maximizing his gain within the limits of constraints. Women, concerned with the family, have fallen outside of their analysis. While models of economic analysis determine whether women earn less than men, they fail to address why. Economics, with its emphasis on mathematical models and econometrics, has shielded its propositions "from challenge on the basis of direct observation and experience." The way economic research has been structured, a researcher has no direct contact with the women studied. The researcher instead deals entirely with secondary data shaped by values of the data collectors. Economic work being done on women is not for women; its purpose is "to derive a function to insert into the overall model of the economy." The ideology, theories, conceptualizations, assumptions, and methods of economics seem "pretty hopeless...from a feminist perspective," but feminists must continue to pursue qualitative work in a discipline that has such enormous influence on policy.

263. Ferber, Marianne A. and Michelle L. Teiman. "The Oldest, the Most Established, the Most Quantitative of the Social Sciences - and the Most Dominated by Men: The Impact of Feminism on Economics." In Men's Studies Modified: The Impact of Feminism on the Academic Disciplines, edited by Dale Spender, pp. 125-140 (Oxford: Pergamon Press, 1981).

Surveying the decade between 1970 and 1980, Ferber and Teiman see small but encouraging gains in the numbers of women working in, teaching, and occupying influential positions in economics. The proportion of women earning Ph.D's in economics rose from five to eight percent between 1970 and 1979. Before 1970, no women had held any of the 375 annual positions on the editorial boards of two official journals; since 1970, 33 women have held these positions. In 1979, three of 28 economic associations had women as presidents. The increased visibility of women will provide role models for female students entering the profession, break down existing prejudices, and allow support networks to develop. Greater participation by women in economics and the issues raised by the women's movement of the 1960s changed economics during the 1970s. During the sixties, economists developed new home economics tools to study the economic behavior of households. These tools, however, assumed the traditional division of labor between husband and wife and looked at the family as unchanging over time. Adapting these same tools to promote progress instead of to stengthen the status quo will lead to constructive models for equal partnerships in which each person has a variety of choices. Researchers are working on ways in which to incorporate household and volunteer work into the Gross National Product (GNP). Over the last few decades, economists have underestimated consistently the numbers of women who would be entering the workforce. Understanding that women substitute market work for housework instead of for leisure has helped explain the change in women's work patterns. Economists have also been trying to explain why women cluster in few occupations, in the lower levels of all occupations, and earn about 60 percent of what men earn. Traditional economists' circular explanation — that women specialize in homemaking because they earn less in the labor market and that their absorption with homemaking results in lower earnings in the labor market — has been replaced with a sensitivity to women's disadvantages in the labor market. Since the publication of Ester Boserup's Woman's Role in Economic Development in 1970, the implications of modernization for women have been better understood. Development without appropriate educational and training programs deprives women of their traditional productive functions and relegates them to helpmates instead of partners in the production process. From their examination of a standard economics textbook through its ten editions between 1948 and 1979, Ferber and Teiman conclude that "progress is being made in raising the consciousness of economists, so that they are more likely to address themselves to women's issues. At the same time their subconscious continues to be rooted in tradition, so that old stereotypical attitudes still permeate much of their work."

264. Greenwood, Daphne. "A Comment on Evolutionary Economics I: Foundations of Institutionalist Thought." Journal of Economic Issues 22: 249-251 (1988).

Greenwood comments on a comprehensive set of papers on institutionalism that the editors of the Journal of Economic Issues brought together. Unfortunately, she says, the papers demonstrate that institutionalist thought is consistent with neoclassical economics in "ignoring gender and family relationships as important economic variables, and...ignoring the differential roles of men and women in the economy." As long as institutionalism focuses on the external world of markets to the exclusion of the internal world of family and gender relationships, Greenwood believes it will fail to make a significant contribution to economic thought.

265. Greenwood, Daphne. "The Economic Significance of 'Woman's Place' In Society: A New-Institutionalist View." Journal of Economic Issues 18(3):663-680 (1984).

The "brand of heterodox economics known as institutionalism," says Greenwood, has worked hard to distinguish itself from the behavioral methodology and conclusions of neoclassical economics. But in its treatment of women and their economic roles, institutional and neoclassical economics remain pretty much the same. Institutionalism has ignored women in spite of the fact that Thorstein Veblen, the founder of the institutional approach, believed that the "changing conditions of production require[d] a greater emphasis on the stereotypically female virtues of nurturing, purposeful activity, and co-operation." As the major points of an institutional analysis, Greenwood lists: 1) "labor market discrimination reflects a segregation of women into traditional non-market work as much as out of the more prestigious areas of market work;" 2) women's lower status in the labor market is an extension of the status accorded their non-market work; 3) patriarchy perpetuates "exploit" over purposeful activity that furthers the life process; 4) feminism is a response to the persistence of traditional ideology in the face of rapid economic and social changes affecting women's lives; and 5) sex role stereotyping in occupations will end when institutions such as the family, the schools, and the media "encourage women of all ages to take new directions rather than simply ceasing to forbid them to."

266. Hartmann, Heidi I. "The Unhappy Marriage of Marxism and Feminism: Towards a More Progressive Union." Capital & Class 8:1-33 (1979).

Hartmann compares the marriage of Marxism and feminism to English common law marriage: Marxism and feminism are one and that one is Marxism. She recommends a healthier marriage or divorce. Marxist analysis provides insights into laws of historical development and capital but its categories are sex-blind. Feminist analysis "has been blind to history and insufficiently materialist" but reveals the "systemic character of relations between men and women." A more progressive union of Marxism and feminism requires "not only improved intellectual understanding of relations of class and sex, but also that alliance replace dominance and subordination in left politics."

267. MacDonald, Martha. "Economics and Feminism: The Dismal Science?" Studies in Political Economy 15:151-177 (1984).

MacDonald claims that economics "has fallen short of other disciplines on all levels relevant to feminism." Women are severly underrepresented in the discipline. Economics lacks even a fringe field devoted to the study of women. The economy as studied by economists does not include the work activities of women. "The feminist idea that women's work is undervalued and thus underpaid is almost impossible for a neoclassical economist to grasp." Institutional and radical paradigms in economics are more promising but interdisciplinary research is essential "in piecing together...a sexual political economy of production." Feminists must reshape economic thinking to understand that the economy is not sex-neutral as has been assumed and to examine the private as well as the public sphere.

268. McFarland, Joan. "Economics and Women: A Critique of the Scope of Traditional Analysis and Research." Atlantis: A Women's Studies Journal 1(2):26-41 (1976).

McFarland contrasts traditional economists' treatment of women with the radical analysis of women's changing role in the economy. Traditional economics concentrates on women in the labor market and examines "why women do what they do not why they do not do something different or what factors might bring about a change." The radical approach asks what economic forces keep women in an inferior position, how these forces can be overcome, and how a society without such discriminatory forces would look. Radical economists explore the relationship between sexism and capitalism in "three realms of a woman's life: in the home, at the workplace and in the marketplace." Neither traditionalists nor radicals seem to be aware of what the other is doing. McFarland urges economists: 1) to include crucial factors, such as availability of day care services and extent of discrimination, in analyses of women's participation in the labor market; 2) to analyze what would happen to growth, employment, and income distribution if women actually were liberated; and 3) to ask specific questions about how women's liberation would affect the demand for labor as well as the supply.

269. Markusen, Ann. "Feminist Notes on Introductory Economics." Review of Radical Political Economics 9(3):1-6 (1977).

Eventually, feminists will develop their own cohesive theory of political economy. For now, however, a feminist analysis of traditional content can "illuminate...women's economic oppression and the weaknesses in conventional economic theory." A feminist analysis: 1) demonstrates that liberation is a struggle against ideology as well as against class, caste, and institutions; 2) demonstrates that feminism is a social struggle not an individual self-improvement program and that neoclassical theory promotes individualism; and 3) dismantles sexist economic arguments and omissions. Central to feminist economic theory is the household as a production unit. As opposed to conventional theory's claims that women prefer and are uniquely qualified for the lower income occupations in which they are grouped, feminist theory exposes the power of the institution to override individual choice. Women's experience counters the conventional theory of demand that says that each person is the best judge of her own preferences, which arise from an innate sense of utility. Feminist theory takes the social formation of tastes into account. Women's experience also identifies the error in marginal productivity theory that relates directly a worker's return to her contribution to production. Empirical facts support the assertion that men are more economically dependent on women than women are on men. The small number of men who remain unmarried all of their lives and the greater speed and frequency with which men remarry attest to the economic value of women's home production.

270. Miller, Edythe S. "Veblen and Women's Lib: A Parallel." Journal of Economic Issues 6:75-86 (1972).

Miller reviews the writing of Thorstein Veblen, the originator of institutionalism, to demonstrate that his views on women "seem almost to have been lifted from the pages of current protest journals." With regard to women's work, cultural conditioning, work and status, women as objects, vicarious leisure, and a woman's place, Veblen's incisive and sympathetic treatment points out the need to take women seriously.

271. Phillips, Anne and Barbara Taylor. "Sex and Skill: Notes Towards a Feminist Economics." Feminist Review 6:79-88 (1980).

Phillips and Taylor argue that "skill definitions are saturated with sexual bias" and that the classification of women's jobs as unskilled and men's as skilled is not related to the amount of training or ability required. Left to its own devices, capitalism might have succeeded in producing an indistinguishable mass of wage laborers. "But patriarchy intervened, and ensured through the development of the family wage system that women's subordinate position within the family be reproduced within waged labor." In their struggle against the process by which all capitalist work is becoming more routinized, male laborers have focused on distinguishing their work from women's work. However, such a segregation "conceals from many men workers the ways in which we are all becoming 'women workers' now." The fact that gender hierarchy enters directly into the development of capitalist relations makes the development of new economic categories and the reorganization of economic struggles themselves essential.

272. Waller, William and Ann Jennings. "On the Possibility of a Feminist Economics: The Convergence of Institutional and Feminist Methodology." Journal of Economic Issues 24(2):613-622 (1990).

Because institutional economics is epistemologically and methodologically similar to feminism, Waller and Jennings believe it has potential to evolve into a feminist economics. Both feminism and institutionalism reject the cartesian, objective, demonstrative approach to reasoning in favor of a dialectical approach. Both reject dualisms, especially the objective versus subjective and public versus private ones. Both believe that knowledge is a social product created in a cultural context. Waller and Jennings advise institutionalists to overcome their cultural blindness and take advantage of the methodologies suggested by feminism to "replace old and inadequate conceptions with more progressive ones."

273. Waring, Marilyn. If Women Counted: A New Feminist Economics. New York: Harper & Row, 1988.

The United Nations System of National Accounts (UNSNA) is used for measuring production and growth throughout most of the world. As Waring demonstrates, by reviewing the derivation of the UNSNA, the census statistics upon which it is based, and the tools used to collect information and develop indicies, women, children, and the environment are not included in worldwide measures of value and production. Women's household, food-related, and reproductive contributions lie outside of the UNSNA's production boundary. Environmental resources, like fresh air and clean water, are also excluded; "yet their destruction and the costs of cleaning up after the destruction are labeled 'growth' and 'production.'" According to Waring, economics' "obsession with numbers and the institutionalization of concepts based on scientific method has been a colonizer." Things which cannot easily be expressed in numbers, for example, the preservation of natural resources, have been colonized. She proposes that Hilkka Pietilä's visual conception of the national economy offers an alternative to the UNSNA that allows work to be assessed by volume (i.e., the number of workers or the number of hours) instead of just by money. Using Pietilä's concept, Waring believes nations' annual budgets would become "a realistic description of the well-being of the community and its environment, a reflection of real wealth and different values...."

9

GEOGRAPHY, ARCHITECTURE AND URBAN PLANNING

INTRODUCTION

When she addressed the students, faculty, graduates, and friends of Vassar College at the school's golden anniversary celebration in 1915, Ellen Churchill Semple (1863-1975), America's most eminent female geographer, beckoned women toward what she called her profession's "open door" (Bushong, 1975). Women's "natural endowments," she claimed, suited them to study the influence of the geographic environment on human development. Neither Semple's natural endowments, however, nor the Cullum Geographical Medal she received from the American Geographical Society protected her against discrimination or succeeded in beckoning substantial numbers of women into her chosen field. Clark University paid Semple $500 less per year than her male counterparts. The percentage of female college and university professors remains extremely low — 10 percent in geography compared with 26 percent in anthropology and 20 percent in sociology (Vetter, B. M. et al., Professional Women and Minorities: A Manpower Data Resource Service, Washington, DC: Scientific Manpower Commission, 1983).

Disciplines concerned with the appearance, use, and design of space have resisted feminist influence. Monk and Hanson (1982) and Zelinsky, Monk and Hanson (1982) complain about the "remarkable degree to which geography remains untouched by feminism" and the slow rate of change in attitudes and perceptions. No review essay on geography and gender, similar to those on sociology, anthropology, political science, and many other disciplines, has yet appeared in the journal Signs (Zelinsky, Monk and Hanson, 1982). Bowlby and Mackenzie (1982) claim that geographers have not met the challenge posed by the feminist critique — "to analyze the part played by gender role differentiation in people-environment relations." In 1985, Johnson wrote that geography's fundamental assumptions had yet to be questioned.

Feminists explain geography's (and other space-related disciplines') stubborn resistance in several ways. Burnett (1973) and Zelinsky, Monk and Hanson (1982) attribute geographers' avoidance of qualitative methodologies using intuition, introspection, or imagination to a strict adherence to empiricist and positivist practices that promise objectivity. In its quest for scientific validation, geography allied itself with geology and its emphasis on the physical, rather than social or political, landscape (Zelinsky, Monk, and Hanson, 1982). Monk and Hanson (1982) suggest that geographical research has single-mindedly pursued a "basis for informed policy and decision making." Such single-minded pursuit takes place within the status quo and will never lead to "alternative structures in which the lot of women is improved." Zelinsky, Monk and Hanson (1982) describe geographers as a conservative group. What, besides a professional conservatism, can account for the Association of American Geographers' decision to continue meeting in states which have not ratified the Equal Rights Amendment.

Feminist geographers, architects, and urban planners not only explain geographical and architectural resistance; they also identify the sexism characteristic of space-related research and design. The Women and Geography Study Group of the Institute of British Geographers (1984) associates the skewed and unbalanced understanding of spatial behavior patterns and perceptions of space with a predominance of male researchers. "Genderblind" premises and practices result when patterns and perceptions developed only by men are treated as universal (McDowell and Bowlby, 1983; Monk and Hanson, 1982). Male researchers generally avoid research themes of direct relevance to women's lives. Traditional sex roles determine the approach when these researchers do take women into account (Monk and Hanson, 1982). Space- and environment-related research has consistently used the household, defined as the nuclear family, as the unit of analysis. Research based on woman as "household surrogate" obscures women as individuals and loses sight of "women's activities in terms of the social injustice perpetuated by sex-role differences." (Tivers, 1978) Interviewing practices and respondent selection guarantee only male representation (Monk and Hanson, 1982). Female practitioners socialized according to the dominant conceptions of space and environment approach the design process in the same way as male practitioners. Only a practitioner with a feminist consciousness will design environments "with women in mind" (Darke, 1984).

A feminist consciousness is crucial to the design of women's space because gender differentiation is socially constructed. Space reflects gender differences, reinforces them, and helps recreate them in new forms (Bowlby, Foord, McDowell and Momsen, 1982; McDowell, 1983). According to Kennedy (1981), female values and priorities would shape a user-oriented, ergonomic, functional, flexible, holistic, and social environment in comparison with the designer-oriented, large scale, formal, fixed, specialized, and profit-oriented male environment that presently exists. Saegert (1980) describes the segregration of urban space into female, domestic, private suburbs versus male, productive, public cities, a segregation that limits women's opportunities and damages their self-definitions. Rural women's domestic role, claims Little (1986), restricts their lifestyles and causes the inequalities they experience. Hayden (1980) proposes a design for housing that overcomes the "traditional divisions between the household and the market economy, the private dwelling and the workplace." Enough of the old, pre-capitalistic ideology of the household as the "pivot of society's relations," as the place where production was organized, resources distributed, and security established, remains to "limit women's ability to function fully within the network of productive relations" dominating capitalist society. Obsolete households mean ambiguous roles for women (Hayford, 1974).

The Women and Geography Study Group of the Institute of British Geographers (1984) says feminist geography "explicitly takes into account the socially created gender structure of society and [is committed to] the alleviation of gender inequality in the short term and towards its removal...in the longer term...." Feminist research must not stop at documenting the differences between men's and women's spatial behavior patterns and perceptions and describing the separation of the public and private spheres. Feminist research must examine the structure of social relations that contributes to female oppression and must confront the theoretical issues raised by an analysis of patriarchy (McDowell, 1983).

Some research comes close to achieving these feminist goals. Palm and Pred (1978) use time-geography modeling to examine women as a subgroup and to isolate the structural bases for family-role inequalities. Peterson, Wekerle, and Morley (1978) propose "action research," which asks what distinguishes women as a group, what defines women's environments, what roles women play and how these roles restrict their freedom, what involvement women have in the design and modification of environments that affect them, and why women lack the power to make decisions concerning the design and use space. Berkeley (1980) questions whether an imagery exclusive to women exists. She believes function rather than form will transform architecture. Increased connections between architects and their clients and the demystification of architectural ideas, skills, and jargon would result in designs more sensitive to the users of the design product and more likely to meet people's practical, social, and aesthetic needs.

Feminist approaches to the study of space support Ellen Churchill Semple's belief that women's strong emotional natures allow them to resist the tendency of modern education to function as a "big mill especially designed for crushing the imagination." (Bushong, 1975) More than imagination may be needed, however, to transform disciplines so completely dominated not only by male definitions and principles but also by male practitioners.

ANNOTATIONS

274. Berkeley, Ellen Perry. "Architecture: Toward a Feminist Critique." In New Space for Women, edited by Gerda R. Wekerle, Rebecca Peterson, and David Morley, pp. 205-218 (Boulder, Colorado: Westview Press, 1980).

Berkeley suggests that feminism could change architecture by increasing the connection between architects and their clients, by making designs more sensitive to their users, and by demystifying architectural ideas, skills, and jargon. "Whether women architects will find their own imagery, special and exclusive to women, is...[a] question," but where Berkeley sees the potential for a feminist transformation of architecture is with function rather than form. She pleads for "an architecture that meets people's needs...and this includes aesthetic needs too."

275. Bowlby, S. R., J. Foord, L. McDowell, and J. Momsen. "Environment, Planning, and Feminist Theory: A British Perspective." Environment and Planning A 14:711-716 (1982).

In a guest editorial in Environment and Planning A, Bowlby, Foord, McDowell, and Momsen describe women's changing economic and social roles over the past few decades, and point out the disparity between these changing roles and "the spatial structure of cities and regions, and the nature of state involvement in facilitating or initiating change." They argue that "the recognition that gender differentiation is socially constructed should change the way in which we examine social processes and spatial organization. Space reflects, reinforces, and helps recreate in new forms these gender differences."

276. Bowlby, S. R. and S. Mackenzie. "Feminism and Geography." Area 14(1):19-25 (1982).

Bowlby and Mackenzie claim that "the feminist critique challenged geographers to analyse the part played by gender role differentiation in people-environment relations...[and] this challenge was not met." Most feminist geographers have done little more than "document 'geographical' features of the inequalities of women" using positivist, liberal approaches that lack "a theoretical perspective which might point to more fundamental causes." Feminist perspectives, like Pat Burnett"s (see annotation below), based on patriarchy and capitalism, are weakened by the treatment of gender differences "not as social constructions, but as natural phenomena." More promising are works that focus on production and the reproduction of labor power that replace "the model of two separate [feminine and masculine] structures with a discussion of gender relations as constituted by women and men in the process of producing society's goods and services and reproducing the labour force."

277. Burnett, Pat. "Social change, the Status of Women and Models of City Form and Development." Antipode 5(3):57-62 (1973).

Burnett says the purpose of her article, one of the earliest attempts at introducing feminist analysis into geography, is to "illustrate how urban growth models in geography have limited explanatory, predictive and prescriptive powers...because of inadequate analysis of social change." She not only describes how four types of urban models fail to deal with women's status in society but also points out that the strict logical empiricism or positivism that guides these models guarantees their inability to identify "hitherto unspecified, alternative sets of premises and conclusions." Good explanations and predictions of urban growth depend upon the "development of intuition, speculation, courage, creative imagination, and empathy...[as well as] the development of facility in handling observation and measurement tools...." Burnett briefly outlines the development of a Marxist-derived theory of "the male psychology of power" that she believes could eliminate the inequalities "of class, race, and sex, together with their expression in contemporary urban systems." A comment by Irene Bruegel follows Burnett's article in Antipode. Bruegel says that the weakness in Burnett's theory of "the male psychology of power" is its view of men and women as opposing social classes. But "womanhood does not transcend social class," and while women are oppressed by the existing structure of cities, such oppression is unequal. A simple male domination theory ignores the fact that "there is a definite class differentiation in women's situation in the city." Bruegel argues that to "understand women's position in society and in the city it is necessary to analyse the institution of private property and the role of the family from a Marxist standpoint."

278. Bushong, Allen D. "Women as Geographers: Some Thoughts On Ellen Churchill Semple." Southeastern Geographer 15(2):102-109 (1975).

Ellen Churchill Semple (1863 - 1931) is probably the most eminent female American geographer. She wrote three highly respected books, taught at Clark University in Massachusetts, at University of Chicago, and at Oxford University Summer School. In 1914, she received the Cullum Geographical Medal from the American Geographical Society "in recognition of her distinguished contributions to the science of anthropogeography." In his article, Bushong reprints sections from Semple's address, "Geographical Research as a Field for Women," to the students, faculty, graduates and, friends of Vassar College on the occasion of the school's golden anniversary in 1915. Semple encouraged women to enter the rich field of geography that lay "waiting for a labor force to develop it, promising an abundant harvest to the tiller." She suggested that, for women, geography was an open door, especially in terms of the need for teachers at all levels. Anthropogeography, the study of the influence of geographic environment on human development, she urged, is particularly suited to women "because of their natural endowment...their power of observation, their capacity for detail work, their patient perserverance in the collection of material, their intellectual humility,...and finally their imagination." Women's strong emotional natures allow them to resist the tendency of modern education to function as a "big mill especially designed for crushing the imagination." In addition, "feminine tastes and the feminine order of mind" prepare women for the careful induction from a broad comparison of data and the wide and various reading anthropogeography demands. It is ironic, in view of Semple's achievements within the field of geography and her belief that women would make better geographers than men, at least in some subfields, that Semple, herself, did not escape from sex discrimination and that the proportion of female geographers remains extremely low. Clark University paid Semple $500 less per year than her male equivalents received (Berman, Mildred, "Sex Discrimination and Geography: The Case of Ellen Churchill Semple," The Professional Geographer 24(1):8-11 (1974)), and, as of 1980, only 9.6 percent of college and university professors were women (see Zelinsky, Monk, and Hanson below).

279. Darke, Jane. "Women, Architects and Feminism." In Making Space: Women and the Man-Made Environment, edited by Matrix, pp.11-25 (London, Pluto Press, 1984).

In her contribution to this collection edited by a group of feminist designers known as Matrix, Darke is less concerned with whether women architects design differently from men and more concerned that architects are out of touch and, in fact, are educated to be out of touch, with those who use their buildings. The built environment reflects social ideals and, therefore, is oppressive for many women. Says Darke, "the relative size and impressiveness of rooms and buildings, the relationship of spaces to each other and the people whose convenience is given priority all help to define what is normal...If a block of council flats looks like a filing cabinet or prison, we are right in thinking that this carries ideas about the status of the people who live there." She ties problems with the environment to the socialization process for architects: just because a woman is an architect doesn't mean she will approach the design process differently. Women with a feminist consciousness can, however, produce an environment "designed with women in mind."

280. Drake, Christine and June Horton. "Comment On Editorial Essay: Sexist Bias in Political Geography." Political Geography Quarterly 2(4):329-337 (1983).

Through a series of examples, Drake and Horton demonstrate the male bias that has characterised political geography. They fault geographers for their "sins of omission," for not asking some of the right questions such as, "to what extent does the organization of political space reflect the priorities, ideas, design, and goals of women?" Gender, they claim, colors perceptions of space and the effect of its political organization as much as nationality and culture. The omission of women, who are not passive and do possess political identity, has resulted in a loss of "insights into geographical realities..." and done real harm "in attempts to promote more just and prosperous societies."

281. Hayden, Dolores. "What Would a Non-Sexist City Be Like? Speculations on Housing, Urban Design, and Human Work." Signs 5(3): 170-187 (1980).

Hayden objects to the principle, "a woman's place is in the home," which has functioned implicitly in the design of housing and urban areas for the last century. Current "dwellings, neighborhoods, and cities designed for homebound women constrain women, [most of whom are employed,] physically, socially, and economically." The "traditional divisions between the household and the market economy, the private dwelling and the workplace," must be overcome in order for women to achieve economic and environmental justice. Hayden proposes the formation of Homemakers Organizations for a More Egalitarian Society (HOMES), small, participatory groups that could work together, to begin to create different housing arrangements. The housing would include private dwellings of various sizes to accommodate people living alone, together, and with children, private fenced outdoor space, collective outdoor space, collective indoor space consisting of laundry facilities, a kitchen providing hot take-out meals and meals-on-wheels, a grocery depot and food cooperative, a garage with collectively owned vehicles, a home help office, and a day care. Such housing arrangements would allow some residents to work in the home area and some to travel to work, and would overcome the limitations of housing designed around "principles of another era."

282. Hayford, Alison M. "The Geography of Women: An Historical Introduction." Antipode 6:1-19 (1974).

Because their lives differ from men's, and because their relations with the earth, its resources, and productive systems are not the same as or even parallel to men's, women form a distinct geographical force. Based on this distinction, Hayford developes the general elements of a geography of women. The rise of capitalism created a major shift in women's roles, moving them "from centrality to the periphery, from being the pivot of society's relations to being nowhere." In an economic and political system in which the household served as the "place through which productive relations were organized, resources distributed, and security...established," women were vitally important in creating the "symbolic and actual center of what was familiar and safe." They were so important, in fact, that some societies imposed stringent controls on women, limiting their external contacts and defining their household-related functions. Under capitalism, the household as a form of organization has become obsolete. Women, however, "can scarcely become obsolete," but their role has become ambiguous: "enough of the old ideology of the household and of its control functions remain to limit [women's] ability to function fully within the network of productive relations which dominate society." Spatial segregation of functions causes women, who lack the means or freedom to move easily, considerable stress.

283. Johnson, Louise. "Gender, Genetics and the Possibility of Feminist Geography." Australian Geographical Studies 23 (April):161-171 (1985).

Johnson describes three phases or dimensions of the feminist critique of geography. The first dimension identified the absence of women, both as geographers and subjects of geographical theories, in the field. The second dimension recognized that conclusions about human behavior had been based on male experiences. The third dimension, which, according to Johnson, "has barely begun in geography," involves "a re-orientation of geographical thinking and practice towards a general consideration of social relations and space, and interventions to create pro-woman social change." This dimension moves the feminist criitque beyond content and choice of variables to a questioning of the assumptions underlying the choice of variables.

284. Kennedy, Margrit I. "Toward a Rediscovery of 'Feminine' Principles in Architecture and Planning." Women's Studies International Quarterly 4(1):75-81 (1981).

Kennedy believes that "there would be a significant difference between an environment shaped by women, female values and priorities, and our present environment shaped mainly by men, male values and priorities." The female principle compared to the male principle would be more user-oriented than designer- oriented, more ergonomic than large scale/monumental, more functional than formal, more flexible than fixed, more organically ordered than abstractly systematized, more holistic/complex than specialized/one-dimensional, more social than profit-oriented, and more slowly growing than quickly constructed. Kennedy emphasizes the need for both principles by underscoring that present problems result from the one-sided dominance of the male principle. While temporarily, to redress the current imbalance, the female principle should take precedence over the male principle, in the long run a balance of the two principles would create the best architecture and the best environment.

285. Kofman, Eleonore and Linda Peake. "Into the 1990s: A Gendered Agenda for Political Geography." Political Geography Quarterly 9(4):313-336 (1990).

In their introduction to a special issue of Political Geography Quarterly, Kofman and Peake review the feminist literature and present "suggested areas of research for a reconstructed and gendered political geography." The areas they suggest include: 1) political participation; 2) public-private dichotomy; 3) public patriarchy and the state; 4) international politics; and 5) politicization and conflict. They are careful to explain that their exploration of the ways gender perspectives challenge traditional models and analyses "is not in any way aimed at erecting a new orthodoxy." The contributors to the special issue attempt to transcend the legacy of dualities "inherited through centuries of Western social and political thought" that have restricted legitimate political activity to groups with power.

286. Little, Jo. "Feminist Perspectives in Rural Geography: An Introduction." Journal of Rural Studies 2(1):1-8 (1986).

In an attempt to be broad-based, Little offers a brief overview of the introduction of feminist perspectives into rural geography. She takes a socialist feminist stand, proposing that "the study of gender relations in conjunction with the analysis of social class [is] most effective for the wider understanding of capitalist society." It is not enough to consider women as a separate social category or population sub-group; the development of feminist perspectives must result in "an appreciation of the importance of gender in all aspects of social relations and the organisation of society in general." She sees women's domestic role as the cause of the inequalities they experience. The caring, domestic image of women projected by rural ideology restricts their lifestyles and limits their choices and experiences. Class and gender power distributions in rural society must be questioned and changed to allow for united political action by women.

287. Little, Jo, Linda Peake and Pat Richardson, editors. Women In Cities: Gender and the Urban Environment. New York: New York University Press, 1988.

In the collection they edit, Little, Peake and Richardson aim "to elaborate the particular contribution that feminist geography can make to the analysis of women's activities and experience and the nature of their oppression in urban areas, and to indicate the kind of research agenda to which it gives rise." Feminist geography, they claim, examines the interrelations between socially constructed gender relations and socially constructed environments. Women, by virtue of being women, don't all live the same lives. Therefore, there is no one feminist perspective. All feminist approaches, however, share the objective "of understanding and improving the position of women in society." Little, Peake and Richardson identify three themes uniting the various approaches in feminist geography: 1) the need to integrate theoretical analysis and political practice; 2) the need to address themes and topics important to women's experiences and daily lives; and 3) the need to increase awareness "of the significance of women's oppression in analyses of social and environmental change in urban areas." Essays in Women In Cities include "Gender and the City: Urban Politics Revisited" by Liz Bondi and Linda Peake, "Balancing Our Space and Time: The Impact of Women's Organisation on the British City, 1920-1980" by Suzanne Mackenzie, "From Corner Shop To Hypermarket: Women and Food Retailing" by Sophia Bowlby, "Women With Young Children: Constraints on Activities in the Urban Environment" by Jacqueline

Tivers, "Hard To Get Around: A Study of Women's Travel Mobility" by Laurie Pickup, and "A Means To Get Out of the House: Working-class Women, Leisure and Bingo" by Rachael Dixey.

288. McDowell, Linda. "Toward an Understanding of the Gender Division of Urban Space." Environment and Planning D: Society and Space 1:59-72 (1983).

McDowell argues that "the nature of the changing interrelationships between production and reproduction, as part of a single inseparable process that varies across space and over time, should be the key focus for a feminist urban studies." While the relatively large number of studies that have been published on women's lives and urban space have been very useful for bringing "gender differences to the research forefront," most of these studies have provided only descriptions and analyses of women's behavior. The separation of the private and public spheres has largely been treated as a given and described rather than questioned and explained. Marxist-feminist and socialist-feminist research has developed "a historical analysis of the origins of women's current oppression and the privatisation of family life in capitalist industrialisation," but this research, too has tended to focus on one side of the private/public dichotomy. Space, like gender, is socially constructed. Land-use policies enforce social relations and gender divisions and function to segregrate "non-conforming uses." The object of feminist research "should not be women alone, but rather the structure of social relations that contributes to female oppression, this involving confrontation with the theoretical issues raised by an analysis of patriarchy...."

289. McDowell, Linda and Sophia Bowlby. "Teaching Feminist Geography." Journal of Geography in Higher Education 7(2):97-107 (1983).

McDowell and Bowlby describe four challenges that feminism poses for existing theoretical and methodological approaches to geography. The first challenge has been feminists' efforts to make women visible by studying women's issues and by examining the differences between men's and women's spatial behaviors and perceptions. Such research has exposed the fallacy of universalizing the conclusions of research that has actually been "genderblind." The second challenge relates to the relationship feminism has exposed among male and female social relations, women's oppression, and created environments: socially created environments reflect social relations and function to reinforce and recreate them. The exposure of such a relationship has led to re-interpretations of the past and present and to suggestions for future environmental changes. The third challenge questions the methods used to conduct research.

"Feminist research in geography entail[s] devising new methods of inquiry that break down routine assumptions about gender roles...and take[s] into account, in a reflexive manner, the gender of the researcher, of the individuals or groups being researched, and the interactions between the two." Typical data collection and statistical categories, such as heads of households, can no longer be seen as providing adequate measures of women's perceptions. The fourth challenge is that feminism involves a commitment to change, "not only change of the larger structures and relations of society but also change of everyday, individual relationships."

290. Monk, Janice and Susan Hanson. "On Not Excluding Half of the Human in Human Geography." Professional Geographer 34(1):11-23 (1982).

Monk and Hanson's article reflects their distress at the remarkable "degree to which geography remains untouched by feminism." They attribute feminism's lack of influence to the fact that over ninety percent of geographers are men, that men have "structured research problems according to their values, their concerns, and their goals," and that positivism, "a method that tends to preserve the status quo," has been the preferred geographical approach. Geographic research has exhibited sexist bias in content, method, and purpose. Sexism in content has resulted from: 1) inadequate specification of research problems; 2) gender-blind theory; 3) the assumption of traditional gender roles; and 4) avoidance of research themes directly related to women's lives. Sexism has permeated geographical methods through: 1) variable selection; 2) respondent selection; 3) interviewing practices; and 4) inadequate secondary data sources. Geographical research has aimed at providing "a basis for informed policy and decision making" primarily within the context of the status quo. The purpose of non-sexist research would be to "define alternative structures in which the lot of women is improved." Human geography will become more fully human when a feminist perspective runs through "all streams" of focus and research.

291. Palm, Risa and Allan Pred. "The Status of American Women: A Time-Geographic View." In An Invitation to Geography, edited by David A. Lanegran and Risa Palm, pp. 99-109 (New York: McGraw-Hill, 1978).

Using Torsten Hagerstrand's time-geography model of society, Palm and Pred illustrate "some of the problems and conflicts which burden women with children, married and unmarried, working outside or within the home." The time-geography model uses terminology and the diagramming of relationships to portray individuals simultaneously in time and space. The use of such a model brings to light the constraints that affect an individual's choices by analyzing how activities are set in space and time and how the settings determine access. Capability constraints are biological and technological factors the individual can command. Examples of capability constraints include the number of hours of sleep needed per day and the method of transportation available. Coupling constraints refer to constraints imposed by the hours during which other people or places are accessible. An example of a coupling constraint is the hours a day care center is open. Authority constraints "restrict access by means of rules, laws, customs, or expectations." When women cannot go out unaccompanied at night they are operating under an authority restraint. "Daily prisms" depicting the range an individual has in the course of her day can be drawn by representing distance and direction along a horizontal axis and time along a vertical axis. Palm and Pred apply time-geography modeling to women in four different situations to demonstrate "why women come to feel restricted and oppressed within the roles they perform...." They believe that "further empirical studies from a time-geographic perspective are essential if we are to understand the serious inequities which exist for women who wish to assume any but the most traditional roles in our society."

292. Peterson, Rebecca, Gerda R. Wekerle, and David Morley. "Women and Environments: An Overview of an Emerging Field." Environment and Behavior 10(4):511-534 (1978).

"Women's increasing self-awareness and rising expectations demand changes in existing environments and in the processes of designing new environments," say Peterson, Wekerle, and Morley. They suggest that "action research" is necessary to bring the issues of women and their environments to the attention of design professionals and policy makers. Four sets of questions must be asked to help define the framework for research on women and environments: 1) how useful is it to distinguish women as a separate group of users in any given environment and how can women's environments be defined? 2) what assumptions are made regarding the roles women will play in particular environments and how do these assumptions limit or restrict women's behaviors? 3) to what extent are women involved in the conscious design and modification of environments? and 4) if women have unique environmental needs but are not involved in environmental design or decision-making, how did this discrepancy come about and how can it be corrected?

293. Saegert, Susan. "Masculine Cities and Feminine Suburbs: Polarized Ideas, Contradictory Realities." Signs 5(3, supplement): S96-S111 (1980).

Culturally, suburbs and cities have been construed as polar opposites and assigned female and male characteristics respectively. This segregration of female, domestic, private, and suburb versus male, productive, public, and urban, which fails to describe the reality of many lives, influences public policy and city planning and serves to limit women's opportunities and damage women's self-definition. Burdened by "double duty at home and work, split loyalties, and too scanty a recognition of achievement in either sphere, [women end up] holding together the necessary areas of life that are organized temporally and spatially to create separation." Individuals cannot satisfactorily overcome the existing segregations on their own; public policy and physical planning must focus on organizing time and space to integrate domestic and productive work and leisure.

294. Tivers, Jacqueline. "How the Other Half Lives: The Geographical Study of Women." Area 10(4):302-306 (1978).

Tivers describes ways in which geographers, most of whom are men, have perpetuated a male-oriented view of society by taking those institutions that express a dominant male role as representative of the whole society. Since the household, i.e., the nuclear family, has been taken by geographers as the unit of analysis, women as individuals disappear. They have been of interest only as "household surrogates" in research that assumes existing family roles as givens and makes no attempt to explain "women's activities in terms of the social injustice perpetuated by sex-role differences." Women must be studied as a sub-group in their own right using frameworks, for example, the "constraint-based" framework of time-geography (see Palm and Pred above), that makes it possible to explore the structural bases for family-role inequalities. Susanne Mackenzie comments on Tiver's article in a subsequent issue of Area (12:47-49 (1980)). She agrees with Tiver's suggestion that women replace households as a population subgroup of their own but suggests a further step: researchers examining the geography of women must ask "what social relations define women's position in contemporary society?" Researchers must move beyond the "empirical measurement of women's spatial perception and activities" and research must be grounded "in a historically informed and politically sensitive understanding of the structural basis of women's position."

295. Women and Geography Study Group of the IBG. Geography and Gender: An Introduction to Feminist Geography (London: Hutchinson, 1984).

The Women and Geography Study Group of the Institute of British Geographers defines feminist geography as "a geography which explicitly takes into account the socially created gender structure of society; and in which a commitment both towards the alleviation of gender inequality in the short term and towards its removal, through social change towards real equality, in the longer term is expressed." Geography, like other disciplines, has focused on the dominant group — white males — and, as a result, has produced a skewed and unbalanced understanding of spatial behavior patterns and perceptions of space. It is not sufficient for feminist geography to document the differences between men's and women's behavior patterns and perceptions. The differences must be explained in light of the social inequalities facing the two genders and suggestions provided for how change might be brought about. The facts that men are "numerically dominant in almost all institutions teaching degree level geography, and also hold most the positions of power, and that female students have faced sexist discrimination, explain the lack of attention that has hitherto been paid to issues concerning women and space." A feminist approach to geographical research will alter the questions asked, "the theoretical context within which empirical data are collected and interpreted, and the methods of data collection and analysis employed." New, more subjective approaches — empathy, intuition, and concern for other's feelings and emotions — must be used to avoid the extent to which "non-involvement can obscure truth." In some cases, the sexist ways in which official statistics have been compiled may impede data collection regarding the actual situations of women (see also Oakley and Oakley in the Sociology chapter). Geography and Gender not only introduces feminist geography but also provides four examples of feminist analysis in urban spatial structure, women's employment, industrial location and regional change, access to facilities, and women and development. "One of the aims of the book is...to redress the balance of introductory geographical material in favor of women."

296. Zelinsky, Wilbur, Janice Monk and Susan Hanson. "Women and Geography: A Review and Prospectus." Progress in Human Geography 6(3):317-366 (1982).

Zelinksy, Monk and Hanson review both the literature on the changing status of female geographers and "writings on the geographical dimensions of women's lives." While their bibliography includes over 225 items, they express concern at the degree to which geography lags behind other scholarly disciplines in filling gaps related to women or in producing the needed "change in attitudes and perceptions, a substantial shift in the angle of vision, a recognition...of the supreme social, and thus geographic, fact that women, as individuals or as a class, exist under much different conditions and contraints in a world quite different from, however closely linked with, that inhabited by men." They point out, for example, that no review essay equivalent to those published in Signs for other disciplines has appeared for the literature of geography and women or gender, and that a collection of papers called Women in Society: A New Perspective edited by Pat Burnett has never made it beyond the mimeographed stage. Zelinsky, Monk, and Hanson attribute geography's slow development in the area of feminist research to several things: 1) geography, "in its pursuit of objectivity, has set for itself very narrow bounds of acceptable scientific endeavour," meaning that other ways of knowing, such as intuition, introspection, or imagination, have been avoided; 2) the small proportion of women geographers, some of whom are in specialties such as physical geography and cartography (women geographers have had to fight against a tendency to attribute to them biological deficiency related to spatial perception and thinking that would weaken their geographical abilities); 3) the conservative nature of geographers as a group relative to the members of other professions (they cite the Association of American Geographers' decision to continue holding meetings in states which had not ratified the Equal Rights Amendmentas proof of such conservatism); and 4) geography's link with geology, resulting in a focus, until recently, on the visible landscape as opposed to the process of society, political economy, or the ecosystem. The authors conclude their review by listing some topics in "which the feminine perspective is altogether absent:" spatial patterns of divorce, urban spatial structure, political and medical geography, and the geography of sport and leisure.

10

COMMUNICATION

INTRODUCTION

Common Themes

Communication encompasses the separate but similar disciplinary areas of media and mass communication studies, linguistics and speech, film studies, and art criticism. Three themes weave through the feminist criticism of these four disciplinary areas. The first theme is that social conditions determine the production of messages (for example, paintings, quilts, films, mass media, speeches, personal conversations). The second theme is that gender itself is a message. The third theme is that meanings are a product of the interaction between a spectator and an image or a listener and a speaker, and that ruptures in an image or a speech provide the opportunity for interpretations that take the spectator's or listener's particular experiences into account.

Feminist critics of research methodology in all four communication disciplinary areas advocate many of the same changes as feminist critics of other disciplines. Dervin (1987), for example, says that feminist scholarship views gender as a "fundamental organizing category of human experience," makes female experience central, promotes social change, is pluralist, cooperative, participatory, and non-hierarchical, and treates the researcher and the researched as equal partners in discovery. A feminist sociologist, philosopher, or biologist could have written these principles.

But feminist communication researchers also relate feminist principles specifically to messages and discourse.

Media and Mass Communications

Within the diciplinary area of media and mass communication studies, feminist scholarship has extended and redirected the central questions the discipline poses by examining the "construction of women's exploitation and subordination materially and ideologically within patriarchy." (Baehr, 1981) Henderson (1989) and Schaef (1989) challenge the profit-oriented, manipulative, and controlling approach of the mass media. Only a "participatory, process-oriented system" (Schaef) will provide minority groups with the access to the media necessary to change "society's group consciousness." (Henderson) All the factors that contribute to the "symbolic annihilation" of women (Tuchman, 1978) — the lack of women news gatherers or distributors, the predominance of male-defined news, the scarcity of female images in the media — offer research opportunities to feminists (Smith, 1982).

Janus (1977) links media sexism to the material conditions of society. She advocates a critical approach to media research. According to the critical approach, divisions based on social class are more important than those based on sex and the well-being of capitalism depends on sexual oppression. Steeves (1987) recommends a socialist feminist approach to research because such an approach emphasizes the connections between women's oppression and other inequities. Oppression is also central to Cirksena's (1987) approach to feminist research on media and communications. Knowledge, information, and language are social constructions that contribute to gender-based inequalities. She proposes consciousness-raising as a feminist paradigm for knowledge accumulation. Press (1989) lists the the alleviation of women's oppression and the centrality of gender in the analysis of individuals and society as qualities that distinguish a feminist approach to mass communications.

All feminist researchers emphasize gender as a central category of analysis. In media and mass communications research, however, feminists have made the unique suggestion that gender is a verb (Rakow, "Rethinking Gender Research in Communication," 1986). Gender, according to Rakow, is a communication practice, work done to maintain a particular gender system. "Communication creates genders who create communication." Similarly, Putnam (1982) says gender is an individually-defined situation rather than a societal characteristic. Communicative behaviors, which are "recipes that evolve from contextual constraints," determine gender.

Traditional research in mass communications has ignored gender or treated men and women as polarized, biological opposites with stable and enduring attributes (Putnam, 1982). Researchers have designed research around preconceived beliefs in the inferiority of women's communication and have rejected data that fails to substantiate their preconceptions

(Putnam, 1987). Feminists, to whom gender is critical, must avoid building their research around accepted assumptions and findings (Foss and Foss, 1983; Spender, 1985). Altman (1987) views with misgiving the publication of feminist theory and research in special issues or sections of journals. While some information, wherever it appears, is better than none, feminism on the margins will not produce change.

Broadening the popular culture canon to include women communicators is an essential feminist activity (Rakow, "Feminist Approaches to Popular Culture...," 1986) because, as Dervin (1987) says, "the very act of not leaving women out" undermines traditional assumptions. Even the traditional canon is subject to "ideological seams." Less powerful groups can use these "seams" or ruptures in media messages designed by the dominant group to understand and cope with their own situations (Radway, 1986). To make significant changes in the media and mass communications disciplines, however, feminist researchers must avoid simply extending or intensifying the kinds of information that already exist. Foss and Foss (1983) advocate holistic research. Unlike research as dichotomy and opposition, which relates only one independent to one dependent variable, holistic research relates and connects as many variables as possible.

Linguistics and Speech Communication

Feminists base their critique of linguistics and speech communication on the belief that speech is a verbal expression of gender. Robin Lakoff (1973) wrote one of the earliest analyses of "Language and Women's Place." She describes women as "linguistically submerged." Spoken words are acceptable, Lakoff points out, as much because of social context and assumptions as because of grammar, syntax, and semantics. In an essay written twelve years after Lakoff's, McConnell-Ginet (1985) praises feminism for restoring language to the sociocultural context from which linguistics extracted it for analysis.

As strongly as agreement with Lakoff's ideas, reaction against them has determined the direction of feminist research in linguistics. Valian (1977) criticizes Lakoff for concluding that women's language is inferior because it differs from men's. Women do not need to adapt their language usage to a male norm; users of oppressive language, rather, need to change. Martyna (1980) rejects Lakoff's advice that the unconscious and widespread use of the male generic pronoun to refer to all members of a sexually mixed group is not worth trying to change. Her research shows that sex-specific uses of the pronoun "he" occur five to ten times more frequently than generic uses. The odds are, therefore, that "he" does not include "she." According to Martyna, resisters, like Lakoff, to changes in sexist language give language symbolic rather than actual importance. Silveira (1980) disagrees with Lakoff's belief that social change creates language change rather than the reverse. Replacing generic masculine words with other forms would "produce long-term reduction in sexist thinking."

Since "language has been literally man made" (Spender,1985), to change their social condition women must change language. Jenkins and Kramarae (1981) agree with the French critic, Claudine Herriman, who encourages women to be "thieves of language." To describe their experiences, women must steal language back from men. Lugones and Spelman (1983) demonstrate the extent to which language can function as a weapon of oppression by writing an article in two different voices, the voice of an Hispana woman and the voice of a white/Anglo woman. Discourse between individuals or groups with different amounts of power can only be productive when it reveals connections that hadn't been obvious before, when it demystifies the world, when it clarifies the responsibility the speakers have for their locations in the world, and when it provides criteria for change.

Feminist analysts of speech communication and linguistics believe that speech is an interaction in which the participants "often have unequal influence and speaking rights." (Kramarae, 1981) Bate and Taylor (1988) show how factoring an analysis of power into definitions, descriptions, and evaluations of women's communication changes the results. For example, men have used differences in language, nonverbal codes, and spheres of interest to justify their domination of work and public leadership. A feminist approach to such differences asks why characteristics associated with males have been defined as dominant, and sees the characteristics associated with women as a "fertile ground" for the development of a new, more affirmative culture. Elshtain (1982) claims that a political discourse centered around the protection of "fragile and vulnerable human existence" could be emancipatory.

Feminist linguistic theories must spell out the connection between language and gender and language and oppression. Cameron (1985) cautions feminists, however, not to blame language for what happens to people. People can change their linguistic practices. Social institutions, therefore, not language, control and oppress the poor, the Black, and the female. Kramarae (1986) says that gender must be the central, organizing force for the study of language not because such an approach will represent progress but rather because it will "produce a linguistic revolution which could affect many women and men."

Film Studies

While they are not immune to becoming trapped in the "patriarchal loop or chain" (Walker, 1984), feminist film studies researchers have, more than feminist researchers in the other three communication disciplinary areas, broken with traditional research approaches and assumptions. The earliest feminist art critics used a sociological approach to evaluate the sex roles adopted by the women represented in various films (Kaplan, 1983). Bergstrom (1988) credits Claire Johnston with moving feminist filmmaking and criticism toward a theoretical and away from a sociological approach. The Camera Obscura Collective (1976) describes the theoretical approach as "textual analysis which brings to the study of film analytical tools derived from...semiology and psychoanalysis."

Feminist film critics borrow from semiotics the idea of signs (Kaplan, 1983). Woman as sign conveys the patriarchal ideology around which social structures are built. Feminists have adopted psychoanalytic theory "as a political weapon" to demonstrate the extent to which "the unconscious of patriarchal society has structured film form." (Mulvey, 1988) Classical Hollywood films include ruptures, gaps, and contradictions in which a feminine voice penetrates an "apparently seamless patriarchal fabric." (Bergstrom, 1988; Walker, 1984)

The most recent developments in feminist film studies extend the idea that both the creator of the film and the spectators participate in producing the film's meaning (Camera Obscura Collective, 1976). de Lauretis (1988) defines a feminine aesthetic based on female spectators whose diverse lives affect their cinematic experience. The Black woman filmmaker, Larkin (1988), insists that feminist film theory must account for, rather than simply acknowledge, historical and social differences between women and their experiences. Gledhill (1988) criticizes the fixed, "once and for all" approaches of psychoanalytic and semiotic frameworks. She proposes their replacement by "negotiation," a struggle between the competing frames of reference held by the film and by the spectators out of which meaning evolves.

Art Criticism

Nochlin's (1973) early essay, "Why Have There Been No Great Women Artists?" had the same effect on feminist art critics as Lakoff's essay, "Language and Womens's Place," had on feminist linguists. Agreement with Nochlin's analysis of the social conditions essential to the production of art and disagreement with her assumption that there have been no great women artists have formed the foundation for much of the feminist analysis of art. Art is more than the translation of personal life into visual terms. Art happens in the context of "temporally-defined conventions, schemata, or systems of notation" which artists learn through study, apprenticeship, or concentrated experiments. For Nochlin, it is not surprising that no great women artists have existed; it is a miracle, rather, that women, denied access to the channels through which artists learn conventions, schemata, and systems of notation, have managed to produce art at all.

Feminist art historians claim that, when Nochlin accepts the statement that no women artists have been great, she is accepting the traditional selection and classification principles that have determined which works belong in art histories and hang in art galleries. The definition of art is too narrow, feminists claim, when it excludes techniques such as needlework and china painting traditionally practiced by women

(Magenta, 1981). Some feminist artists argue for a female imagery — separate from male imagery and subject to different critical standards — based on the biology and sexuality of the female body (Magenta, 1981).

Dalton (1980) cautions that the meaning of images depends upon the context in which they appear. Most women see art filtered through "male-controlled selection procedures." She advises feminists to create alternative systems of mass communication or, at least, to appropriate what they want and need from existing systems. Women should practice both traditionally female art forms (for example, knitting) and traditionally male ones (for example, photography). Kuhn (1985) explores Dalton's concern in greater detail. She raises some feminist questions about images and how they mean: what sort of activity is looking and what does it have to do with sexuality or with gender or with power or with knowledge? is a spectator addressed as male or female? is femininity constructed through representation? why are images of women's bodies so prevalent? An examination of images alone will not provide answers to these questions. The use and exchange value of images depends upon context, on the particular time and place of their consumption.

Barry and Flitterman (1987) distinguish feminist art working against the patriarchy from art produced by women in a male-dominated society. Feminist art involves the spectator in the production of meaning by exploiting social contradictions. Art that ruptures traditionally held ideas about women raises questions about the social construction of femininity and sexual differences and engages the spectator in a process of discovery. Such feminist textual practice, unlike art which glorifies female power, exalts crafts, or tries to stand outside of the dominant cultural order, can produce social change.

The Extent of Feminist Influence

Some feminist critics of the communication disciplines celebrate feminism's influence on the establishment. Even though women's art still has less chance of hanging on a gallery wall than men's art, Magenta (1981) sees "tangible success" in the increasing number of women artists, critics, and art historians. Other feminist critics are less enthusiastic. According to Cirksena (1989), feminist perspectives have left the "central body of knowledge which is the core of the discipline of communications research" untouched.

ANNOTATIONS

297. Altman, Karen E. "Conversing at the Margins: A Polemic, or Feminism and Communication Studies." Journal of Communication Inquiry 11(1):116-117 (1987).

Altman points out that, during 1986 and 1987, three communication journals featured feminist theory and research: Communication (volume 9, number 1, 1986), Quarterly Journal of Speech (the book review section of volume 72, number 3, 1986), and Journal of Communication Inquiry (volume 11, number 1, 1987). While in some ways such visibility is encouraging, Altman views it as a sign of marginalization. Relegating to the margins feminisms' concern with power relations and its identification of language, meaning, or knowledge as sites of power struggles, is an effective way for the dominant orders to prevent it from producing change. Separating the feminist dialogue into special volumes or sections conveys the sense that it operates in isolation away from the mainstream practices. While conversing at the margins is better than not conversing at all, Altman recommends that feminists organize to be heard across the discipline.

298. Baehr, Helen. "The Impact of Feminism on Media Studies - Just Another Commercial Break?" In Men's Studies Modified: The Impact of Feminism on the Academic Disciplines, edited by Dale Spender, pp.141-154 (Oxford: Pergamon Press, 1981).

Baehr says that feminist scholarship has influenced media studies in two major ways: 1) it has attempted to extend and redirect some of the central questions being posed within the discipline; and 2) it has created a special area concerning women's relationship to the media. As a result of feminism, a crucial debate of media studies has shifted. Discussions of the ideological role of the media in capitalist society now involve an examination of the "construction of women's exploitation and subordination materially and ideologically within patriarchy." Baehr faults much of the feminist research in media studies for its reliance on the "behaviourist...'direct-effects' model," which presents "a simplistic, unidirectional and reductive connection between media and behaviour by arguing that the media determine and directly affect how we see ourselves and how we behave 'as women' in society." She suggests that media studies researchers turn to feminist film critics for more sophisticated analyses of "the mechanisms film employs to produce meanings...." If the media is understood as "a system of representation [that functions as] a point of production of definitions," questions can be asked which will promote the "struggle towards the creation of alternative modes of media production and distribution and progressive images." While the special study of women may be a temporary necessity to securing "firm feminist grounding," Baehr cautions against institutionalizing a separate strand of women's media studies. Such separateness could easily lead to ghettoization and a subordinate status within the mainstream.

299. Barry, Judith and Sandy Flitterman. "Textual Strategies: The Politics of Art Making." In Framing Feminism: Art and the Women's Movement 1970-1985, edited by Rozsika Parker and Griselda Pollock, pp. 313-320 (New York: Pandora, 1987).

Barry and Flitterman describe four categories of art in order to demonstrate that "a more theoretically informed art can contribute to enduring changes by addressing itself to structural and deep-seated causes of women's oppression rather than to its effects." Each of the four categories proposes different answers to the question "Action, by whom, and for what purpose?" The four categories include: 1) art as a glorification of essential female power; 2) women's art as a form of sub-cultural resistance (i.e., exalting crafts); 3) women's art as entirely outside of the dominant cultural order; and 4) artistic activity as textual practice which exploits existing social contradictions. Only the fourth category represents feminist art working against patriarchy instead of just women making art in a male-dominated society. Feminist art evolves from a consideration of "how the representation of women is produced, the way it is understood, and the social conditions in which it is situated." Art in the fourth category transforms the spectator into an active producer of meaning "by engaging the spectator in a process of discovery rather than offering a rigidly-formulated truth." By rupturing traditionally held ideas about women, such art works examine the social construction of femininity and sexual difference. A theoretical approach breaks with "the dominant notion of art as personal expression, instead connecting it with the social and political and placing the artist as producer in a new situation of responsibility for her images."

300. Bate, Barbara and Anita Taylor. "Themes and Perspectives in Women's Talk." In Women Communicating: Studies of Women's Talk, edited by Barbara Bate and Anita Taylor, pp. 303-314 (Norwood, New Jersey: Ablex Publishing Corporation, 1988).

To remedy the "striking absence" of studies on women's communication with one another, the editors produced this collection. Given the unexamined assumptions that characterize the literature on gender and communication, Bate and Taylor stress the need to distinguish sex (i.e., the physical features that differentiate men and women) and gender (i.e., learned and socially evaluated feminine and masculine behaviors). "Communication," they say, "is the means by which most children learn to connect their physical selves with actions that are expected for one sex more than the other." Bate and Taylor present four perspectives which have been the "bases for defining, describing, and evaluating the communication of women." Each of these perspectives has partriarchal and feminist interpretations. The biological perspective assumes that biological differences result in communication differences. Traditionally, this has led to a link between male size and protective or aggressive behavior and female size and quiet, passive behavior. Feminists claim that women's reproductive capacity equips them with a tendency towards intimacy and support. According to the cultural perspective, different assumptions, languages, nonverbal codes, and spheres of interest make men and women develop differently. This perspective has often been used to justify men's domination of the world of work and public leadership and women's role as mother and homemaker. On the negative side, feminists see gender conditioning and socialization as inhibiting for both sexes as adult communicators; on the positive side, they see women's unique perspective as a fertile ground for the development of a new, more affirmative female culture. The power perspective concentrates on each participant's control or efficacy in a communication situation. Traditionally, power has been viewed hierarchically, meaning that one communicator must have more power than the other. Feminists view power as empowerment related to sharing and exchange; both communicators can be equally and creatively powerful. The rhetorical perspective holds that speakers make communication choices based on what will achieve their goals in particular situations. Studies from this perspective have tended to focus on men because few women could be found in public speaking contexts. Feminists have begun to apply the rhetorical perspective to private communication settings where women have dominated. On examining the studies collected for their volume, Bate and Taylor conclude that "women communicating with each other try to nourish joint values and to pursue goals cooperatively."

301. Bergstrom, Janet. "Rereading the Works of Claire Johnston." In Feminism and Film Theory, edited by Constance Penley, pp. 80-88 (New York: Routledge, 1988).

The works of Claire Johnston to which Bergstrom refers include "Notes on Women's Cinema," BFI Pamphlet, 1973; With Pam Cook, "The Place of Woman in the Cinema of Raoul Walsh," Edinburgh pamphlet on Raoul Walsh, 1974 (reprinted in Feminism and Film Theory, pp. 25-34); "Femininity and the Masquerade Anne of the Indies," Edinburgh pamphlet on Jacques Tourneur, 1975; and, "The Work of Dorothy Arzner, BFI Pamphlet, 1975 (parts of this pamphlet are reprinted in Feminism and Film Theory, pp. 36-56). Bergstrom credits Johnston with laying the groundwork for several important areas of feminist film research: 1) a theoretical rather than a sociological approach to feminist filmmaking and criticism; 2) a recognition that feminist theory and criticism are central to feminist filmmaking; 3) an emphasis on understanding how women have been represented in classical narrative film rather than rejecting Hollywood films from consideration; 4) the introduction of topics such as woman-as-sign and fetishism; and 5) the rejection of the notion that political films could not be pleasurable. Johnston developed and attempted to demonstrate what Bergstrom calls "the rupture thesis." According to the rupture thesis, in many classical films, particularly some by women directors such as Dorothy Arzner, ruptures, gaps, and contradictions disrupt the "apparently seamless patriarchal fabric...." It is in these disruptions that a feminine voice can be found. Bergstrom argues that the ruptures and gaps Johnston identified were often the result of "highly interpretive readings," and that "rupturing activity is characteristic of classical text, [and even] in large part a precondition of the pleasure it provides."

302. Byars, Jackie. "Reading Feminine Discourse: Prime-time Television in the U.S." Communication 9:289-303 (1987).

Byars brings the work of Nancy Chodorow (The Reproduction of Mothering: Psychoanalysis and the Sociology of Gender, Berkeley: University of California Press, 1978) and Carol Gilligan (In a Different Voice: Psychological Theory and Women's Development, Cambridge, Massachusetts: Harvard University Press, 1982; see annotation in Psychology chapter) to bear on her analysis of contemporary American television. In particular, she draws on Chordorow's and Gilligan's theory that women's and men's ways of thinking and communicating are distinctly different. A serious problem with much textual analysis, claims Byars, is the belief that "dominant textual patterns dominate reading." Strong feminine discourses are consistently going on within prime-time television, proving that "television does not present a monolithic and invulnerable discursive system." Cinematic language is "not essentially gender-bound," and the gender of the spectator makes a difference. Researchers grossly underestimate the complexity of mainstream texts and their role in the ideological process if they ignore the feminine discourse that already exists.

303. Camera Obscura Collective. "Feminism and Film: Critical Approaches." Camera Obscura 1:3-10 (1976).

The Camera Obscura Collective describes the methodology that feminist film critics have found useful as "textual analysis which brings to the study of film analytical tools derived from recent advances in areas such as semiology and psychoanalysis." According to textual analysis, both the originator of the text, i.e., the filmmaker, and the spectator participate in the production of meaning. The film or text is recognized as a "social phenomenon which is created and understood through language..., a social space through which various languages (social, cultural, political, aesthetic) circulate and interact." Perceptions of a representation, in which ideology is inscribed, seem natural but are culturally determined. Drawing on the theory of French psychoanalyst, Jacques Lacan, feminist textual analysis compares films with dreams and the unconscious and seeks to determine the "ways in which the dominant partiarchal view conditions us at the levels of psychic structures...."

304. Cameron, Deborah. Feminism & Linguistic Theory. New York: St. Martin's Press, 1985.

Cameron defines a feminist linguistic theory as one that spells out the connection between language and gender identity and between language and women's oppression. All feminist linguistic theories must take a clear stand on four basic questions: 1) what exactly is meant by language? 2) what is meant by women's (or men's) language and how is the link between gender and language to be understood? 3) what is the relation of language to reality? and 4) what is the relation of language to disadvantage? Language can mean writing or speaking, and it can be used to refer to words, or syntax, or content, or custom. Cameron identifies three main frameworks by which feminists relate women's identity and position to language: 1) the subculture and gender role framework associates different speech with different roles; 2) the dominance framework associates women's speech with their powerlessness; and 3) the sexuality framework links language to gender identity "through its intimate connection with the body and sexual desire." She dismisses all three frameworks for lacking the complexity necessary to link "ways of speaking and writing to our multifaceted identifies as women." Cameron believes that personality, desire, behavior, and self are constructed in interactions with the world, and that language is only one factor among many involved in the construction process. Feminists must avoid blaming language for what happens to people. Holding language responsible for disadvantages ignores the fact that social institutions create inequities which harm the poor, the Black, and the female. No perfect feminist speech or language exists or can be created. "The most positive effect of changing our linguistic practice will be to destroy the pernicious belief that we have to be controlled or oppressed by our language."

305. Cantor, Muriel G. "Feminism and the Media." Society 25(5):76-81 (1988).

The intention of Cantor's article is to review the license challenges initiated by feminists to force broadcast stations to end their discrimination against women both in terms of employment and media content. She describes briefly the women's media reform movement that began in 1963 when the Equal Pay Act was passed and the Feminine Mystique by Betty Friedan was published. Cantor believes that the "most important effect of th[is] reform movement was its contribution to a new focus in the research process." Feminists learned that it is possible to use research for political as well as educational and informational purposes.

306. Cirksena, Kathryn. "Politics and Difference: Radical Feminist Epistemological Premises for Communication Studies." Journal of Communication Inquiry 11(1):19-28 (1987).

Cirksena believes that the radical feminist perspective is most pertinent to an analysis of communication processes. She defines the radical feminist approach as one which rejects as an end goal equality for women in the existing social structure, one which maintains that a socialist revolution will not end women's oppression, one which takes gender as a primary organizing force in social relations, and one which incorporates racism, classism, and other forms of oppression into its analyses. Particularly relevant to communication, are the radical feminist assertions that knowledge and information are socially constructed, that language contributes to gender-based inequalities, and that differences exist which challenge methodological and political positions based on the universality of the human condition. Cirksena suggests that consciousness-raising, with its supportive structure for validating women's experiences and interpretations of their own lives, could serve as a feminist paradigm for knowledge accumulation.

307. Cirksena, Kathryn. "Women's Liberation from Spirals of Silence: The Need for Feminist Studies in Mass Communication Research." In Communications at the Crossroads: The Gender Gap Connection, edited by Ramona R. Rush and Donna Allen, pp. 46-58 (Norwood, New Jersey: Ablex Publishing Corporation, 1989).

According to the "spiral of silence" theory developed by Elisabeth Noelle-Neumann ("The Spiral of Silence: A Theory of Public Opinion," Journal of Communication, Spring, 1974), fear of isolation motivates people to monitor the prevailing climate of opinion from the mass media in order to determine what views they should express.

As a result of such monitoring, social movements can prevail or be swept away. Cirksena urges feminist communication scholars to take a special interest in the "spiral of silence." Feminist perspectives have not had any significant effect on "the central body of knowledge which is the core of the discipline of communications research..." and most work remains "gender-blind." All theories need to be reevaluated in light of three central questions: 1) how does the theory obscure, silence, or render invisible the experiences of women of various races, classes, abilities, and ages? 2) how does the theory perpetuate stereotyped and biased thinking about women as a group that limits individual women's options and potential? and 3) how would including an analysis of the power relations inherent in society's gender divisions change the arguments central to a given theory? These questions would focus research on diversity rather than on generalization and on the needs of the women being studied rather than on the needs of the researcher. "Gender correctives" must be applied to communication research, claims Cirksena, not only to redress the previous neglect of women but also to improve our overall understanding of communication.

308. Cooper, Pamela J., Lea P. Stewart, and Sheryl A. Friedley. "Twenty Years of Research By and About Women in Major Communication Journals: 1967-1986." ACA Bulletin (January, 1989): 46-61.

Cooper, Stewart and Friedley update and add to the findings of Foss and Foss, who examined "The Status of Research on Women and Communication" in 1983 (see annotation below). With the goal of examining the place of women's research in mainstream communication literature, Cooper, Stewart and Friedley analyzed all issues of the nine publications of the national and regional communication associations for the years 1967 to 1986. Out of a total of 5,879 articles, 240 or 4.1 percent dealt with communication and gender. The percentage of articles dealing with gender increased over time: .7 percent of the articles published in 1967 as compared to 7.5 percent of the articles published in 1986 dealt with gender. Sixty-nine percent of the articles were written soley by men and 11.7 percent were co-authored by men. Only 14.2 percent of the articles were written solely by women. However, the percentage of male authorship is decreasing compared with the increasing percentage of female authorship: women wrote 8.2 percent of the articles in 1967 and 18.9 percent in 1986. Cooper, Stewart and Friedley encourage the communication disciplines to ensure that women are not underrepresented in journal publications. "Women will never be equally successful in our field unless they are equally represented in our journals."

309. Dalton, Pen. "Feminist Art Practice and the Mass Media: A 'Personal' Account." Women's Studies International Quarterly 3(1):55-57 (1980).

Art images' and representations' final meanings, says Dalton, "depend upon the context in which they appear." Most women have access to feminist art only through "male-controlled selection procedures and filters" such as television, films, or magazines. Dalton believes that since women are not powerful nor rich enough to create alternative systems of mass communications, they "need to use what [they] have to appropriate what [they] want" within the existing system. Feminists must work within the mass media to gain access to control. Young women must be encouraged to practice both traditionally female art forms such as knitting and embroidery and traditionally male ones such as photography and film. "Ideally, this could lead to a re-evaluation of the traditional feminine areas and an infiltration of women into the areas" which establish artistic context.

310. de Lauretis, Teresa. "Aesthetic and Feminist Theory: Rethinking Women's Cinema." In Female Spectators: Looking At Film and Television, edited by E. Deidre Pribram, pp. 174-195 (London: Verso, 1988).

de Lauretis defines a feminine aesthetic not in relation or reaction to the masculine, dominant aesthetic but rather in terms of women's heterogeneity. Spectators gain in power and importance as emphasis shifts from the text to its reception by women as diverse individuals. When films address women as social subjects whose lives affect their cinematic experience they address spectators as female.

311. Dervin, Brenda. "The Potential Contribution of Feminist Scholarship to the Field of Communication." Journal of Communication 37(4):107-120 (1987).

According to Dervin, feminist scholarship arises out of a discomfort with the way positivist and critical/cultural scholarship deal with gender, sexuality, and the experience of women. The "very act of not leaving women out" undermines some basic assumptions, for example, that men are normal and women are abnormal. Feminist scholarship views gender as a fundamental organizing category of human experience, makes female experience central, tends to be activist and to promote social change, is usually conducted in a cooperative, participatory, interdisciplinary, non-hierarchical way, is pluralist in that it draws on whatever methods are appropriate, and is self-reflective about the relationship between the researcher and the researched. Dervin attempts to explain why "the field of communication is a latecomer to feminist scholarship" by the field's traditional reliance on scientific rather than humanistic disciplines and by "the time [the field of communication] needed to confront itself." Now that the confrontation has occurred, Dervin believes that communication, because it is a "ragamuffin" field, will be influenced more strongly and more permanently than "rigid, staid" fields like psychology and sociology. Communication deals with cognitive events and must answer the question of how to account for individuality and structure at the same time. Feminist scholarship begins to have a presence at the point at which communicators "deal with the making of meaning within structures." Communication scientists, like other scholars, need to hear women's voices because these voices represent over fifty percent of reality and also because they are voices which speak from outside of the power structure. Feminists' greatest contribution, says Dervin, is "that they have turned everything into a problem." The traditional constraints and conceptions of what science is all about are broken apart by a fundamental questioning of how to collect data, how to make observations, how to draw conclusions, and how to determine research relationships.

312. Doane, Mary Ann, Patricia Mellencamp, and Linda Williams. "Feminist Film Criticism: An Introduction." In Re-Vision: Essays In Feminist Film Criticism, edited by Mary Ann Doane, Patricia Mellencamp and Linda Williams, pp. 1-17 (Frederick, Maryland: University Publications of America, Inc., 1984).

In an introduction to their collection of essays, Doane, Mellencamp and Williams examine what feminist re-vision has accomplished in film studies over the last decade. They point to the tendency for feminist film to become an area of study rather than "a sphere of action." While assimilation of feminist study within an institution, such as the university, is dangerous, feminists have approached all the major film related activities — filmmaking, festival organizing, scholarship — with a remarkable degree of cooperation and collaboration. "Feminist film theory, given the 'illegality' — by the standards of traditional academic discourse — of its two components (feminism and film studies), is in a unique position" to challenge traditional modes of knowledge production and epistemology. Because of the lack of women filmmakers (as compared to women authors), feminist film critics have focused on psychoanalytic and semiotic methodologies that "could account for the absence of 'woman as woman'." By the mid-1970s, two divergent traditions of feminist film theory and practice had emerged: 1) a tradition of portraying women's truth on the screen even if the truth were conveyed according to dominant forms of representation; and 2) a tradition convinced that women's truth could only be told using radically different forms of representation. These two traditions represent the double bind in which feminist theorists often find themselves. They can continue to analyze and document various instances of women's absence and repression in traditional cinema or they can attempt to define a feminine cinema, "risking a recapitulation of patriarchal constructions and a naturalization of 'woman'." Initially, feminists rejected difference, since the differences between men and women formed the basis for women's oppression. More recent feminist film theory, however, has begun to delineate and specify difference as liberating, "as offering the only possibility of radical change."

313. Elshtain, Jean Bethke. "Feminist Discourse and Its Discontents: Language, Power, and Meaning." Signs 7(3):603-621 (1982).

Elshtain criticizes theories of discourse proposed by several Western political theorists and by contemporary feminist thinkers because they "interdict by definition any possibility that speech might serve libertory purposes." Some discursive modes she finds promising include "psychoanalytic discourse informed by feminist sensibilities," the notion of the "ideal speech situation" proposed by Jürgen Habermas, Carol Gilligan's discussions of female moral reasoning, and Sara Ruddick's idea of "maternal thinking." Elshtain believes that "for women to affirm the protection of fragile and vulnerable human existence as the basis of a mode of political discourse and to create the terms for its flourishing as a worthy political activity...would signal a force of great reconstructive potential." Feminists must move beyond a view of discourse as domination or as unavoidably masked and toward "speech as part of an emancipatory effort, a movement toward social clarity and self-comprehension." (see also Elshtain in the Political Science chapter)

314. Foss, Karen A. and Sonja K. Foss. "The Status of Research on Women and Communication." Communication Quarterly 31(3):195-204 (1983).

Foss and Foss surveyed all issues to date of eleven major speech communication journals in order to survey and summarize the research on women. They conclude that research on women and communication has been "building on accepted assumptions and findings by contributing additional data in these same directions." Foss and Foss divide the literature into historical treatments on women, sex differences, women and the media, education and pedagogy, and surveys and integrative works. They recommend that more research is needed on the discourse of women not famous in politics, on communication aspects of the women's movement, and on the impact of media images on the viewing, listening, or reading public to pull together the diverse findings in communication and sex differences and to question, evaluate, and attack traditional research methodologies, assumptions, approaches, and frameworks. For example, approaching research from the perspective of relation and connection rather than dichotomy and opposition would lead to a holistic examination of as many factors as possible instead of the effect of just one independent variable on one dependent one. Revolution, not extension or intension, is needed to carry research on women and communication forward.

315. Gledhill, Christine. "Pleasurable Negotiations." In Female Spectators: Looking At Film and Television, edited by E. Deidre Pribram, pp. 64-89 (London: Verso, 1988).

To relate the "feminine spectator" as constructed by the text to the female audience constructed by the social and historical categories of gender, class, race, etc., Gledhill proposes the concept of negotiation. The term negotiation "implies the holding together of opposite sides in an ongoing process of give-and-take." Meaning is not imposed on an audience nor passively imbibed by the audience "but arises out of a struggle or negotiation between competing frames of reference, motivation, and experience." A process which subjects ideology to continual negotiation and renegotiation is more consistent with the contradictions and diversities central to feminist theory than the fixed, "once and for all" approach of psychoanalytic-semiotic frameworks.

316. Godard, Barbara. "Translating and Sexual Difference." Resources for Feminist Research 13(3):13-16 (1984).

Since a translator is "an active participant in the creation of meaning," and since males and females occupy two different linguistic spheres, Godard suggests that there is a relationship between translation and gender Using examples of translations of women's French poetry to English by men and by women, Godard demonstrates that female translators actively engage in "naming and writing the life of the body," while male translators "frequently [fail] to comprehend the full range of this experience...." Because the "translator's engagement with a text is a profound one that changes one's ways of seeing the world," the question of translation and sexual difference deserves further attention.

317. Gregg, Nina. "Reflections on the Feminist Critique of Objectivity." Journal of Communication Inquiry 11(1):8-18 (1987).

Feminists object to the claim that meaning and knowledge exist apart from personal experience and context. They claim that women's lives serve as the source of knowledge. Objectivity as the sole criterion for truth "is sexist in its methodological tendency to equate a male perspective with a human perspective." The objective stance has produced "methodologies for locating, defining, and ranking difference and opposition rather than methodologies for recognizing and explaining relatedness." Objects of study cannot function as agents of knowledge. Feminist communication research examines all forms of cultural production (for example, appearance, cinema, novels) and focuses on "communication as the production of meaning in everyday life." Criteria of feminist research include: 1) the recognition of subjects as agents of knowledge; 2) the acknowledgement of the context of research and the conditions of its production; 3) descriptions of the values of the researcher, the research question, and the subjects; 4) the relation of knowledge to practice not to truth; and 5) an expression of how the research results will be made available to women as tools of liberation. The goal of feminist research is not only to change the explanations of the world but also to change the world itself.

318. Henderson, Hazel. "Eco-feminism and Eco-communication: Toward the Feminization of Economics." In Communication at the Crossroads: The Gender Gap Connection, edited by Ramona R. Rush and Donna Allen, pp. 289-304 (Norwood, New Jersey: Ablex Publishing Corporation, 1989).

Current economic theory, states Henderson, fails to handle information adequately. Information is not a material commodity and is not subject to the zero-sum, competitive, one winner-one loser dynamic of the marketplace. Accurate, innovative information becomes more valuable the more it is shared. The old economic formula defined inputs to production as land, labor and capital; in the future formula, inputs should be capital, resources, and knowledge and the output should be "healthy people and bio-regions on a peaceful, healthy, equitable, ecologically-viable Planet." When they operate as businesses concerned primarily with profits, the mass media fail to provide an outlet for communication by diverse groups. Sponsors and private owners censor the information the public receives. Minority opinion groups must have access to mass media and thereby, to "society's group consciousness" or they will continue to behave aberrantly to get attention. As the most powerful education system, mass journalism must accept its responsibility to reconnect the individual to the community and to the state. The process of communication must embrace the principles of interconnectedness, redistribution, change, complementarity, heterarchy (as opposed to hierarchy), and indeterminancy (openness to many viewpoints).

319. Henley, Nancy M. Body Politics: Power, Sex, and Nonverbal Communication. Englewood Cliffs, New Jersey: Prentice-Hall, Inc., 1977.

The belief in "the personal is the political" takes on a new dimension when understood in the context of nonverbal communication. Everything people do in their personal lives — including gestures, expressions, postures, eye contact — reflects their participation in a power system. In Western culture, nonverbal behavior is trivialized and ignored. As a result, "it constitutes a vague stimulus situation" highly susceptible to interpretation according to the status quo. However, nonverbal behavior is a major medium of communication whose topic is power. Henley recommends that the overall approach to nonverbal research must be changed. Nonverbal research must avoid: 1) blaming the victim; 2) rationalizing the status quo; 3) seeing racial and sexual groups as different species; and 4) cultural, racial, sex, and power biases. Nonverbal research must: 1) watch for unconscious biases throughout the research process (in the makeup of the research team, the framing of the research question, the subjects, objects, and setting in which the research takes place, research procedures, interpretation, writeup, and the distribution of the results); 2) use broad research samples, which study both social class and sex as factors; 3) study power and status as they are expressed in nonverbal behaviors; and 4) examine ways in which nonverbal communication resembles language (for example, is nonverbal communication sensitive to genderlects, acquisition, bilingualism, and sex difference and sexism). Henley advises women not to abandon their nonverbal style just because it differs from the style of the oppressors. "Any valuable qualities displayed by those in power must be carefully separated from the ugly characteristics that come with power."

320. Janus, Noreen Z. "Research on Sex-Roles in the Mass Media: Toward a Critical Approach." The Insurgent Sociologist 7:19-31 (1977).

The critical approach toward which Janus believes mass media research needs to move is based on two major points: 1) the most fundamental social division is the division between classes not the division between men and women; and 2) sexual oppression is linked to the material conditions of society and is necessary to the operation of capitalism. As profit-motivated industries, the mass media have both designed messages to correspond to roles women play and attempted to "mold women according to their needs to sell products." New images of women in the media reflect changes that are "consistent with the needs of the ruling class," and do not represent real progress. The liberal feminist approach to media research deals only with media's passive responses to social movements, thereby encouraging marginal or cosmetic change. Using a critical approach to broaden their understanding of sexism in the media, feminists could bring about fundamental changes in media and in society itself.

321. Jenkins, Mercilee M. and Cheris Kramarae. "A Thief in the House: Women and Language." In Men's Studies Modified: The Impact of Feminism on the Academic Disciplines, edited by Dale Spender, pp. 11-22 (Oxford: Pergamon Press, 1981).

Jenkins and Kramarae borrow their title from the French critic, Claudine Herriman, who said women must be thieves of language. They must steal words back and redefine them to include female experiences. Jenkins and Kramarae distinguish between two different types of research on sex differences in language and communication. The first type merely reports sex differences and gives "hypothetical reasons for these differences based on common gender stereotypes...." Research of this type often includes gender as a variable but fails to take differences between men's and women's experiences into account in the research design. The second type actually focuses on an investigation of sex differences and offers a variety of explanations for their occurrence. In taking a feminist perspective on the study of women and language, researchers must: 1) evaluate cautiously basic assumptions males have made about speech; 2) integrate elements related to recurring everyday speech patterns (the micro level) with elements related to institutional structure (the macro level); 3) study the attitudes, intentions, and identities of speakers by learning about speakers' relationships to groups; 4) recognize that studies are interpretations not reconstructions of reality; and 5) determine the meaning of gender for speakers. "Feminism has made a difference in what we study, how we study it, with whom we study, and who reads what we write...Women can now sustain the publication of books and articles that deal with [their] own experiences."

322. Kampen, Natalie and Elizabeth G. Grossman. Feminism and Methodology: Dynamics of Change in the History of Art and Architecture. Working Paper No. 122, Mellon Faculty Development Program (Wellesley, Massachusetts: Wellesley College Center for Research on Women, 1983).

Kampen and Grossman believe that the field of art history has not just lacked consciousness. Rather, it is "based on assumptions which make it impossible for women's roles and images ever to be interpreted correctly." Questionable assumptions include: 1) a notion of time as fundamentally linear and progressive, and of periodicity as absolute; 2) a vision of reality with a hierarchical organization; 3) the view that competition is part of human nature; and 4) the association of greatness with talent, rather than with socially constructed measures. Feminist art history has rediscovered women artists, granted dignity to the study of objects defined as decorative and functional, and insisted that gender, race, class, ethnicity, and sexual preference are essential variables in artistic creation. According to Kampen and Grossman, the fact that "feminist work in one discipline may have almost no impact on another" proves that problems cannot be solved by consciousness-raising. Direct action must be taken against "the structures that maintain the assumptions that are antithetical to a feminist history."

323. Kaplan, E. Ann. "Is the Gaze Male?" In Women & Film: Both Sides of the Camera, edited by E.Ann Kaplan, pp. 23-35 (New York: Methuen, 1983).

Kaplan distinguishes feminist criticism of the representation of female sexuality in literature, painting, film, and television from other critical movements. Typically, critical movements in art criticism have developed in reaction to some dominant theoretical position. Feminist criticism, "as a new way of reading texts, emerged from the daily, ongoing concerns of women re-evaluating the culture in which they had been socialized and educated." Early feminist art critics used a sociological approach to evaluate the sex roles women occupied in various works. While this content-oriented approach was valuable for initiating the feminist critical process, it had its limitations, which feminist film critics were among the earliest to point out. Feminist film critics have brought both semiotics and psychoanalysis to bear on their examination of how meaning is produced in films. From semiotics, feminist film critics borrowed the idea of signs. Women, and other participants in Hollywood films, function as signs which "convey the patriarchal ideology that underlies our social structures...." Certain questions must be asked within the psychoanalytic framework of Oedipal processes in order for feminists to "find the gaps and fissures through which we can insert woman in a historical discourse that has hitherto been male-dominated...." These questions include: is the gaze necessarily male? could things be structured so that women own the gaze? would women want to own the gaze? and, what does it mean to be a female spectator? Kaplan concludes that it is not the gaze that is male but rather the position of owning and activating the gaze which has been defined as the masculine position. Women have the possibility to change themselves and possibly effect social change "because they have not been processed, as have men as little boys, through a clearly defined, and ultimately simple, set of psychic stages."

324. Kramarae, Cheris. "A Feminist Critique of Sociolinguistics." Atlantic Provinces Linguistic Association Journal 8:1-17 (1986).

Kramarae proposes that, for the next decade, linguists use gender as the central, organizing focus for the study of language. She suggests that the following questions be asked of any study: 1) How do the women/men identify themselves? What are their social alliances, identities, goals? 2) What does the researcher know of the political and economic inequalities of the women/men? What are their social, political, and economic resources? What are the norms and expectations of the speakers and the constraints for researchers? 3) What are the traditional attitudes toward the speech of the women/men studied? 4) What has the feminist literature said about this or related topics? What is the applicable Black, Latin, lesbian, and gay literature? 5) What are the implications of the study results for women's language use? For men's language use? 6) How is the researcher related to the women/men whose speech/writing she is studying? Why have these speakers been chosen? 7) What sex, class, age, and race stereotypes or assumptions are involved? and 8) How would the research be different if it involved only women or only men, or both women and men? Drawing on Alice Walker who distinguishes progress, which affects few, from revolution, which affects many, Kramarae encourages the focused use of gender in sociolinguistic work — not because it would represent progress but rather because "it would produce a linguistic revolution which could affect many women and men."

325. Kramarae, Cheris. Women and Men Speaking. Rowley, Massachusetts: Newbury House Publishers, 1981.

In Women and Men Speaking, Kramarae describes four frameworks that she has found useful when discussing language and gender. All four deal with social relations but differ in terms of the analyses they provide and the theories on which they are based. The "women as a muted group" framework assumes that women perceive the world differently from men, that men's system of perception is dominant, and that women must translate their own models of expression into male models in order to participate in society. Because language has been formulated by men, it serves them better than it serves women. The reconstructed psychoanalytic framework begins from the writings of Freud but goes beyond them by challenging the conception of women as "lack of" or mere complement to men and by emphasizing men's and women's different relationships to language. The speech styles approach grows out of attempts to understand the relationship between linguistic groups. It is useful for "examining the dynamics of the intergroup speech behavior of women and men, including change in that behavior." The strategy framework views speech as socially situated action. Speech as strategy is linked with women's position in industrialized society as separated spacially and ideologically from men's. Principles of language usage will reveal principles of social relations. Underlying all four frameworks is the assumption that "language structure is a social form which affects and is affected by the rest of the social life of its speakers. Speech is an interaction in which participants often have unequal influence and speaking rights."

326. Kramer, Cheris, Barrie Thorne, and Nancy Henley. "Perspectives on Language and Communication." Signs 3(3):638-651 (1978).

In their review essay, Kramer, Thorne and Henley examine the literature on language and gender from four different perspectives: 1) sex differences and similarities in language use, speech, and nonverbal communication; 2) sexism in language structure and content; 3) relations between language structure and language use; and 4) efforts and prospects for change. Few expected sex differences have actually been substantiated by speech studies, and findings of difference between the sexes have been emphasized while the lack of difference has been ignored. What appear to be sex-based differences may actually be power imbalances between speakers. The study of language, when seen in its proper social context, can provide insight into gender as a social and cultural construction. Men have generally controlled what is labeled, what ordering and classifying systems will be used, what words will be cataloged in dictionaries, and have placed prohibitions against women as public speakers. Studies have indicated that gender marking in language, for example, the generic use of he and man, influences people's behavior. The language development of female and male children may differ because of a girl's need "to shift her expectations to try to include herself in masculine pronouns." Language establishes, reflects, and maintains the asymmetrical relationship between men and women. An oppressor's language creates problems of concept formation and expression for the oppressed. Even when women and men use the same words, the same pronunciations, and the same intonation in the same situation, they will be interpreted differently. Language usage changes must be made along with other changes related to women and communication, for example, the prejudice against women as public speakers and language innovators and the nature of nonverbal behaviors, such as head patting.

327. Kuhn, Annette. The Power of the Image: Essays on Representation and Sexuality. London: Routledge & Kegan Paul, 1985.

In five essays, Kuhn explores some of the basic questions feminists ask about how images make meaning: what relation does spectatorship have to representations of women? what sort of activity is looking? what does looking have to do with sexuality? with masculinity or femininity? with power? with knowledge? how do images of women speak to the spectator? is the spectator addressed as male or female, masculine or feminine? is femininity constructed in certain ways through representation? why are images of women's bodies so prevalent in our society? The answers to these questions cannot be found only through examining and analysing images because meanings do not reside in images. Images have use value and exchange value based on context, on the particular time and place of their consumption. "All representations are constructive in their own right:...they construct meanings through their own particular codes and conventions."

328. Lakoff, Robin. "Language and Woman's Place." Language in Society 2:45-80 (1973).

"Language and Woman's Place" is an early classic in the area of language and gender. Lakoff uses examples to demonstrate that "the marginality and powerlessness of women is reflected in both the ways women are expected to speak, and the ways in which women are spoken of." She describes women as "linguistically submerged" because language works against their treatment as "serious persons with individual views." The acceptability of a sentence is not a simple yes/no grammatical decision. It is a combination of factors like phonology, syntax, and semantics but also of the social context in which an utterance is expressed and "the assumptions about the world made by all participants in the discourse." Lakoff intended by her article to generate controversy and to stimulate additional research on women and language; she succeeded in both intentions. As a linguist, Lakoff emphasizes that "social change creates language change, not the reverse," and, thus, cautions feminists against seeing language changes as panaceas. She advises against investing a lot of energy into changing pronominal neutralization, i.e., using the male form (he, him, or man, or mankind) to refer to all members of a sexually mixed group. Such neutralization is too unconscious, too common, and too mixed throughout the language to change. Lakoff, using male speech as the norm, describes women's speech patterns as more tentative and more trivial than men's (see Valian in this chapter for a reaction to Lakoff).

329. Larkin, Alile Sharon. "Black Women Film-makers Defining Ourselves: Feminism in Our Own Voice." In Female Spectators: Looking At Film and Television, edited by E. Deidre Pribram, pp. 157-173 (London: Verso, 1988).

"As a Black woman film-maker," says Larkin, "my objective is to contribute to the development of our own definitions." Because of racism, larger divisions exist between Black women and white women than between Black women and Black men. Unless white women address their current and historical participation in and benefits from white supremacy, feminism will continue to maintain institutional racism. Feminist film theory must go beyond acknowledging historical and social differences between women and their experiences by actually accounting for these differences. One film at a time, Larkin says, Black women film-makers hope "to change minds, widen perspectives and destroy the fear of difference."

330. Lugones, María C. and Elizabeth V. Spelman. "Have We Got a Theory For You! Feminist Theory, Cultural Imperialism and the Demand for 'The Woman's Voice'." Women's Studies International Forum 6(6):573-581 (1983).

Lugones and Spelman use two different voices — the voice of an Hispana woman and the voice of a white/Anglo woman — to illustrate that "only when genuine and reciprocal dialogue takes place between 'outsiders' and 'insiders' can...the outsider's account" be trusted. They list several ways of talking or being talked about that are helpful, illuminating, empowering, and respectful as opposed to imperialistic, ethnocentric, and disrespectful. A theory or account can be helpful if: 1) it enables one to see connections between parts of one's life that hadn't been obvious before; 2) it helps one locate oneself concretely in the world rather than adds to the mystification; 3) it helps one understand the extent to which one is responsible or not for being in the location in the world one is in; 4) it provides criteria for change and makes suggestions for resistance that go beyond reflecting the values and situation of the theorizer; and 5) knowing what the theory means and believing it to be true have some connection to resistance and change.

331. Magenta, Muriel. "Feminist Art Criticism: A Political Definition." Journal of the Theory and Criticism of the Visual Arts 1:89-98 (1981).

Magenta claims that feminist art criticism and the feminist art movement have impressed their influence permanently on "the art establishment and the character of post-modern art." The two objectives of the movement have been: 1) to make known women's contributions to past and present art traditions; and 2) to invalidate existing attitudes which define women's artistic contributions as minor. The feminist strategy has been to develop a network of separate structures, for example, art organizations, publications, and educational programs, for women art professionals. Feminist art historians are working to develop a "well-documented history of art by women ...in order to provide a factual evaluation of works of art created by females." They question the male-oriented means of selection and categorization of materials that has led to the inclusion of artists in art histories and of works in art exhibitions. Feminists have broadened aesthetic concepts of fine art to include content, media, and processes traditionally used by women (for example, needlework, china painting). Some feminists have promoted the idea of a female imagery, an aesthetic centered around the female body and sexuality. Although a work of art created by a woman still has less chance of hanging on a gallery wall than one created by a man, the tangible success of the feminist art movement is evident when one compares the number of women artists, critics, and historians represented in art periodicals with the number represented a decade ago.

332. Martyna, Wendy. "Beyond the 'He/Man' Approach: The Case for Nonsexist Language." Signs 5(3):482-493 (1980).

Martyna clarifies the arguments of opponents of language change and synthesizes the case against sexist language. "Nonsexist language," she argues, "would not only reflect a move toward a nonsexist ideology; it would also function in itself as one form of social equality." An inability to separate generic and specific meanings creates ambiguity. A context which prohibits a generic interpretation creates exclusion. Martyna's research shows that, in educational materials, sex-specific uses of "he" occur five to ten times more frequently than generic uses of "he." On encountering "he," therefore, a reader's best guess is that "he" does not include an implicit "she." Resistance to changes in sexist language seems to be related to "a general cultural reluctance to acknowledge the power of language in our lives, an insistence that language is of symbolic rather than actual importance."

333. McConnell-Ginet, Sally. "Feminism in Linguistics." In For Alma Mater: Theory and Practice in Feminist Scholarship, edited by Paula A. Treichler, Cheris Kramarae, and Beth Stafford, pp. 159-176 (Urbana, Illinois: University of Illinois Press, 1985).

According to McConnell-Ginet, an academic feminist is a feminist scholar when scholarship informs her feminism and feminism informs her scholarship. Linguists offer feminists some useful tools for the study of language. Linguistics specifies "precise formal characterizations of expressions speakers (and writers) use" and supplies "some methods and procedures for the collection and analysis of language uses." Using these linguistic tools, feminist scholars have studied language as an indicator of social structure and cultural values, language use as a significant factor in maintaining and transmitting male-centered values and views, and language change as an instrument for achieving social, cultural, and political changes. Feminist scholarship has shown the inadequacy of traditional linguistic structures by restoring "language to the sociocultural context from which [it was] extracted for analysis." The interrelationships feminists are uncovering among language, thought, and sociocultural systems may force linguists to revise their theories of language.

334. Mulvey, Laura. "Visual Pleasure and Narrative Cinema." In Feminism and Film Theory, edited by Constance Penley, pp. 57-68 (New York: Routledge, 1988).

Mulvey appropriates psychoanalytic theory "as a political weapon" to demonstrate "the way the unconscious of patriarchal society has structured film form." A woman on the screen is erotic but at the same time signifies castration due to her own lack of a penis. As a defense against the threat of castration, spectators unconsciously use voyeurism and fetishism. Feminists, therefore, must reject the forms of classical cinema because they are based on male fantasy which is detrimental to women and because they center around woman as passive recipient of the aggressive male look. To combat the satisfaction, pleasure, and privilege of the male spectator, feminist cinema must "free the look of the camera into its materiality in time and space and the look of the audience into dialectics, passionate detachment." After the publication of "Visual Pleasure and Narrative Cinema" (which originally appeared in 1975), Mulvey was asked consistently why in her essay she had always referred to the spectator as male thus ignoring the women in the audience. In response, Mulvey wrote "Afterthoughts on Visual Pleasure and Narrative Cinema Inspired by Duel in the Sun" (originally published in 1981, but also included in Feminism and Film Theory, edited by Constance Penley, pp. 69-79 (New York: Routledge, 1988)). In "Afterthoughts," Mulvey concedes that classical cinema did provide a place for the female spectator. This place, however, is a "phantasy of masculinzation at cross-purposes with itself, restless in its transvestite clothes."

335. Nelson, Marie Wilson. "Women's Ways: Interactive Patterns in Predominantly Female Research Teams." In Women Communicating: Studies of Women's Talk, edited by Barbara Bate and Anita Taylor, pp.199-232 (Norwood, New Jersey: Ablex Publishing Corporation, 1988).

Nelson uses teacher-researcher teams involved in the qualitative program evaluation of a university writing center to demonstrate interactive as opposed to hierarchical research and work patterns. Interactive patterns, or "women's ways," emphasize collegiality, a noncompetitive atmosphere, a supportive environment, emotional openness, and equal status among all participants. Unlike hierarchies, "women's ways" encourage rather than exclude the weak. Cooperation, rather than competition, works to the mutual benefit of all researchers and the goals of the research. Although she uses the term "women's ways" to indicate that interactive patterns are more typical of women as they are socialized than they are of men, Nelson claims that such "ways" are distributed evenly across genders. Successful research is predicated upon "both task and group maintenance functions...[upon] producing quality results and [a] maintenance climate and interpersonal skills."

336. Nochlin, Linda. "Why Have There Been No Great Women Artists?" In Art and Sexual Politics: Women's Liberation, Women Artists, and Art History, edited by Thomas B. Hess and Elizabeth C. Baker, pp. 1-43 (New York: Macmillan Publishing Co., Inc., 1973).

Asking a simple question such as "Why have there been no great women artists?" can, says Nochlin, "create a chain reaction, expanding to encompass every accepted assumption of the field..." of art history. By attempting to answer the question either by "dig[ging] up examples of insufficiently appreciated women artists throughout history" or by proposing different standards of greatness for women's art than for men's, feminists betray a misconception of what art is. Great art is much more than "the direct, personal expression of individual emotional experience — a translation of personal life into visual terms. The making of art involves a self-consistent language of form, more of less dependent upon, or free from, given temporally-defined conventions, schemata, or systems of notation, which have to be learned or worked out, through study, apprenticeship, or a long period of individual experimentation." Asking the right questions about the conditions for producing art reveals the miracle involved in the fact that any women or Blacks have managed to achieve artistic excellence. As an example of social conditions affecting women's artistic achievement, Nochlin discusses women artists' lack of access to nude models during a period extending from the Renaissance until near the end of the nineteenth century, a period when "careful and prolonged study of the nude model was essential to the production of any work with pretensions to grandeur." No matter what a woman's individual talent or genius, it has been institutionally impossible for her to achieve excellence or success equal to men's. Nochlin's essay, an early classic in feminist art history, provoked numerous responses, some of which are included in Art and Sexual Politics.

337. Pollock, Griselda. Vision and Difference: Femininity, Feminism and Histories of Art. London: Routledge, 1988.

Vision and Difference is a collection of essays by Pollock which "represent[s] a contribution to a diversified and heterogeneous range of practices which constitute the feminist intervention in art's history." The essays deal with feminist art history and Marxism, woman as sign, sexuality and representation, and the spaces and signs of femininity. Pollock emphasizes the need to go beyond the question, "have there been great women artists?" The criteria for artistic greatness in art have already been male defined. "Shifting the paradigm of art history involves...much more than adding new materials — women and their history — to existing categories and methods...[it means] wholly new ways of conceptualizing what it is we study and how we do it." The traditional art historical narrative pictures a gifted (male) individual creating a discrete work of art which is then admired by art lovers. Pollock argues against treating works of art as objects and for a broader view which considers the "totality of social relations which form the conditions of the production and consumption of objects designated as art." When art is viewed as practice, art history analyzes the nature and the conditions of that practice. Feminist interventions "demand recognition of gender power relations, making visible the mechanisms of male power, the social construction of sexual difference and the role of cultural representations in that construction."

338. Press, Andrea. "The Ongoing Feminist Revolution." Critical Studies in Mass Communication 6(2):196-202 (1989).

Press encourages feminists to build not just criticism of communication studies but rather a critique. Criticism remains "locked into the epistemological framework of those disciplines, and their methods of inquiry, which should be its object." It assumes the criteria it uses for evaluation. A critique takes the criteria as part of its object and poses "a fundamental epistemological challenge to the disciplines from which it emerges." Because they fear the repression that has accompanied theorizing up until now, feminists have been reluctant to specify what feminist theory is or should be. Press believes, however, that "specifying some of the unitary qualities of feminist theory" is essential for feminism to function effectively as a disciplinary critique. Two unitary qualities Press suggests include the primacy of gender in analyzing individuals and society and the alleviation of women's oppression. A feminist critique of the communication field must "question customary methods of investigation — whether quantitative or qualitative, empirical or critical — as well as the theoretical categories and paradigms the field uses to define its terms, to couch its problems."

339. Putnam, Linda L. "In Search of Gender: A Critique of Communication and Sex-Roles Research." Women's Studies in Communication 5:1-9 (1982).

Putnam's article grew out of her attempts to understand her own ambivalence about teaching and researching gender-related communication. She traces her discomfort to the assumption of bipolarity and mutual exclusivity between the sexes. "Duality," she complains, "characterizes conceptual and operational definitions of gender, the nature of research questions, and the measurement tools we employ." The very language system links masculinity and femininity to biological opposites and destroys any meaning in the concept of androgyny. Inadequate theorizing about male-female communication also results from the tendency to treat gender as a stable and enduring attribute of an individual that is constant across situations. "The situational contingencies that give rise to bracketing and interpreting behaviors in sex-stereotypic ways" must be understood for research on male-female communication to advance. Putnam borrows from Karl Weick to suggest strategies for developing research questions that attack "taken-for-granted assumptions" about gender and communication. The first strategy is to reverse "figure and ground relationships." Gender, for example, could be viewed as an individually-defined phenomenon (figure) instead of a societal characteristic (ground) so that gender definitions would be based on individual choices and modes. The second strategy is to reverse causes and effects. Most research assumes that gender influences communication or that communication reflects gender. A cause-effect reversal would see gender as determined by communicative behaviors. The third strategy for breaking out of limiting assumptions is "to treat communicative behaviors as recipes that evolve from contextual constraints." A fourth stategy involves concentrating on the similarities of opposites, finding, for example, the similarities between individuals who define themselves as extremely feminine and those who define themselves as extremely masculine. The fifth strategy involves finding complexity in phenomena that appear simple. To avoid the tautological thinking that characterizes much of the research on gender and communication, Putnam emphasizes the need to re-orient the questions and to degenderize behaviors.

340. Radway, Janice A. "Identifying Ideological Seams: Mass Culture, Analytical Method, and Political Practice." Communication 9:93-123 (1986).

Based on her belief that "the content of any message, whether textual or behavioral, is not simply found in that message but is constructed by an audience interacting with that message," Radway defends romance reading as a way that women think through their condition. Both the fact that romances provide women with temporary relief from "the constant physical and emotional demands of being a mother," and the fact that the heroes they seek are nurturant, tender, and kind indicate "ideological seams" that offer space for political intervention. Any ethnographer brings assumptions and understandings into the activities of observation and description, thus imposing interpretation at every step. Once the ethnographer knows "how romance readers understand their reading and the context that gives it meaning," she can present a feminist stance to those readers with the idea that they might "benefit from seeing differently." Messages designed by the dominant group can be used by less powerful groups to analyze their material situation and express their discontent.

341. Rakow, Lana F. "Feminist Approaches to Popular Culture: Giving Patriarchy Its Due." Communication 9:19-41 (1986).

Rakow points out two problems with the popular culture canon, which examines the "quality and changing nature of culture, the rise of the mass media, and the political implications of capitalist-industrialization:" 1) the canon contains no women; and 2) the analyses of social power ignore patriarchy and obscure an understanding of the relations between women and men. She describes works written in the early 1900s by Charlotte Perkins

Gilman and Beatrice Forbes-Robertson Hale. These authors are examples of women popular culture writers who have been excluded from the canon, and the exclusion leads Rakow to conclude that "the history of feminist approaches to popular culture remains to be written." Rakow summarizes the approaches to popular culture that feminists have taken over the last twenty years. She categorizes the approaches into four groups: 1) images and representations approach; 2) recovery and appraisal approach; 3) reception and experience approach; and 4) cultural theory approach. The images and representations approach developed because "women's most significant relationship to popular culture has been in providing its major images...." Feminists who take this approach ask what the images of women are and what these images reveal about women's position in culture, whose images they are, who they serve, and how they mean, and what the consequences of the images are likely to be. Those taking the recovery and reappraisal approach ask how women have managed to express themselves in a male dominated culture, why women's creativity has been overlooked, how women's creativity differs from men's, and what women's stories and myths might be. Recovery and reappraisal feminists call for a re-evaluation of the criteria that establish artistic canons and determine artistic and social merit. Readers and viewers of cultural products are the focus of feminists who take the reception and experience approach. "Women's encounters with popular culture may be an important site where...ruptures [between women's experiences and the social forms of expression to them] can be made visible...." The organization and production of culture occupies feminists who take the cultural theory approach, and their goal is to understand and change social relations. While these four different feminist approaches can be identified, Rakow sees two assumptions upon which all feminist popular culture researchers agree: women have a particular relationship to popular culture that differs from men's, and understanding how popular culture operates for women and for patriarchal culture is vital if women are "to gain control over their own identities and change both social mythologies and social relations."

342. Rakow, Lana F. "Feminist Studies: The Next Stage." Critical Studies in Mass Communication 6(2):209-215 (1989).

Rakow lists four processes that will change feminist scholarship in communication from a presence in the field to a transforming force. The first process is monitoring the status of feminist scholars. Will feminists obtain jobs or receive tenure without "travel[ling] under some guise in order to be marketable and promotable." The second process is intervening in the field's discourses. Feminists must beware of becoming simply another paradigm in a pluralist field. Discourses must account for feminist work and concerns, and feminists must avoid entrapment in the language and categories they are trying to change. Collaborating with other feminists is the third process. Rakow suggests replacing the "intellectual one-upmanship and competition" of research with a collective pursuit of knowledge and a respect for diversity. Only soul-searching will uncover the reasons why feminist scholarship in communications is so white. As the fourth process, feminists must envision the transformations they want and need. Collective visions for a different world will allow feminists to move away from the falsehoods that exist without claiming to have found the truth.

343. Rakow, Lana F. "Looking to the Future: Five Questions for Gender Research." Women's Studies in Communication 10:79-86 (1987).

Rakow illustrates the five questions gender researchers need to ask themselves by describing her research project on women's use of the telephone in a small midwestern town. She states unequivocably that there cannot or should not be "any other direction for gender research to go but in the direction of feminist scholarship." Gender researchers must first ask themselves why they are doing the research. Following unexamined assumptions, researchers have tended to prove sex differences that label women as deficient. Studies must be conducted for women, and participants must be involved in their design and benefit from the results. Gender researchers must inform their research by feminist theory, thus challenging old assumptions. They must ask themselves what their own assumptions are that need to be questioned. Unquestioned assumptions obscure and justify women's oppression. Instead of being assumed, gender itself must be studied. Rather than being biologically determined, gender "is an on-going accomplishment...[which] does not cause communication practices; gender is a communication practice." Maleness must not be assumed as the norm making femaleness deviant. Gender researchers must decide what methodologies to use. "A belief in 'objectivity' and the goal of prediction and control of attitudes and behavior are not compatible with feminist research." In gender research, researchers are what they study. Their subjectivities result from their genders, races, classes, and other sensibilities. An awareness of these subjectivities can prevent researchers from drawing conclusions about all groups based on the study of only a particular group.

344. Rakow, Lana F. "Rethinking Gender Research In Communication." Journal of Communication 36(4):11-26 (1986).

Rakow examines the assumptions behind social science research related to gender and the approaches to gender in speech, interpersonal, and mass communication studies. Traditionally, gender has been "operationalized as a pregiven category that can account for measurable differences in women's and men's...communication behavior...." Often, the results of such research advise women to correct their speaking and interaction deficiencies or criticize the media for contributing to women's deficient socialization. In keeping with feminist approaches to gender, Rakow argues that gender should be seen as a verb. Gender, in other words, is "work we do to construct and maintain a particular gender system...Communication creates genders who create communication." Research that assumes the concepts of gender and communication, concepts that it should be setting out to explain, should no longer be conducted.

345. Reinhardt, Nancy S. "New Directions for Feminist Criticism in Theatre and the Related Arts." Soundings 64(4):361-387 (1981).

Compared to feminist film criticism, feminist theatre criticism is not well developed. Reinhardt outlines three explanations for the discrepancy between film and theatre criticism: 1) film is a twentieth century as opposed to an ancient medium, which makes it more responsive to new perspectives and challenges; 2) the content of film is more blatantly sexist; and 3) theatre is essentially "a public, social and hence a male-dominated art...[which] has been run by and for men throughout most of its history and has, for the most part, reflected current political and social realities, deferring to the taste of the political majority." Audience participation has an effect on theatre that it can never have on films. Reinhardt describes how a feminist perspective might be applied to dramatic genre and physical production. In terms of genre, she suggests that the structure and domain of tragedy are derived from the structure of patriarchy. In terms of physical production, she advises theatre historians to re-examine the position of women in productions of earlier centuries. They will be found, she suggests, "kept to the sides, in the recesses, or placed on display for the male viewer." Just as they have colonized stage and audience space, men have colonized theatre criticism and theatre history.

346. Schaef, Anne Wilson. "Old Systems and Shifting Paradigms: Can the Media Facilitate Needed Change?" In Communications at the Crossroads: The Gender Gap Connection, edited by Ramona R. Rush and Donna Allen, pp. 279-288 (Norwood, New Jersey: Ablex Publishing Corporation, 1989).

In this essay, Shaef applies (loosely) the themes developed in her earlier publications (Women's Reality, 1981; Co-dependence: Misunderstood and Mistreated, 1986; When Society Is an Addict, 1987) to women's involvement in communication and the media. She describes five myths that support the predominant addictive and nonparticipatory White Male System: 1) it is possible for people to become gods in the sense of having complete control over themselves, other people, and nature; 2) the White Male System represents reality; 3) the White Male System is superior; 4) the White Male System knows and understands everything, and therefore, defines the epistemology of our culture and our world; and 5) it is possible to be logical, rational, and objective. Communication and the media in the White Male System exist to manipulate and control. Women (and men) must work toward a participatory, process-oriented system as an alternative to the destructive White Male System. The media will be crucial as the means through which alternatives will be communicated. Women and minorities, those who are not totally engulfed in the prevailing White Male System, must gain control of media access in order for system change to occur.

347. Silveira, Jeanette. "Generic Masculine Words and Thinking." Women's Studies International Quarterly 3(2-3):165-178 (1980).

"Feminist questions are often theory's basic unanswered questions," says Silveira. This is demonstrated by linguistics' failure or unwillingness to deal adequately with the relationship between unmarked words (i.e., words, such as man or kleenex, that name both a category and a member of that category) and typicality. Silveira cites research that has revealed a people=male bias, which means that males are assumed to be more typical of the people category than are fems (throughout her article, Silveira refers to females as fems in order to remove the male form from a word associated with women). Using examples, she demonstrates that the generic and specific word man exhibits more people=male bias than the rest of the language. Feminist researchers have demonstrated a causal relationship between the use of the generic man and he and people=male bias in both the receiver of the generic term and the producer of the word. Results of studies also suggest that people=male bias increases the use of the generic man/he. Silveira believes that unmarked words cause a generic=specific bias independently of whether bias causes those words. Replacing generic masculine words with other forms, therefore, would be likely to change language and "produce long-term reduction in sexist thinking." People think creatively when they can integrate the abstract with personal experience. The people=male bias produces a sex difference in people=self bias; unlike men, women feel alienated from people concepts and are consequently disadvantaged in achieving this integration. While social reinforcement coerces women into using generic masculine terms, they are less comfortable with such use and resist.

348. Smith, MaryAnn Yodelis. "Research Retrospective: Feminism and the Media." Communication Research 9(2):145-160 (1982).

Smith reviews selected feminist literature on the media published during the 1970s. Based on a 1978 study by Gaye Tuchman, Arlene Kaplan Daniels, and James Benét called Hearth and Home: Images of Women in the Mass Media (see Tuchman in this chapter), Smith proposes a research model for analyzing women and the media. The major hypotheses established by Tuchman, Daniels, and Benét are that the mass media reflect dominant social values in a symbolic manner and offer programs that will appeal to the largest audience, and that women are subject to symbolic annihilation (condemnation, trivialization, or absence) in the media. The symbolic annihilation of women can be traced to the scarcity of female media processors, the male-defined process of news definition and limited access for women to the media, the scarcity of dominant female images in the media, and the educational, political, legal, and economic factors that determine media context. Each of these contributors to women's symbolic annihilation has offered and continues to offer opportunity for feminist scholars to define research questions of importance.

349. Spender, Dale. Man Made Language. Second edition. London: Routledge & Kegan Paul, 1985.

Spender works in her book to demonstrate that "language has been literally man made." One of the repercussions of male dominance of language is that women's language has been defined as deficient. Research conducted in this male supremacist environment has begun with the premise that women's language is inferior. When evidence has left this assumption unproven, it has not been rejected but rather the evidence explained away on the basis that researchers were looking in the wrong place. Spender concedes that feminist research is also biased. "The choice of what to believe or not to believe," she says, "is not between 'biased' and 'objective' research: the issue is which set of biases takes more of the evidence into account." Spender suggests that research concern itself with "the relative silence of over half the population." Questions framed in relation to the silence of women lead both to an examination of the language which excludes and denigrates them and to an examination of their access to discourse. Maria Black and Rosalind Coward review Spender's book and offer an alternative analysis in an article called "Linguistic, Social and Sexual Relations: A Review of Dale Spender's Man-Made Language," published in Screen Education 39:69-85 (1981).

350. Stanback, Marsha Houston. "Language and Black Woman's Place: Evidence from the Black Middle Class." In For Alma Mater: Theory and Practice in Feminist Scholarship, edited by Paula A. Treichler, Cheris Kramarae, and Beth Stafford, pp. 177-196 (Urbana, Illinois: University of Illinois Press, 1985).

"In short," Stanback summarizes, "neither contemporary research on language and gender nor that on Black communication coherently describes Black women's communicative experiences." Over the past ten years, a considerable amount of information has been added to our understanding of middle-class white women's communication. Little, however, has been added with regard to the communication among working class, Black, and other minority women. Stanback uses her own research on college educated middle-class Black women to demonstrate that their "communicative experiences within their own cultural group form a striking contrast to those of middle-class white women." When making generalizations about women's speech, both gender and culture must be taken into account.

351. Steeves, H. Leslie. "Feminist Theories and Media Studies." Critical Studies in Mass Communication 4(2):95-134 (1987).

Steeves reviews and critiques the feminist media literature using a framework that classifies studies according to their radical feminist, liberal feminist, Marxist feminist, or socialist feminist approach. In sum, radical feminism argues for separate women's media environments where they can use their own language. Liberal feminism believes that changes within the existing system can be made that will give women freedom of expression and equality. Marxist feminists claim that the capitalist mode of production must change before women's situation can change. Socialist feminists emphasize the need to expose and change all oppressive ideologies whether based on gender, class, or race. Feminist theories assume women are oppressed and seek to understand why by suggesting possible solutions, for example, separatism, reproductive control, individual action, equitable parenting, changes in language, etc.

Steeves urges that "research be used to augment...theory as well as to seek ways society and mass media can be altered." The socialist feminist approach appears to be the most viable because of the connection between women's oppression and other inequities.

352. Treichler, Paula A. and Ellen Wartella. "Interventions: Feminist Theory and Communications Studies." Communication 9:1-18 (1986).

In their introduction to an issue of the journal, Communication, Treichler and Wartella review briefly the present status of communication research, discuss feminist contributions to communication studies, which have not been incorporated into on-going arguments within the field, and describe the feminist cultural studies approach, which "formulates old questions in new ways, raises new questions, and suggests a promising agenda for research." Feminist cultural studies evolves from feminist theory and the critical and interpretive study of culture. It is interdisciplinary, drawing from feminist criticism, communication, anthropology, American studies, sociolinguistics, and other disciplines. Feminist cultural studies goes beyond women in the profession issues or images of women in the media to explore questions about the nature of representation, sexual difference and identity, the relationship between ideology and material conditions, the relationship between the personal and the political, the ultimate subjectivity of research, and the critical intersections of race, class, ethnic background, and gender.

353. Tuchman, Gaye. "Introduction: The Symbolic Annihilation of Women by the Mass Media." In Hearth & Home: Images of Women in the Mass Media, edited by Gaye Tuchman, Arlene Kaplan Daniels, and James Benét, pp. 3-38 (New York: Oxford University Press, 1978).

In her introduction to a collection of papers on "the depiction of sex roles in the mass media and the effect of that portrayal on American girls and women," Tuchman defines the mass media's treatment of women as a national social problem. Central to her discussion are the reflection hypothesis and symbolic annihilation. The reflection hypothesis says that the mass media reflect dominant societal values. These values appear symbolically, not as literal portrayals, in television and other media. "Representation in the mass media announces to audience members that this kind of family (or social characteristic) is valued and approved." When something, for example, women, is not represented in the media, or is condemned or trivalized, that something is annihilated symbolically. Women are portrayed by the media as unimportant and ineffectual, with limited lives divorced from economic productivity. When over forty percent of the American labor force is female, a message which socializes young women and men to view women as inaccurately limited has severe national consequences (see also Smith above).

354. Valian, Virginia. "Linguistics and Feminism." In Feminism and Philosophy, edited by Mary Vetterling-Braggin, Frederick A. Elliston, and Jane English, pp. 154-166 (Totowa, New Jersey: Rowman & Littlefield, 1977).

Valian's paper is a response to two articles by Robin Lakoff, "Language and Woman's Place," and "Why Women Are Ladies" (see Lakoff in this chapter). She criticizes Lakoff's use of data about language to draw conclusions about the utility of men's and women's speech, her failure to distinguish between speech and language, and her faulty analysis of the relationship between linguistic and social change. Valian argues for the superiority of women's speech based on some of the differences Lakoff identifies between it and men's speech. For example, while Lakoff sees women's use of finer color distinctions as trivial detail, Valian sees it as greater percision and accuracy. Lakoff concludes that, since men and women speak different languages, women must learn a different language in order to overcome their oppression. Valian dismisses this contention of different male and female languages because its logical extension is "that people speak a different language from one minute to the next, and that everyone is a polyglot." Instead of women learning a different language, all oppressive language usage needs to be eliminated. Lakoff encourages women to accept the use of the generic "he" on the grounds that it will be difficult for people to change. Valian believes that linguists should not be answering political questions by telling us "to learn to live with a certain amount of oppression, or to try not to think of it as oppression...." Linguists should be helping to implement the feminist strategy of eliminating sexist and oppressive language.

355. Walker, Janet. "The Problem of Sexual Difference and Identity." Wide Angle 6:16-23 (1984).

Walker surveys the ways in which feminist film theory has appropriated psychoanalytic theory. One use of psychoanalysis is the investigation of oppression within classical narrative cinema, an oppression resulting from the fact that cinema is a partriarchal institution. Feminist film theory also uses "the gaps and lacunae within (primarily Freudian) psychoanalytic theory" to explore the notion of femininity. According to this type of analysis, Hollywood films are interrogated for "subversive moments when the film's' unconscious surfaces in the form of heretofore repressed femininity, or moments when the film presents contradictory notions of femininity." The third use of psychoanalytic theory in feminist film theory involves a critique of the limitations of psychoanalysis as used in the first two approaches. "The project," says Walker, "is to characterize filmic representation of woman's (sexual) pleasure and of a generalized notion of her existence." Feminist film critics must beware of the "patriarchal loop or chain," the ease, that is, with which "critical discourse about the cinema in general is elided into an extension of that institution."

11

SCIENCE

INTRODUCTION

Science and Culture

The feminist critique of science explores the interaction of nature and culture in the production of scientific knowledge (Keller, 1987). Hubbard (1988) insists that scientific research, teaching, and communication are political. Scientists claiming objectivity and neutrality are dishonest because social context determines what researchers notice and accept as real (Hubbard, 1979). Keller (1985, 1986) links gender, which feminists have defined as " a socially constructed and culturally transmitted organizer of our inner and outer worlds," with parochial social, political, and emotional commitments that shape the scientific enterprise.

Natural knowledge reflects what Fee (1986) calls " gender-based dominance relations." According to Rosser (1988), science can never be free from the values of the society in which it is developed. Gender, as well as race, class, and sexual preference, are basic, prevasive factors that influence everything researchers examine and interpret. Because science is a social product, a sexist society will produce a sexist science (Fee, 1981).

The Razor's Edge

As feminists rush to demonstrate that science is gendered, cautions Rosser (1988), they must avoid claims that good science is gender-neutral. Such claims depend upon the same false dichotomy for which feminism has taken traditional science to task. Keller (1980) calls feminism's charge that science suffers from masculinist distortions " a vitally threatening razor's edge." By focusing on the characteristics of good science — objectivity, theory, receptivity to the material — feminists can avoid associating traditional scientific behaviors with men.

Perhaps because they have focused on what is male rather than what is good about traditional science, feminist critiques have failed to account for science's successes (Keller, 1987; Levin, 1988). Koertge (1980) supports traditional science as " one of the most important allies of oppressed peoples," and argues that a patriarchy which produces such a science should not be dismissed. Besides, what is the alternative? Feminists have not yet described, in concrete terms, what a feminist science would be like (Levin, 1988).

Lowe (1981) and others (Birke, 1986; Sayers, 1987) argue that when women's roles change in the larger social context, women scientists will change science. Until society is no longer sexist, feminists will develop critiques rather than an alternative science itself (Fee, " Is Feminism a Threat to Scientific Objectivity?" 1981).

Types of Feminist Critiques

Feminist critiques of science cluster into four types. Rose (1986) calls the earliest type " why so few." In her 1965 article called " Women in Science: Why So Few?" , Alice Rossi blames social values, rather than women themselves, for the scarcity of women scientists. Vivian Gornick (1983) approaches the same problem from the opposite direction. Through interviews with more than one hundred women scientists, she illustrates the consequences of existing in an environment where rewards are likely to be few.

The " recovery of Hypatia's sisters" approach unearths the work and accomplishments of women scientists. Ruth Hubbard (1979) describes Rosalind Franklin's role in the discovery of DNA and James Watson's all-too-successful attempts to deny her credit. " Gynocentric science," as Ruth Ginzberg (1989) points out, has always existed. If men had practiced them, cooking, housekeeping, and midwifery would be science instead of art and would be sanctioned by institutions and degrees instead of discredited as trivial or superstitious.

The third type of feminist critique, which Rose (1986) calls " contestation of patriarchal science," attacks studies that find a biological basis for gender discrimination. Ruth Bleier (1978; 1979; 1984; 1987) exposes the false assumptions underlying sex differences research. She advises scientists to quit wasting time justifying preconceptions and start investigating why, when sex differences are so small, participation rates of women and men in scientific fields differ so radically.

It is in terms of the fourth approach, the critique of epistemology, that feminists come closest to outlining what a feminist science would involve. Arditti (1980) claims that women can give science a soul. When research consequences are as important as the research itself and when the worth of knowledge is evaluated against scientists' own experience, science will be a tool for human liberation. Both Rose (1983) and Benston (1982) describe women's contribution in terms of care. Women scientists will dissolve the separation between the knower and the known, what Schweickart (1983) calls the " master/slave dialectic between self and other," in favor of a " context of care and responsibility for both natural processes and other creatures." (Benston)

Stanford (1986) calls on psychologist Carol Gilligan (see Psychology chapter) to support her contention that science would benefit from a relationship perspective. Unlike objectivity and analysis, which isolate variables from their environments, the relationship perspective values context. Hein (1981) goes one step further. When women apply the contextual mode, science will stop dominating nature.

Rosser (" Teaching Techniques to Attract Women to Science," 1989) says that a feminist science will expand the kinds of observations that are scientifically acceptable. While she is careful to define it as part of good rather than simply feminist science, Keller (1980) advocates receptivity to research material over imposing an answer. Science is power, says Wallsgrove (1980), so scientists insist that their method is a step-by-step logical process of neutral observation. In reality, all scientists use intuition and analogy and interpret results out of pre-existing frameworks — characteristics usually defined as female.

The Challenge

Harding (1986) sums up feminism's epistemological challenge: to explain how research motivated by politics can increase the objectivity of an inquiry. It is a challenge Koertge (1981), Levin (1988), and others doubt that feminism can meet. But Fee (1986) and Potter (1989) are more optimistic. They argue that feminists are not alone. Gender-dominance is only one factor in a broader analysis that examines the effects of race, class, and sexual preference on the production, scope, and structure of natural knowledge. Hubbard (1988) believes that women as political beings, not as gendered ones, will contribute something new to science.

Perhaps Keller (1982) is the most optimistic of all. Feminists need not imagine a different science into being, she claims. The history of science offers the " thematic pluralism" necessary for the development of a " new consciousness of the potentialities lying latent in the scientific project."

ANNOTATIONS

356. Arditti, Rita. " Feminism and Science." In Science and Liberation, edited by Rita Arditti, Pat Brennan, and Steve Cavrak, pp. 350-368 (Boston: South End Press, 1980).

Emphasizing that the personal is the political, Arditti traces the history of women in science, describes her own scientific experiences, and advises women scientists to share their experiences with one another. By bringing together intellect and emotion, by making research consequences as important as research, and by using their own experiences to evaluate critically the worth of knowledge, women can give science a soul and transform scientific research into a communion with the universe and a tool for human liberation.

357. Benston, Margaret. " Feminism and the Critique of Scientific Method." In Feminism in Canada: From Pressure to Politics, edited by Angela R. Miles and Geraldine Finn, pp. 47-66 (Montreal: Black Rose Books, 1982).

Benston describes science as both a methodology and an ideology. Scientific knowledge results when an objective observer measures abstract quantities from nature. Objectivity provides scientists with the power to control and manipulate the natural world. Benston claims that distortions and limitations result because present science originated from a hierarchical, class-based, sexist society. A feminist approach involves investigating the effect that the male/female split has had on the practice of science. Feminist science will take into account " both subjectivity and the interactions between the knower and the known in a context of care and responsibility for both natural processes and other creatures."

358. Birke, Lynda. Women, Feminism and Biology: The Feminist Challenge. New York: Metheun, 1986.

Because biological arguments are so often offered to justify women's oppression, biology is relevant to feminists. Five lines of feminist inquiry into biology include: 1) critiques of biological determinism; 2) the argument that gender is socially rather than biologically constructed; 3) an examination of reproductive technology to determine if it is oppressive or liberating for women; 4) an examination of the association between science and masculinity and nature and feminity; and 5) an examination of the production of scientific knowledge. Birke predicates changes within science on changes within society. She criticizes the scientific method as reductionist. Only certain methodologies can yield truth and knowledge and what counts as scientific knowledge is tied to who produces the knowledge and how the research is structured. Feminist science would support conclusions found by using a variety of methodologies and would make scientific knowledge accessible to society at large. Competition in science must be replaced by cooperation, for which nature can serve as a model. Instead of dominating nature, scientists must strive to establish an interaction with organisms and their environments. A feminist science implies constraints on what science does. Birke suggests that too little attention has been paid to human differences and the accompanying differences in biological constraints. " Any attempt to 'rethink' biology, to move towards more progressive ideas about the role and significance of human biology, has to take...differences in biological experience and needs into account."

359. Bleier, Ruth. " Bias in Biological and Human Sciences: Some Comments." Signs 4(1):159-162 (1978).

Bleier criticizes research on primates and rodents as " flawed by the assumption of male investigators, who view animal behavior...in the light and language of their own experiences, values, and beliefs." Referring to the accusations of partiality frequently directly toward feminist researchers, Bleier says " it is a pity that the sensitivity to bias comes so late."

360. Bleier, Ruth. " A Polemic on Sex Differences Research." In The Impact of Feminist Research in the Academy, edited by Christie Farnham, pp. 111-129 (Bloomington, Indiana: Indiana University Press, 1987).

Bleier believes that " the natural sciences may well be the last of the research disciplines to feel the impact of critical feminist scholarship." Biological scientists have been active investigating and developing theories related to the " dominant cultural representations of women as biologically flawed for the skills our society values." Biologists base this sex differences research on the false assumptions: 1) that measureable, consistent differences in achievement, behavior, and cognitive abilities exist; 2) that such differences are universal; and 3) that such differences have a biological basis. According to Bleier, no facts substantiate biological differences in achievement and cognitive functioning; the scientific case for gender differences is based on individual and social values and consists of unsubstantiated conjectures built upon one another like " the infinite series of images produced by two facing mirrors." She analyzes the sex differences literature in aggressivity, brain asymmetries, and mathematical/visuospatial ability to demonstrate that: 1) scientists who assume a set of arbitrarily assigned cultural differences design studies to measure such differences and look to biology for their origins; 2) measurable cognitive differences between males and females are too small to be attributable to biology; 3) studies of brain functions cannot explain cognitive abilities, intelligence, or consciousness and, therefore, cannot explain sex differences; 4) too little is known about the interaction of biology and environment in terms of development for biologists to draw conclusions about sex differences. Instead of justifying cultural preconceptions, scientists should be attempting to understand why, when sex differences in intellectual abilities are so small, participation rates of women and men in scientific fields differ so radically. Bleier concludes that it is not biology but rather " the cultures that our brains have created that most severely limit our visions and the possibilities for the fullest development of each individual."

361. Bleier, Ruth. Science and Gender: A Critique of Biology and Its Theories on Women. New York: Pergamon Press, 1984.

Bleier exposes the " elaborate mythology of women's biological inferiority" that traditional science has created to explain women's subordinate social position. She points out that scientific theories defending the status quo typically emerge in response to social movements advocating change. Good science " requires what women in general have: the ability to listen and hear, to be aware and perceptive, to understand and appreciate process and interaction." The feminist critique of science differs from other critiques in its emphasis on a plurality of views. Feminist science involves a " collective approach to knowledge of nature and ourselves and the survival of both."

362. Bleier, Ruth. " Social and Political Bias in Science: An Examination of Animal Studies and Their Generalizations to Human Behaviors and Evolution." In Genes and Gender, edited by Ruth Hubbard and Marian Lowe, pp. 49-69 (New York: Gordian Press, 1979).

In research on sex hormones and behavior, male aggression and dominance, and animal models, Bleier identifies " parochial androcentrism and sexism." Studies are interpreted to confirm the investigators' preconceptions. She places herself among feminists who view human culture as a male creation. " All that remains to do" to demystify and deconstruct traditional scholarship, says Bleier, " is to write and speak ourselves into being: to construct a new language, a new scholarship, and a new knowledge that is whole."

363. Bonner, Jill C. " The Cult of Objectivity in the Physical Sciences." In Choices for Science: Proceedings of a Symposium Sponsored by the Mary Ingraham Bunting Institute of Radcliffe College, April 11, 1980, pp. 52-57 (Cambridge, Massachusetts: Bunting Institute, 1980).

Bonner defines the objective criteron for evaluating the career achievements of a scientist as " present qualifications in relation to the level of opportunity experienced." She advocates a professional structure that brings the most able scientists to the top regardless of color, sex, race, or any other secondary characteristics such as mobility. According to Bonner, physical scientists who practice scientific objectivity are often blind to their lack of objectivity in other areas.

364. Fausto-Sterling, Anne. " Women and Science." Women's Studies International Quarterly 4(1):41-50 (1981).

Fausto-Sterling asks why there are so few women scientists and what science would be like if there were as many women as men practicing it. When science is understood as an ideological construct with narrowly-defined boundaries, the fact that any women have managed to become scientists becomes the interesting question. Science has been designed to accomodate an ideologically defined male role. Women, with their female characteristics, will continue to find this role uncomfortable. While women could change to become more male, Fausto-Sterling believes more is to be gained by altering the patriarchal structure of science. A science in which women can comfortably practice will be a more accountable science and one that is accessible to society at large.

365. Fee, Elizabeth. " Critiques of Modern Science: The Relationship of Feminism to Other Radical Epistemologies." In Feminist Approaches to Science, edited by Ruth Bleier, pp. 42-56 (New York: Pergamon Press, 1986).

Feminist scientists have revealed the pro-masculine bias within the epistemological assumptions, methods, theories, " facts," and interpretations of existing science and argued for an alternative science to which women, because of their different experience, have privileged access. Fee finds inadequate the " post-Freudian psychoanalytic object relations theories" used by feminists to support their assertion that women see the world differently. Object relations theory with its concentration on the family tells only about the reproduction of power relations rather than their origins. She posits power as the central issue in criticizing science and assigns gender a secondary role as " but one of a series of dominant/dominated relationships whose intersections must be analysed and placed at the center of a feminist politics." Three separate literatures all criticize science: 1) Black and Indian liberation literature, which calls science white and European; 2) Marxist literature, which calls science bourgeois; and 3) feminist literature, which calls science male. These three critiques need to be brought together through an examination of power relations as articulated by race, class, gender, and nationality. A single feminist science representing the interests of women as a group cannot exist. There is, however, " a feminist perspective on science that shows the ways in which gender-based dominance relations have been programmed into the production, scope, and structure of natural knowledge, distorting the content, meaning, and uses of that knowledge."

366. Fee, Elizabeth. " Is Feminism a Threat to Scientific Objectivity?" International Journal of Women's Studies 4:378-392 (1981).

The radical feminist critique locates the problem with science and technology " in the particular character of our production of scientific knowledge." Fee emphasizes that science is a social product and that a sexist society will produce a sexist science. Until society is no longer sexist, feminists will produce feminist critiques of science rather than feminist science itself. The feminist science Fee envisions will eliminate " artificial distinctions between the production and use of knowledge, between thought and feeling, between subject and object, or between expert and non-expert." It will also incorporate the experiences of respondents into collective definitions of problems and methodology.

367. Fee, Elizabeth. " Is There a Feminist Science?" Science and Nature 4:46-57 (1981).

Fee argues against making women more scientific and for making science less masculine and, thus, more human. She charges the radical feminist critique of science with determining aspects of science and objectivity that need to be questioned without " abandoning the ideal that we can come to an ever more complete understanding of the natural world through a collective and disciplined process of investigation and discovery." For a feminist science to develop: 1) social resources must be devoted to liberating women; 2) studies must be conducted of the funding, organization, and social production of scientific knowledge; and 3) science must be accepted as " an historically determined human activity." Fee advocates the " use of the analytic methods of Marxist theory" to develop " alternate ways of creating knowledge...."

368. Ginzberg, Ruth. " Uncovering Gynocentric Science." In Feminism & Science, edited by Nancy Tuana, pp. 69-84 (Bloomington, Indiana: Indiana University Press, 1989).

Ginzberg suggests that gynocentric science has always existed. Because it has not been labelled as " Science," it has often been difficult to recognize. She points to the " arts" of midwifery, cooking, and homemaking as examples of activities that, practiced by men, would have been labelled as sciences. Gynocentric sciences will be difficult to identify because: 1) women's work has often not been recorded in historical records; 2) gynocentric science has often been an oral rather than a written tradition; 3) traditional science has been sanctioned by institutions, degrees, and other formal structures while the certification and transmission of women's knowledge has not been organized hierarchially; and 4) gynocentric science has often been suppressed and discredited as erroneous, superstitious, and harmful.

369. Goodman, Madeleine J. and Lenn Evan Goodman. " Is There a Feminist Biology?" International Journal of Women's Studies 4(4):393-413 (1981).

Scientists sensitive to feminist concerns who ask logical, epistemological, and conceptual questions of the research on sex differences can expose " the biases of pseudo-science...[and] mark out a distinctive and scientifically sounder path for human biology." Goodman and Goodman stress that feminist biology should not simply be counter-bias to " anti-feminism which passes itself off as biology." A feminist biology must develop a balanced picture of sexual realities, which is in keeping with scientific objectivity.

370. Gornick, Vivian. Women in Science: Portraits from a World in Transition. New York: Simon and Schuster, 1983.

Gornick interviewed more than one hundred women scientists in an attempt to understand what happens to the nerve, self-confidence, and creativity of those who have continually to prove themselves in an environment where their rewards are likely to be few. Among many discoveries and conclusions, one of Gornick's is particularly interesting: " the world looks different to one who stands on the border advancing only slowly toward the interior than it does to one whose feet have always been moving directly and confidently toward the center."

371. Haraway, Donna J. " In the Beginning Was the Word: The Genesis of Biological Theory." Signs 6(3):469-481 (1981).

Haraway reviews four books to analyze their contributions to the debate about biological determinism. The books reviewed include David Barash, The Whisperings Within: Evolution and the Origin of Human Nature (New York: Harper & Row, 1979); Michael Gregory, Anita Silvers, and Diane Sutch, eds., Sociobiology and Human Nature: An Interdisciplinary Critique and Defense (San Francisco: Josey-Bass, Inc., 1978); Ruth Hubbard and Marian Lowe, eds., Genes and Gender (Staten Island, New York: Gordian Press, 1979); and Ruth Hubbard, Mary Sue Henifin, and Barbara Fried, eds., Women Look at Biology Looking at Women (Cambridge, Massachusetts: Schenkman Publishing Co., 1979). She believes that feminist biologists are " contesting for a voice," contesting for the power to name. She warns feminists developing a " theory of representation to avoid the problem of epistemological anarchism. An epistemology that justifies not taking a stand on the nature of things is of little use to women trying to build a shared politics." As they take the power to name, feminists must avoid the patriarchal tendency to name only by subordinating.

372. Harding, Sandra. " The Instability of the Analytical Categories of Feminist Theory." In Sex and Scientific Inquiry, edited by Sandra Harding and Jean F. O'Barr, pp. 283-302 (Chicago: University of Chicago Press, 1987).

Harding advises feminists to " embrace the instability of the analytical categories; to find in the instability itself the desired theoretical reflection of certain aspects of the political reality in which we live and think; to use these instabilities as a resource for our thinking and practices." A normal science with methodological assumptions that all feminists accept would be a " delusion." Feminist theories must avoid encouraging us to " fanatize about how we could order reality into the forms we desire." Discomforts, rather than clear solutions, are the keys to new kinds of theorizing.

373. Harding, Sandra. The Science Question in Feminism. Ithaca, New York: Cornell University Press, 1986.

By her title, Harding asks if feminists " can locate anything morally and politically worth redeeming or reforming in the scientific world view, its underlying epistemology, or the practices these legitimate." While Harding points out the lack of a developed feminist theory, she also praises feminist lines of inquiry (i.e., equity studies, studies of the uses and abuses of science, critiques of pure science, readings of science as a text, and epistemological studies) for providing a truer picture of science. Feminism's epistemological problem is to explain how research motivated by politics can increase the objectivity of an inquiry. Harding describes three explanations: 1) feminist empiricism, which sees sexism as a social bias that scientists who adhere strictly to scientific norms can avoid; 2) feminist standpoint, which argues that dominance obscures full understanding while subjugation encourages it; and 3) feminist postmodernism, which is skeptical of the universal claims of science. She suggests open acknowledgement and appreciation of the tensions that appear in feminist critiques of science. These tensions include: 1) the unnecessary choice between criticizing bad science and science-as-usual; 2) the apparent opposition between constructing a successor science and deconstructing traditional science; 3) the conflict between a unitary and a fragmented conception of feminist voice; 4) the choice between reform affirmative action measures and the revolution necessary to change society's gender divisions; and 5) the opposition between the scientist as a craft worker and modern science. Turning the notion of value-free objectivity on its head, Harding says that " the paradigm models of objective science are those studies explicitly directed by morally and politically emancipatory interests — that is, by interests in eliminating sexist, racist, classist, and culturally coercive understandings of the nature of social life."

374. Hein, Hilde. " Women and Science: Fitting Men to Think About Nature." International Journal of Women's Studies 4:369-377 (1981).

Hein answers the question of why so few women have been scientists with the claim that men have created conceptions of women and of science that are incompatible. Men, the knowing subjects, define women as nature and approach the natural world as their object of study. Women, who derive their identity from their environment, differ from men, who distinguish themselves from it. Applying the female contextual or relational mode could move science away from the objective pursuit of dominance over nature. By insisting that their experience of self and nature constitutes the norm, men have made women seem incapable of science and " inhibited [them] from articulating with any clarity the distinctive patterns of their own mode of thinking."

375. Heldke, Lisa. " John Dewey and Evelyn Fox Keller: A Shared Epistemological Tradition." In Feminism & Science, edited by Nancy Tuana, pp. 104-115 (Bloomington, Indiana: Indiana University Press, 1989).

Heldke describes the epistemological tradition shared by Keller and Dewey as the " Coresponsible Option." Coresponsible implies that inquiry is an activity that occurs between two " things" that have obligations to respect and care about one another. Option suggests that the tradition provisionally accepts theories, claims, and beliefs whose obsolescence can always be imagined. She supports the Option as one that can avoid the " dualistic and hierarchical binds into which many traditional epistemologies place us." While both Dewey and Keller agree that inquiry is a connecting activity, Dewey concentrates on the ways inquirers affect the course of nature while Keller concentrates on the importance for inquirers to " remember both their connection and their separation from the things into which they inquire."

376. Hubbard, Ruth. " The Emperor Doesn't Wear Any Clothes: The Impact of Feminism On Biology." In Men's Studies Modified: The Impact of Feminism on the Academic Disciplines, edited by Dale Spender, pp. 213-235 (New York: Pergamon Press, 1981).

Science " stands in sharp contrast to feminist principles," says Hubbard, because it invalidates much of people's daily experience. Assumptions about the world determine the questions scientists ask and the answers they will accept. Scientific language, heavy with the use of passive voice, " masks authority and authorship." Hubbard advises feminists to ask what a woman is. She believes that biology is not women's destiny and it may not even be their biology. To rethink women's evolutionary history, some feminists have constructed estrocentric theories. These theories, however, resemble androcentric ones and accept behavior as biologically determined. A scarcity of raw data will confront feminists seeking facts by " paring away the mythology." Perhaps the most valuable step feminists can take toward developing a more accurate evolutionary history is to expose and analyze male myths.

377. Hubbard, Ruth. " Reflections on the Story of the Double Helix." Women's Studies International Quarterly 2:261-273 (1979).

Hubbard begins her article with a " brief excursion into autobiography" because " the admission and description of our personal involvement with our subject must be part of the picture." In order to describe Rosalind Franklin's role in the discovery of DNA structure and the extent to which she was denied credit by James

Watson, Hubbard explains her own philosophical approach to science. “ What we see out there and our interpretation of it,” she says, “ depend on the larger social context that determines what we actively notice and accept as real.” Hubbard calls for an analytic approach that acknowledges “ the role of our subjective participation in the science we construct.”

378. Hubbard, Ruth. “ Science, Facts, and Feminism.” In Feminism & Science, edited by Nancy Tuana, pp. 119-131 (Bloomington, Indiana: Indiana University Press, 1989).

Hubbard asks how we could “ have a science that is more open and accessible, a science for the people.” Even though fact making is a social process, science as currently practiced is made by the chosen for the chosen. Feminists seeking to change science must do more than simply become scientists. They must encourage science to recognize that reality consists of objective facts and of scientists' perceptions of the facts. Hubbard praises the women's health movement as the most concrete example of a different kind of science.

379. Hubbard, Ruth. “ Some Thoughts About the Masculinity of the Natural Sciences.” In Feminist Thought and the Structure of Knowledge, edited by Mary McCanney Gergen, pp. 1-15 (New York: New York University Press, 1988).

Hubbard doubts that women as gendered beings have something new or different to contribute to science but she believes that women as political beings do. No public accountability is built into science. It is made “ by a self-perpetuating, self-reflexive group: by the chosen for the chosen.” While feminists have begun to question the standard male-centered descriptions and analyses of science, Hubbard urges them to go deeper and also challenge underlying premises. The particular, context-stripping definition of objectivity operates to make science an exclusive practice. Hubbard suggests that the social sciences, where context-stripping is impossible, rather than the controlled world of classical physics, serve as the model for how to do every kind of science. “ Feminist methodology is about [recognizing] the 'indisputable unity' between subject and object.” Feminist science must insist on the political nature and content of scientific work, teaching, and communication and “ it must expose the errors and dishonesty of the claim of scientific objectivity and neutrality.”

380. Imber, Barbara and Nancy Tuana. " Feminist Perspectives on Science." Hypatia 3:139-156 (1988).

Feminists agree about the need to reclaim women's place in the history of science, about the need to critique sexism in science, and about the need " for a feminist presence in the formulation of epistemology and methodology." But they have not reached agreement about which feminist concerns are valid components of scientific inquiry or about the role of politics in science. Imber and Tuana believe that feminists must clarify the concept of difference and the role difference should play in feminist theory and that they must articulate ways to ensure a participatory science.

381. Irigaray, Luce (translated by Carol Mastrangelo Bové). " Is the Subject of Science Sexed?" In Feminism & Science, edited by Nancy Tuana, pp. 58-68 (Bloomington, Indiana: Indiana University Press, 1989).

Irigaray proposes that the language of science is neither asexual nor neutral. Understanding the laws that determine what language is acceptable will reveal the sexed logic governing science as a whole.

382. Keller, Evelyn Fox. " Feminism and Science." Signs 7(3):589-602 (1982).

Keller argues that feminist thought can help to clarify the distorted substructure of science and improve objectivity. She describes a range of feminist critiques of science: 1) the liberal critique objects to the unfair employment practices that have created a science dominated by men; 2) a slighty more radical critique suggests that the predominance of male scientists has resulted in bias in the choice and definition and problems and in the design and interpretation of experiments; and 3) the truly radical critique that questions the " very assumptions of objectivity and rationality that underlie the scientific enterprise," that challenges the truths and conclusions of science on the grounds that they reflect the judgment of men. Keller defines the task of feminist theorists as distinguishing " that which is parochial from that which is universal in the scientific impulse, reclaiming for women what has historically been denied to them; and legitimat[ing] those elements of scientific culture that have been denied precisely because they are defined as female." The addition of critical self-reflection to the inquiry process will enable scientists to separate objective effort from " objectivist illusion." History rather than imagination can provide the vision of a different science. The history of science offers the " thematic pluralism" necessary for the development of a " new consciousness of the potentialities lying latent in the scientific project."

383. Keller, Evelyn Fox. " Feminism as an Analytic Tool for the Study of Science." Academe 69(5):15-21 (1983).

Keller calls feminism " a form of attention." This attention questions the division of the world into masculine and feminine, objective and subjective, public and private, and inquires into the " simultaneous construction of both gender and science." This attention focuses on the author of the scientific text and his particular subjectivity. Keller proposes a psychosociology of science, that is, the use of psychological, historical, and scientific analyses to develop " an understanding of the ways in which psychodynamics and social norms interact in the construction and acceptance of claims to scientific knowledge." The aggressive language of science expresses the scientist's desire to dominate nature and to separate himself from the immediate objects of the emotional world. " The major task of a feminist critique of science," Keller concludes, " [is] to excavate the erotic dimension of science and restore it to its proper place in both the rhetoric and practice of science."

384. Keller, Evelyn Fox. " Feminist Critique of Science: A Forward or Backward Move?" Fundamenta Scientiae 1:341-349 (1980).

Keller calls the charge " that scientific thought suffers from masculinist distortions" a vitally threatening razor's edge. The assertion that the scientific questions asked, the data sought, and the interpretations made are all a product of male articulation risks affirming the definitions imposed by patriarchal tradition of masculine as objective and scientific and feminine as subjective and anti-scientific. Objectivity, theory, and truth, according to Keller, are universal goals. Their most obvious distortion is the extent to which they have been characterized as masculine. Feminism must restore legitimacy to " feminine" modes of being and give women back an identity that is not distorted by " patriarchal caricature." Receptivity to the material, for example, as opposed to imposing an answer, is not necessarily a female trait but is a characteristic of a good scientist, regardless of sex. Feminists will subvert the aim of their critique if they accept masculine and feminine as natural categories.

385. Keller, Evelyn Fox. " Gender and Science." In Discovering Reality, edited by Sandra Harding and Merrill B. Hintikka, pp. 187-205 (Boston: D. Reidel, 1983).

The history and sociology of science are silent on the association between objectivity and masculinity. Taken to its logical conclusion, this dangerous association implies that, if more women were scientists, science would be different and undermines the formal view of science as determined only by its own logical and empirical methodology. Keller explains the silence by describing the association as a " mythlike belief" that determines thinking by its " subterrean potency." She draws on theories from psychoanalysis and cognitive psychology to suggest " a network of interactions between gender development, a belief system which equates objectivity with masculinity, and a set of cultural values which simultaneously elevates what is defined as scientific and what is defined as masculine."

386. Keller, Evelyn Fox. " The Gender/Science System: Or Is Sex to Gender as Nature Is to Science?" In Feminism & Science, edited by Nancy Tuana, pp. 33-44 (Bloomington, Indiana: Indiana University Press, 1989).

Keller draws historical, epistemological, and political parallels between feminist studies and science studies. Feminist studies assume that women are made not born; science studies assume that science is not and can never be a " mirror of nature." Since gender is not sex, feminists are struggling to define what gender is; similarly, since science is not nature, scientists are struggling to define what science is. Feminists must ask if gender is a category different from or even prior to categories such as race or class; scientists must ask if scientific claims to knowledge are any better than social scientific or humanistic claims. Feminists and scientists know one truth: " that neither nature nor sex can be named out of existence. Both persist, beyond theory, as humbling reminders of our mortality." Keller emphasizes the relationships among gender, science, and power, particularly the way constructions of gender and science are used to structure " our conceptual and political landscape of power."

387. Keller, Evelyn Fox. " Making Gender Visible in the Pursuit of Nature's Secrets." In Feminist Studies Critical Studies, edited by Teresa de Lauretis, pp. 67-77 (Bloomington, Indiana: Indiana University Press, 1986).

Feminism has revealed gender to be " a socially constructed and culturally transmitted organizer of our inner and outer worlds." This viewpoint provides feminist scientists with a tool for descontructing and reconstituting conventional knowledge. Defining nature as mysterious and female and nature's invisibilities as threats to male power, modern science has undertaken to make exterior the interior and to make visible the invisible. Exposing and bringing into light " female interiority" would " dissolve its threat entirely." Keller suggests that feminist theorists need to develop and explain " what changes in meaning...would accrue...from abandoning gender altogether in [the] construction and de(con)struction of nature."

388. Keller, Evelyn Fox. Reflections on Gender and Science. New Haven: Yale University Press, 1985.

Keller uses a feminist analysis to preserve the objectivity that science teaches. Feminism rejects the division of the personal from the political and exposes the scientific as the personal. The question becomes, according to Keller, " how the making of men and women has affected the making of science." Feminist critics of science must be careful not to reject the commitment to " experimental replicability and logical coherence" that makes science effective as they reject " parochial social, political, and emotional commitments" that subvert the scientific enterprise. Keller traces the evolution of the feminist criticism of science from the exposure of women's underrepresentation in the discipline (see Rossi below) to an examination of the consequences of their underrepresentation. More women scientists will shift the focus away from division and toward difference between individual scientists and between scientists and the objects they study.

389. Keller, Evelyn Fox. " Women and Science: Two Cultures or One?: Commentary on Hein, Lowe, Fee, and Goodman and Goodman." International Journal of Women's Studies 4(4):415-419 (1981).

Keller's essay responds to several papers presented at a symposium called " Women and Science: Two Cultures or One," held at the American Academy for the Advancement of Science meetings in Toronto in January, 1981. Keller says that early feminist critics of science focused on the entrance of more women into science because asserting that science is " genderized" in production or product risks supporting the argument that has been used to exclude women from its practice. She sees the introduction of more women into science as a necessary first step. Sexual polarities and the sexual division of intellectual labor must be abandoned. Scientific ideology is rooted in a larger economic, political, and social context; changes in science will evolve from changes in the larger context. Models for how a different science might look can be found in the history of science, particularly in the contributions of women scientists of the past. To understand the ways " science has traditionally both reflected and contributed to the social and political structures we wish to change," the feminist critique must work hand in hand with other social analyses.

390. Keller, Evelyn Fox. " Women in Science: An Analysis of a Social Problem." Harvard Magazine 76:14-19 (1974).

In this article, Keller focuses on the social and cultural factors (for example, stereotyped female and male development, sexual harassment, lack of role models and other institutional barriers to women's professional achievement) that have led to a predominantly male science. The myth that there are male and female ways of knowing discourages women from entering fields characterized by analytical thinking and produces one-sided descriptions of scientific goals (i.e., scientists " attack" problems and " conquer" nature). " More creative, more imaginative and...more humanistic science" will be practiced when scientists of both sexes use their " full, unhampered mind[s]."

391. Keller, Evelyn Fox. " Women, Science, and Popular Mythology." In Machina Ex Dea: Feminist Perspectives On Technology, edited by Joan Rothschild, pp. 130-146 (New York: Pergamon Press, 1983).

Keller asks " what would it mean for science to change its self-conception and ideological commitments, and still be considered science." She uses object relations theory to examine the psychological basis for the belief that science is to male as nature is to female. Pervasive parenting and cultural arrangements demand of males a two-fold separation to establish self-identity and to develop a male gender identity. " ...Separating subject from object, objectivity itself comes to be associated with masculinity." An autonomous, objectivist, and masculine science appeals to those psychologically comfortable with such characteristics. On the basis of her interviews with Barbara McClintock, Keller suggests that science is not the monolithic structure it sometimes seems to be. Scientists consistently practice alternatives to the dominant mythology about science and these alternatives " are consonant with and perhaps even essential to the scientific enterprise as a whole." Feminists must understand how science has reflected and contributed to social and political structures they wish to change. According to Keller, " change depends less on the introduction of a specifically female culture into science than on the rethinking of sexual polarities and the abandonment of a sexual division of intellectual labor altogether."

392. Keller, Evelyn Fox. " Women Scientists and Feminist Critics of Science." Daedalus 116(4):77-91 (1987).

The schism that has arisen between feminist critics of science and practicing scientists illuminates a crucial question that the former must address: how exactly do nature and and culture interact in the production of scientific knowledge? Practicing scientists tend to hear in feminist critiques the accusation that science is masculine, that science mirrors culture, and that women should not practice traditional science. Because, as Keller points out, science will only change from within, feminists seeking to change the way science is done must respect practitioners by acknowledging the reliance of scientific knowledge on nature and the " remarkable record of technological success that science can claim."

393. Kimball, Meredith M. " Women and Science: A Critique of Biological Theories." International Journal of Women's Studies 4:318-338 (1981).

Kimball rejects the X-linked genetic theory, hormonal theories, and brain lateralization theories because they have no scientific basis. Scientists waste time debating the origins, magnitude, or existence of sex differences. The question they need to ask is, " why is it that the difference in the participation rates of women and men in scientific fields is so large when sex differences in intellectual abilities are so small?"

394. Koertge, Noretta. " Methodology, Ideology, and Feminist Critiques of Science." PSA 1980 2:325-359 (1981).

Koertge says feminists are right when they insist that science as a corpus of knowledge is not divorced from the intellectual and social backgrounds of individual scientists but she doubts that feminists can come up with a new epistemology. She reviews the feminist critique of science, including the " revolution-by-infiltration strategy," which believes that science will change as more women practice it, and the approach which claims that the " basic methodological concepts of the scientific enterprise are irreparably chauvinist." Koertge believes that science, as it has traditionally been practiced, " is one of the most important allies of oppressed people." She argues that, if patriarchy is necessary for science to be carried out the way we know it, then patriarchy cannot be dismissed.

395. Levin, Margarita. " Caring New World: Feminism and Science." American Scholar 57(1):100-106 (1988).

Levin sums up her reviews of feminist critiques of science by saying that " feminist ideology has been seesawing between the claim that women's unique viewpoint will bring a different conceptual framework to bear on the world, and the claim that women will bring a better, truer set of concepts." Three basic errors weaken feminist critiques: 1) accepting the genderized origins of scientific knowledge doesn't mean that science itself must be rejected; 2) feminist critiques have yet to deal with the fact that science is successful; and 3) feminists have offered no concrete account of what a feminist science would be like. Feminists have suggested revisions in scientific language. Changing vocabulary, however, does not necessarily change ideas. Overall, Levin believes that the feminist critique of science is an empty enterprise.

396. Longino, Helen. " Can There Be a Feminist Science?" In Feminism & Science, edited by Nancy Tuana, pp. 45-57 (Bloomington, Indiana: Indiana University Press, 1989).

Longino prefers to focus on science as process and practice rather than as content and product. There is no feminist science but there are feminists doing science. She argues against a clear distinction between " constitutive values," the source of rules for what constitutes acceptable scientific practice and method, and " contextual values," personal, social, and cultural norms and preferences. " The deep metaphysical and normative commitments of the culture in which it flourishes" affect science. Thus, neither masculine science nor feminist science are necessarily bad science. Instead of worrying about eliminating bias, feminists, according to Longino, " must expand [their] scope to include the detection of limiting and interpretive frameworks and the finding or construction of more appropriate frameworks." In principle, it is possible for a feminist to do science. In practice, however, it is not possible, unless and until feminists change present conditions.

397. Longino, Helen and Ruth Doell. " Body, Bias, and Behavior: A Comparative Analysis of Reasoning in Two Areas of Biological Science." Signs 9(2):206-227 (1983).

Feminists do not need to condemn science as an enterprise. Rather, say Longino and Doell, feminists have " a variety of tactical responses" open to them as they expose the masculine bias in science. They distinguish between sexist science that uses poor methodology and sexist science as science as usual. Improving methods will improve the former science but only a paradigm shift will improve the latter. To be effective, feminist critiques of science must differentiate the existence of male bias from its mode of operation. Longino and Doell demonstrate the methodological approach they advocate by analyzing the scientific literature on evolutionary studies and studies of the hormone control of behavior. Their approach involves an examination of the logical aspects of theory construction to determine what counts as evidence and how the evidence relates to the hypothesis it supports. Once a feminist critic of science understands the way masculine bias operates in a particular scientific context, she can respond in one of three ways: 1) by adopting and applying " gynocentric" or unbiased assumptions; 2) by determining if androcentric language creates or misdescribes its object; or 3) by searching for sexist motivations outside of the research methodology itself (for example, in the research program itself).

398. Lowe, Marian. " Cooperation and Competition in Science." International Journal of Women's Studies 4(4):362-368 (1981).

Lowe suggests that scarce resources " breed competitiveness and an instrumental orientation toward relationships" in science. She rejects causal arguments for differences in female and male scientific behavior and associates women's " blocked aspirations" with cooperation, an emphasis on peer solidarity, and a questioning of the meaning of success. Unless women's role changes in society at large, there is little hope that women scientists will change the social framework of science.

399. Merchant, Carolyn. " Critiques and Contentions: Isis' Consciousness Raised." Isis 73(268):398-409 (1982).

Merchant says that a feminist history of science " involves a female perspective on science, nature and society," a challenge to traditional scientific roles, and a consciousness of women's subordination and exclusion from historical literature. A feminist approach to science suggests alternative interpretations of the rise of science, professionalization, and the scientific world view. Approaching science from a feminist persective redefines periods of scientific change.

400. Namenwirth, Marion. " Science Seen Through a Feminist Prism." In Feminist Approaches to Science, edited by Ruth Bleier, ppl.18-41 (New York: Pergamon Press, 1986).

Namenwirth calls on feminism to improve the " contemporary science system." She sides with feminists who call for moderate rather than radical changes to patriarchal science. The objectivity, repeatability, and verifiability characteristic of science identify properties things have in common; such analytical thinking, however, cannot detect the idiosyncratic or the particular. Researchers understand best when they apply their minds in a variety of ways. Scientists must know how their work will be applied, prevent detrimental applications and promote beneficial ones, " cope responsibly" with research by-products such as pollution, and promote accurate and realistic descriptions of research in the media.

Science as an establishment must reward thorough, honest, and cooperative research and penalize careless, dishonest, and self-serving research. The publish-or-perish mentality must be replaced by a system favoring high-quality, thoroughly researched publications. The science curriculum must include the history and sociology of science and emphasize uncertainty and honesty over " bluff and bluster."

401. Potter, Elizabeth. " Modeling the Gender Politics in Science." In Feminism & Science, edited by Nancy Tuana, pp. 132-146 (Bloomington, Indiana: Indiana University Press, 1989).

Feminists need a way to understand science that will allow them to show how sex, race, and class influence the way scientific theories are formulated. A useful model of science, says Potter, will expose masculinist interests and demonstrate their link to scientific theory and practice. It will also explain how good science can be androcentric and sexist.

402. Rose, Hilary. " Beyond Masculinist Realities: A Feminist Epistemology for the Sciences." In Feminist Approaches to Science, edited by Ruth Bleier, pp. 57-76 (New York: Pergamon Press, 1986).

Rose divides feminist writing on science into four categories: 1) the " why so few?" category, which explores the sparcity of women scientists; 2) the " recovery of Hypatia's sisters" category, which recovers the work and accomplishments of women scientists; 3) the " contestation of patriarchal science" category, which invalidates science aimed at establishing a biological justification for gender division; and 4) the " feminist critique of epistemology" category, which reevaluates and critizes scientific assumptions and methods. She claims that none of this literature shows why women are excluded from science and proceeds, using a materialist theory of labor, to show " how this exclusion is rooted in material reality, and...[what its] consequences [are] for a feminist epistemology of science...." Rose asks in whose interests the exclusion of women from science occurs. Women's paid work " echoes just what she does at home." Feminist materialism recognizes that the capitalist and patriarchal modes of production control women's work and lives. Because of their distinctive social position, women's work is " doublesided," incorporating both labor and love. A feminist epistemology derived from women's doublesided approach to work " must represent a more complete materialism, a truer knowledge." Characteristics of this truer knowledge include transcending dichotomies, insisting on the scientific validity of the subject, and emphasizing holism and complexity rather than reductionism and domination.

403. Rose, Hilary. " Hand, Brain, and Heart: A Feminist Epistemology for the Natural Sciences." Signs 9(1):73-90. (1983).

Rose argues for an end to the patriarchal division of labor that has created a science whose " telos is nuclear annihilation." Feminists must seek to incorporate " caring labor and the knowledge that stems from participating in it" into scientific forms and knowledge systems. In their focus on " caring labor," feminists take their critique of science one step beyond the radical critiques of the 1970s, which argued against the separation of mental and manual labor in production. Only through undoing the divisions established between hand, brain, and heart will scientists transform their discipline to exist in harmony with nature.

404. Rose, Hilary. " Making Science Feminist." In The Changing Experience of Women, edited by ELizabeth Whitelegg, Madeleine Arnot, Else Bartels, Veronica Beechey, Lynda Birke, Susan Himmelweit, Diana Leonard, Sonja Ruehl, and Mary Anne Speakman, pp. 352-372 (Oxford: Martin Robertson, 1982).

The division of labor between men and women has excluded women from science. Men have produced or manufactured things; women have reproduced by performing " nurturant caring tasks involving people." Radical critiques of science have focused on the division between manual and intellectual labor. Feminist critiques bring caring labor into the equation. Feminism began in consciousness raising groups where women shared their experiences. Feminist theory and methodology derive from the sharing of personal experience and bring together " subjective and objective ways of knowing the world." Appropriate numbers of women scientists are needed to " achieve a liberatory science."

405. Rosser, Sue V. " A Call for Feminist Science." International Journal of Women's Studies 7(1):3-9 (1984).

Rosser encourages feminists to use actively methods and theories that will result in a richer and more complete science rather than simply to attack defensively nonscientific assumptions and data that support biological determinism. Female scientists have not yet developed feminist scientific theory because a relatively small percentage of women is engaged in scientific research and teaching, innovations in theory that women have suggested have often been ignored, and the language and constructs of science constrain women scientists from thinking creatively. Science, says Rosser, " needs to consider alternative interpretations of data, new subjects and areas for exploration, and females as experimental subjects."

406. Rosser, Sue V. " Feminist Scholarship in the Sciences: Where Are We Now and When Can We Expect a Theoretical Breakthrough?" In Feminism & Science, edited by Nancy Tuana, pp. 3-14 (Bloomington, Indiana: Indiana University Press, 1989).

Rosser reviews feminist scholarship in the sciences. She divides the scholarship into six areas: 1) teaching and curriculum transformations; 2) history of women in science; 3) current status of women in science; 4) feminist critique of science; 5) feminine science; and 6) feminist theory of science. Rosser believes that " to untangle the complicated interrelationships between feminism and science," more feminist scientists, historians, and philosophers are needed.

407. Rosser, Sue V. " Good Science: Can It Ever Be Gender Free?" Women's Studies International Forum 11(1):13-19 (1988).

Rosser believes that " good science cannot be free from the values of the society in which it is developed." In claiming that good science is gender neutral, feminist scientists insist on a dichotomy between biology and environment or nature and nurture. Ironically, this false dichotomy is precisely the basis for feminist critiques of traditional behavioral, neuroscientific, and endocrinological research. A gender-free science assumes either that: 1) science really is objective and that scientific experiments can be run without gender, class, race, historical period, or sexual preference bias; or 2) gender, race, class, and/or sexual preference are not basic, pervasive factors influencing the very core of one's being, one's life experiences, and one's interpretations of those experiences. Rosser contends that until " we have many feminists in top-level research and decision-making positions in science for a considerable period of time," we cannot imagine how a feminist science might differ from a traditional one.

408. Rosser, Sue V. " Introductory Biology: Approaches to Feminist Transformation in Course Content and Teaching Practice." Journal of Thought 20(3):205-217 (1985).

Science is a " masculine province," says Rosser, because it excludes women and it is biased in practice and assumptions. While feminists have not yet " developed the theoretical base which will revolutionize biology," they have proposed methods and theories which produce a more accurate science and have made practicing and future scientists aware of science's lack of objectivity and androcentric bias. Introductory courses must include materials that take a feminist approach.

409. Rosser, Sue V. " Teaching Techniques to Attract Women to Science: Applications of Feminist Theories and Methodologies." Women's Studies International Forum 12(3):363-377 (1989).

Rosser promotes teaching as an important means to attract more women into science. Among her many suggestions for changes in the classroom, the following relate most closely to research: 1) expand the kinds of observations that are scientifically acceptable; 2) take gender into account as a crucial variable; 3) use both qualitative and quantitative methods and data; 4) include women as subjects in experiments; 5) emphasize a relationship with the objects of experiments; 6) use gender-neutral language; 7) encourage students to expose and examine their own research for sexist, racist, classist or other kinds of biases; and 8) link scientific discoveries to moral and practical applications.

410. Rossi, Alice. " Women in Science: Why So Few?" Science 148:1196-1202 (1965).

In one of the earliest feminist criticisms of science, Rossi lists four strategies for increasing the number of women scientists: 1) educate both men and women to all of the adult roles, for example, work, parenting, and leisure; 2) stop discouraging women's career aspirations by advising them to be realistic; 3) use " house-care service firms" to reduce women's household obligations; and 4) encourage men to be more sensitive to and articulate about themselves and women. Underlying her strategies is the assumption that social values rather than women themselves are at fault for making science an unhospitable enterprise for women.

411. Rothschild, Joan. " Afterword: Machina Ex Dea and Future Research." In Machina Ex Dea: Feminist Perspectives on Technology, edited by Joan Rothschild, pp. 213-225 (New York: Pergamon Press, 1983).

About technology, feminists agree that a male bias, which must be confronted and changed, pervades research and analysis. Rothschild lists three directions in which feminist research on technology points: 1) historical analysis, which will relate gender-based patterns of technological invention and use to wider technolgical and social developments; 2) women and work, focusing especially on health hazards, biological reproduction, and how women feel about technological change; and 3) epistemology and values, which questions the connection between the domination of nature and the domination of woman as underlying factors in Western science and technology. Rothschild acknowledges that feminists are not alone in questioning the directions of technology. They contribute uniquely, however, by " bringing the female back into the technological picture" and by using a holistic and experiential approach to transform scholarly inquiry " to be greater than the sum of its female and male parts."

412. Sayers, Janet. " Science, Sexual Difference, and Feminism." In Analyzing Gender: A Handbook of Social Science Research, edited by Beth B. Hess and Myra M. Ferree, pp. 68-91 (Newbury Park, California: Sage Publications, 1987).

Feminists are justifyably ambivalent about science, which has both constructive and destructive effects. On the one hand, feminists rely on scientific rather than religious or moral arguments to debate questions of sexual difference and equality. On the other hand, they reject science for its failure to take women's needs and interests into account. Research conducted on women has often abused subjects whose socio-economic status is such that they have no recourse for retribution. The remedy for scientific bias against women lies with women's greater participation in public life, with " women gaining equal status and power with men in science and society in general." Greater equality will influence the priorities, the methodolgies, and the results of scientific research.

413. Schweickart, Patrocinio. " What If...Science and Technology in Feminist Utopias." In Machina Ex Dea: Feminist Perspectives on Technology, edited by Joan Rothschild, pp. 198-211 (New York: Pergamon Press, 1983).

Schweickart appreciates feminist utopias because they explore alternative worlds organized around feminist values and they offer women a " liberating experience." Traditional science " in patriarchy" operates on a " master/slave dialectic between self and Other." Feminist utopias either redefine science and technology (as in Marge Piercy's Woman On the Edge of Time (New York: Fawcett Crest Books, 1976) or Ursula Le Guin's The Dispossessed (New York: Avon Books, 1974)) or claim that the technological domination of nature has no social place (as in Dorothy Bryant's The Kin of Ata Are Waiting for You (New York: Random House, 1971) or Sally Gearhart's The Wanderground (Watertown, Massachusetts: Persephone Press, 1979)). Feminist utopias stretch " our sense of what is possible and what is natural, to see what we could be in a better world."

414. Stanford, Barbara Dodds. " Re-naming and Re-searching Reality." Science for the People January/February: 5-9, 27 (1986).

Describing science as " an obsolete structure with a hierarchy clinging to privileges it no longer deserves," Stanford blames the lack of women scientists on " fundamental weaknesses in the prevailing scientific paradigm and the resistance of the scientific power-structure to change." She uses Carol Gilligan (see Psychology chapter) to defend a relationship perspective that rejects objectivity and analysis, which isolate variables from their environments. The relationship between science and society must be reexamined and a new paradigm developed. Women do not need to become successful in traditional scientific ways; they need to transform science.

415. Tuana, Nancy. " Re-presenting the World: Feminism and the Natural Sciences." Frontiers 8(3):73-78 (1985).

A review of the texts best suited for classroom use in re-presenting the scientific world from a feminist perspective, Tuana's article includes a valuable bibliography. She describes three processes involved in feminist re-presentation: 1) recovering the work of women scientists to gain them recognition and to increase awareness of women's silencing; 2) uncovering institutional biases against women to document the exclusion of women and to expose the relationship between bias and content; and 3) re-visioning scientific methodologies to reveal the connection between values and science.

416. Wallsgrove, Ruth. " The Masculine Face of Science." In Alice Through the Microscope: The Power of Science Over Women's Lives, edited by Linda Birke, Wendy Faulkner, Sandy Best, Deirdre Janson-Smith, and Kathy Overfield (Brighton Women's Science Group), pp. 228-240 (London: Virago, 1980).

" Science is power," says Wallsgrove, " so science is defined as masculine." Those in power, oppressors, despise qualities of the oppressed, fear finding these qualities in themselves, and, ultimately, fear those they oppress. Wallsgrove claims that three characteristics of science are associated with oppression: 1) detachment, which separates the scientists from nature and can lead to discovery for its own sake; 2) the insistence that the scientific method is a step-by-step logical process of neutral observation when, in reality, all scientists proceed by intuition and analogy, interpreting results on the basis of a pre-existing framework; and 3) faith in logic and its ability, eventually, to predict and control all facets of life and nature.

SUBJECT INDEX

The Subject Index includes proper names and titles referred to in chapter introductions and within the body of annotations. Numbers in parentheses refer to annotation entry numbers; plain numbers refer to pages.

AUTHOR INDEX

The Author Index includes the names of the authors and editors of the annotated sources. In double names, the name listed last (for example, Kanter as in Rosabeth Moss Kanter) determines the entry point, except when names are hyphenated (for example, Fausto-Sterling as in Anne Fausto-Sterling). Numbers in parentheses refer to annotation entry numbers.

About the Authors

CONNIE MILLER is associate librarian and coordinator of computer-assisted information services at Indiana University. She is the author of several articles and of the book *The Technical and Cultural Prerequisites for the Invention of Printing in China and the West* (1983).

CORINNA TREITEL is a doctoral student in History and Philosophy of Science at Indiana University. Her interest in feminist issues and politics influences her scholarship as well as her life.